THE NEW PORTUGUESE TABLE

THE NEW
PORTUGUESE TABLE

Exciting Flavors from Europe's Western Coast

DAVID LEITE

Photographs by Nuno Correia

CLARKSON POTTER/PUBLISHERS

NEW YORK

FOR VOVÓ COSTA, WHO WAS
ALWAYS HAPPIEST IN THE KITCHEN

Copyright © 2009 by David Leite
Photographs by Nuno Correia, copyright © 2009

All rights reserved.
Published in the United States by Clarkson Potter/Publishers,
an imprint of the Crown Publishing Group, a division of Random House, Inc., New York.
www.crownpublishing.com
www.clarksonpotter.com

CLARKSON POTTER is a trademark and POTTER with colophon
is a registered trademark of Random House, Inc.

Photographs on pages 1, 8, 11, 15, 17, 18, 20, 25, 27, 30, 31, 32, 49, 54, 64, 78, 95, 108,
117, 130, 141, 147, 153, 154, 186, 191, 202, 230 courtesy of the author.

Library of Congress Cataloging-in-Publication Data
Leite, David.
The new Portuguese table / David Leite. — 1st ed.
p. cm.
Includes index.
1. Cookery, Portuguese. I. Title.
TX723.5.P7L44   2009
614.59469—dc22   2008051283

ISBN 978-0-307-39441-5

Printed in China

Design by Stephanie Huntwork

2 4 6 8 10 9 7 5 3 1

First Edition

CONTENTS

———+———

INTRODUCTION

CONFESSIONS OF A LATE-BLOOMING LUSOPHILE

Let me set the record straight: for the first thirty-two years of my life, I wanted nothing to do with Portugal, its food, or its culture. For anyone else, that wouldn't have been a problem, considering that during the 1960s and 1970s Portugal wasn't exactly on most people's radar. But coming from a Portuguese family, I was hard-pressed to ignore my heritage. When I was growing up in Fall River, Massachusetts, smack in the middle of America's biggest Little Portugal, there was always a clutch of immigrants from São Miguel, one of the nine Azorean islands and my family's homeland, crowded around our chrome-and-green Formica table. Eating. *Always* eating. And while the tawny smoke of their strange-smelling cigarettes curled itself around the ceiling light, I sat in my parents' closet stuffing Hostess cupcakes into my mouth, praying to be blond and blue-eyed, with a last name of Fitzgerald or Abernathy.

But when my maternal grandmother, vovó Costa, died in 1992, so did many of her specialties, such as *sopa de galinha*, her famous pink chicken soup, and *recheio com chouriço*, a moist stuffing studded with big chunks of garlicky smoked pork sausage. It was then that I grew curious about my family's food. I stole my mother's "cookbook," a green-leather telephone address book—which I still have—where she had dutifully logged some of my grandmother's dishes, in her perfect cursive handwriting. Later, poking around my mother's kitchen while she was cooking, I fervently jotted down whatever she did, because the last thing I wanted, as she likes to put it, was "for any deathbed recipe-dictation sessions to be cut short by the big guy upstairs."

A few years later, when I visited Portugal for the first time, I spent most of my vacation on São Miguel. Although smitten by the volcanic landscape and the ease of the Old World culture, I was riveted by the food. What hit me was that even though many dishes shared their names with those of my family, none was remotely similar. And to my mind, they weren't just different, they were wrong. Utterly, stupendously *wrong*. Until then, Portuguese food was one thing and one thing only: the dishes put in front of me by the women who love me. Period. Even more disturbing was that I'd never imagined that any dish my family cooked could be made better by someone else. That trip launched me on a journey of discovery—of the food of my heritage and of myself—that included my becoming a Portuguese citizen in 2004.

During the past twelve years, I've grazed my way through every region of Portugal, the island of Madeira, and most of the Azorean archipelago. In 2007, even with the slumping dollar, I snagged an apartment in the luxe neighborhood of Sé, in Lisbon. With that as my home base, I set out. But I was always in such a rush, to learn more, see more, eat more, that one day I tripped over my luggage and, unbeknownst to me, severed my Achilles tendon. Apparently, hunger trumps pain, because I walked on it for two months, limping up mountains with my friend Portuguese food scholar Janet Boileau in search of the perfect São Jorge cheese, down vertiginous steps in the Alfama district with ex-pat Amy Herrick sniffing out my next great meal, and across my apartment for another handful of Advil.

But all this traveling wasn't without some sadness. After listening to a lifetime's worth of my family's stories of Portugal, I had an indelible and, admittedly, romanticized image of the country and its people. That's why, at first, whenever I arrived somewhere new, I expected to find the town fool and his donkey who was smarter than him; the fat priest who indulged in the sin of dessert pilfering from the *pastelaria* when he thought the baker wasn't watching; or family dinners after the yearly *matança*, or pig slaughter, when the cooks would triumphantly carry out platters of hard-earned food.

That Portugal was gone.

When I decided to write this book, I had to rejigger my thinking. At first I felt that if I wrote about what I was experiencing—exciting cutting-edge food, up-and-coming restaurants, a nascent TV food culture, elegant home entertaining—I was betraying my family, being unfaithful to the old ways.

It was while sitting around the dinner table of my friend José Vilela, eating falling-off-the-bone partridge escabeche (see page 123) with a spice profile that unmoored the dish from its traditions, that I felt an internal crowbar-pop that finally freed me. Classically, the dish is nothing more than partridge simmered in oil and vinegar. But José felt comfortable reaching for spices with Indian and Asian flavors now so popular in Portugal, to enhance and refresh, not obliterate, this ancient recipe.

All around the table were his idiosyncratic, argumentative, and wickedly funny friends, debating the merits of one restaurant over another, the need for home sous-vide machines, the benefits of Portugal's short-grain Carolino versus long-grained Agulha rices. At that moment it was clear to me what I had to do: embrace *this* meal, *this* dining scene, *this* Portugal. Just because the Portuguese pantry and table had changed since my father left in 1958 didn't mean Portugal was any less authentic. And neither was I less true to my heritage for wanting to write about this vibrant new culture.

From then on, I ventured out with an even bigger appetite for food and knowledge. I now, it seemed, had twice as much to learn, see, and eat. Discovering the similarities and differences between classic and contemporary dishes obsessed me. Bacalhau à Gomes de Sá (page 103), a traditional casserole of layered salt cod, potatoes, and onions, and a modern dish of Olive Oil–Poached Fresh Cod with Roasted Tomato Sauce (page 84) vied for my attention. I saw how traditions were loosening—but not being forsaken—as cooks took a freer hand with the classics. For example, *almôndegas*, or meatballs, traditionally made from beef, pork, or a combination of both, were whipped up by my friend Teresa Cota Dias using lamb perfumed with cumin and orange zest (see page 150).

While researching turkey, a New World bird (see page 120), I was extraordinarily moved to uncover the Portuguese roots of some of my family's dining traditions surrounding Thanksgiving—traditions we followed because that's what we had been taught, without any idea of where they'd originated.

To keep it all straight, I carried a camera, tape recorder, and a now-battered pocket notebook, where I jotted down menu items, drew maps of dinner plates in restaurants and home kitchens, and transcribed quotes from cooks, professional and not, in my pidgin Portuguese. I embarked upon what I'm sure will be the closest thing to a glittery social season I will ever experience: once the word was out, I was feted at people's homes; received invitations to restaurant openings and hearty dinners at centuries-old country estates; was ferried about countless villages by proud residents to sample the local cuisine; supped with some of the most influential and intelligent dining critics and journalists in Portugal; and was even consulted about the menu of one of Lisbon's hotly anticipated restaurants.

When I returned home at the end of 2007 and was promptly wheeled into surgery for my ankle, I had a stash of recipes and stories that became this book—a chronicle of the Portuguese table that picks up the narrative where my family left it, in that smoky room so many years ago. Does it have classics? Certainly. And family favorites? Absolutely. But there are also many new recipes about which my grandmother, if she were alive today, would say, *"Gosto muito."* I like them very much.

I hope you do, too.

PORTUGAL PARSED

A QUICK REGIONAL GASTRONOMIC TOUR

—+—

Portugal has been called a lot of things—diminutive, minuscule, a pipsqueak even—but one thing it's never been called is insignificant. About the size of the state of Indiana, it measures a meager 349 miles from north to south, a trip ambitious travelers can pull off in a day. Yet its major historical provinces offer wild extremes of temperature, weather, and terrain that for centuries have resulted in an amazing variety of some of the finest foods on the Iberian Peninsula. Distinctive and artisanal, these foods have shaped local diets, customs, and traditions, many of which have remained virtually unchanged for generations. Anyone with good sense and a better palate would do right to reserve at least a month to make that 349-mile trek.

Despite its size, Portugal has contributed mightily to world cuisine. During the Age of Discovery (fifteenth to seventeenth centuries), under the watchful eye of Henry the Navigator and, later, the explorers Bartolomeu Dias, Vasco da Gama, and others, Portugal forged expeditions along the African coast and, eventually, to the East. The result? Formerly exotic spices such as cinnamon, pepper, nutmeg, and cloves were brought back to European kitchens and filled Portuguese coffers with unparalleled wealth. At about the same time, Pedro Álvares Cabral sailed westward, reaching Brazil, and opened up routes that introduced the continent, and the world, to many New World ingredients that have become hallmarks of Portuguese cooking, including chile peppers and potatoes.

But to appreciate the contemporary Portuguese table, it's necessary to understand the new Portuguese Paradox: since joining the European Community in 1986, Portugal has found itself straddling two eras, nearly one hundred years apart. New ingredients, techniques, and chefs have flooded into the country while the old guard continues to march on, oftentimes oblivious to the radical changes occuring around it. Case in point: Grab a table at the tony 100 Maneiras, a waterfront restaurant just west of Lisbon praised for its Portuguese-inspired fusion menu crowded with foie gras, black pig carpaccio, and all types of seafood risottos, then glance out at the water. Chugging by are small, dilapidated fishing boats, weighted down with the day's catch. Onboard are living anachronisms: some men mending heaps of nets by hand, others gutting fish, and still others, with caps drawn, catching a few moments of sleep before reaching home—as if they've somehow willed away the past one hundred years.

At the same time, cooks are using the country's iconic ingredients—fish right off the boat, vegetables picked from backyard gardens, and deeply smoked meats—in innovative ways. And it's this dichotomy that's redefining the cuisine of Portugal, a delicious frisson that's felt differently throughout the land. Although classic dishes still hold sway over much of rural Portugal, many of them are being tweaked and reinterpreted in metropolitan areas, as well as sharing menu space with new dishes that build upon tradition to bring exciting modern cooking to the fore. There has never been a more thrilling time to eat and drink one's way through Portugal.

So here's a peripatetic look at the eleven historical provinces, from north to south, plus Madeira and the Azares, along with just some of their traditional specialties—without which there wouldn't be a modern Portuguese cuisine.

ATENÇÃO ⟩⟩ *Portugal's historical provinces and wine regions don't overlap perfectly; some of the wine regions spill over into several provinces. In order to give you concise information as you travel through the country, I've grouped the most important wine producers by provinces. This way you can learn about and enjoy the food and wine of each area.*

MINHO *(meen-yoo)*

If Portugal ever had an emerald province, it's the Minho. Tucked inconspicuously between the Minho River, which marks the northernmost border between Portugal and Spain, and the Douro River to the south, the region benefits from idyllic temperatures (55° to 75°F), warm Atlantic breezes, and a good amount of rain. The result is commercial farms and home gardens bursting with vegetation, as well as a prodigious amount of vineyards that produce the famous *vinho verde*, or green wine. Perhaps because of its distance from any major metropolitan center, the Minho is considered Portugal's most traditional region: a place where men with ox-drawn carts still work the field and unattended herds of cattle leisurely cross pencil-thin roads at will, tossing half-lidded glances at any impatient driver cheeky enough to lean on his horn. In the distance, backdrops of burnished granite mountains, a haven to many endangered animal and plant species, silently preside over the region.

What to Eat
Caldo verde (puréed potato-onion soup swimming with slivers of kale and slices of sausage); *rojões* (cubes of pork or pork belly fried with cloves and cumin until crisp); *broa de milho* (hearty corn bread); the Carnival specialty *cozido à Portuguesa* (a boiled dinner of pork, chicken, beef, potatoes, blood sausage, chouriço, and cabbage); *sopa dourada* (in this region, at least, layers of delicate sponge cake covered with *ovos moles*, or thickened sweetened egg yolks).

What to Drink
Vinho verde (literally, "green wine") is the go-to drink. This crisp, slightly effervescent wine, which comes in red, rosé, and primarily, white, is meant to be drunk while still young, or green, hence the name. Producers: Adega de Monção, Anselmo Mendes, António Esteves Ferreira, Casa de Vila Verde, Quinta da Aveleda, and Quinta de Serrade.

TRÁS-OS-MONTES (trahzh oozh *mawn*-tizh) and ALTO DOURO *(ahl-too doh-roo)*

Hidden in the northeast corner beyond the Marão, Gerês, and Alvão mountain ranges, Trás-os-Montes ("behind the mountains") is brutally cut off from the warmer Atlantic winds that favor the neighboring Minho. In place of lush green vegetation and undulating hills of vineyards, this desolate and punishingly untamed region is blanketed by moors of heather, dense forest, and scraggy brush, suitable for hardy herds of sheep, goats, and pigs. This is meat country.

The Alto Douro, in the south, near the mighty Douro River, is less forbidding, as the peaks slope down to the river and are dotted with wealthy *quintas*, or large estates. The reason? Cut into the hills, ziggurat-style, are what some say is the most expensive real estate in Portugal: hectares upon hectares of land that produce the finest grapes that go into the country's liquid gold—port wine. So important is this area that in 1756 it became the first wine region in the world to be demarcated, or defined, serving as a model for the wine industry.

What to Eat
Presunto (smoked ham, especially from the towns of Chaves and Lamego); creamy Monte cheese; *feijoada* (stew of kidney beans plus nearly every part of the region's pigs fattened on sweet chestnuts); *sopa de castanhas piladas* (chestnut soup); and, arguably, the most confusing Portuguese dessert: *toucinho do céu* (literally "bacon from heaven"). This sweet has

nary a pork product in it, although some claim it had some originally. A dense flan, it's rich with egg yolks, pumpkin, and ground almonds.

What to Drink
Wines from CARM, Casa Ferreirinha, Lemos & Van Zeller, Niepoort, Quinta da Carolina, Quinta do Crasto, Quinta do Noval, Quinta do Sobreiro de Cima, Quinta do Vale Meão, and Quinta do Vallado.

DOURO LITORAL (*doh*-roo lee-too-*rahl*)

The heart of the Douro Litoral is Portugal's second-largest city, Porto. As the name implies, everything—from the colorful boats that bob in the Douro River outside the port lodges of Vila Nova de Gaia to the economy to the food served to both hungry vineyard workers and elegant tourists—is fueled by port wine and the busy harbor from which it's shipped.

Although the weather is favorable to many crops, if it weren't for the ingenuity and back-breaking work of generations of Portuguese, little would grow. The solid schist slopes of the inland valley, as in the Alto Douro, are so steep and impassable that everything from small whitewashed cottages and their tiny gardens to immense terraced vineyards are carved into the mountains. Still, trees bowed heavy with peaches, plums, quince, apples, almonds, pears, and figs—the stuff that preserve dreams are made of—manage to flourish.

What to Eat
Tripas à moda do Porto (slow-cooked casserole of tripe, pigs' feet, chicken, sausages, navy beans, vegetables, and a good dose of cumin); *bacalhau à Gomes de Sá* (casserole of potatoes, sautéed onions, and salt cod garnished with slices of hard-boiled eggs and black olives); *pastéis de bacalhau* (salt cod fritters); and *bolo de amêndoa* (almond cake made from flour, sugar, eggs, and blanched almonds).

What to Drink
Port, of course. Some producers: A. A. Ferreira, Calem e Filho, Croft, Delaforce, Fonseca, Graham, Niepoort, Quinta do Noval, Ramos Pinto, Taylor-Fladgate, Sandeman, and Warre.

PORT PRIMER

Legends abound regarding the creation of port wine—from acts of god to the efforts of mercenary Liverpudlian merchants trying to find a replacement for the fine wine in Britain that disappeared because of a French embargo. But the fortified wine, which is the dictionary definition of a postprandial drink, was in reality the product of good business and better weather. British merchants were regularly adding brandy to Portuguese wine to prevent spoilage while in transit to England. Then in 1820, particularly favorable conditions made for a superb, naturally sweet wine, one that Britain couldn't resist. Seeing an opportunity, Portuguese producers began adding more brandy to their wines earlier in the fermentation process to mimic the sweeter, higher alcohol content of that blessed year. Eventually they refined the process, creating a wine similar to what we know as port.

VINTAGE PORT

The finest and rarest of all ports. Vintage ports make up a mere 2 to 3 percent of all port production. The wines are made only in extraordinary years, called "declared" years (hence the term "vintage") when the growing season has all the conditions for making an exquisite and lasting wine. When that happens, grapes from *only* that year and from *only* the finest vineyards can be used by producers to make the port. The wines are aged in barrels for two years and then bottle-aged for as long as several decades, giving the port its defining depth, richness, and character. Vintage ports are never filtered, so they need to be decanted.

LATE-BOTTLED VINTAGE PORT (LBV)

The name is a bit misleading. LBVs aren't as tony as they sound, for they don't have the same complexity as vintage ports. Although they are made from grapes from a single vintage, LBVs are produced in a "nondeclared" year. These delicious, plummy-tasting wines are barrel-aged for four to six years and then are ready to be drunk.

TAWNY PORT

Hands-down the world's bestselling ports. Blending finely aged superb ports from different years, some a century old, is what lends tawny port its nutty flavor with overtones of vanilla, butterscotch, and caramel. And the name? Because of long barrel-aging, the wine's color lightens from a deep red to an orange brown. Tawny ports are designated on the bottle as ten, twenty, thirty, and more than forty years old. *Colheita* is the Portuguese term for an extraordinary rare tawny port made from a single vintage.

RUBY PORT

This is a good entry-level port. It's a blend of good but not stellar ports from different years that are barrel- or tank-aged for no more than three years and receive little bottle aging. Therefore, it has a straightforward character with spicy, red-fruit flavors.

WHITE PORT

These dry or sweet wines, made from white grapes, are aged briefly in wood and have a mild nutty, slightly sweet taste. Served chilled with a twist of lemon or a splash of soda, they make an excellent aperitif.

BEIRA LITORAL (*bay*-rduh lee-too-*rahl*), BEIRA BAIXA (*bay*-rduh *buy*-shuh), and BEIRA ALTA (*bay*-rduh *ahl*-tuh)

Beira Litoral, Beira Baixa, and Beira Alta—collectively known as the Beiras—cut a huge swath through central Portugal. Second in size only to the vast Alentejo, the Beiras run from the mountains abutting Spain in the east to the Atlantic in the west. The provinces got their respective names because, as you travel east, the region rises precipitously like half of a giant bell curve, from balmy sea (*litoral* means "coast") to squat hills (*baixa* means "low") to soaring, thickly forested mountains (*alta* translates as "high"). But, more important, the provinces act as a curtain between the lush green regions to the north and the summer-parched provinces to the south. And because of their sheer size, they offer perhaps the wildest changes in topography (including Serra da Estrela, the highest point on the mainland, topping out at 6,532 feet), the greatest differences in culture, and the widest variety of food.

What to Eat
Cheese, including queijo da Serra (unctuous runny sheep's-milk cheese), Requeijão (soft and ricotta-like), Castelo Branco (similar to Serra), and peppery Rabaçal; *cabrito assado* (roast kid rubbed with plenty of garlic, then doused in rich brandy before cooking); *chanfana de cabrito* (red wine–based kid stew); *leitão* (roast suckling pig); and *torresmos* (here, pork cracklings).

What to Drink
Wines from Adega Cooperativa de Cantanhede, Adega Cooperativa de Mealhada, Álvaro Castro, Campolargo, Casa de Santar, Caves São João, Companhia das Quintas, Filipa Pato, Luís Pato, Quinta de Cabriz, Quinta do Encontro, Quinta dos Carvalhais, and Quinta dos Roques.

ESTREMADURA (ess-treh-muh-*doo*-ruh)

Literally translated as "boundary," Estremadura was once the extreme southern border of Christendom. The rest of the country was at the time under the hands of the Moors, from the eighth to the eleventh century. But even with their endless occupation, the Moors were unable to conquer this long and sinuous coastal province, etched by sandy beaches to the west and rugged cliffs to the south, all bisected by the languid Tejo River, on which Lisbon sits. Estremadura's name could just as easily be translated as "seafood": it has a rich history of classic fish dishes and specialties that fed the bodies and spirit of the Portuguese even before they had to defend themselves against the Moors.

What to Eat
Sopa de mariscos and *caldeirada de peixe* (shellfish stew and fish stew, respectively); *bacalhau à Brás* (clouds of softly scrambled eggs encasing bits of salt cod and crispy matchstick potatoes); *açorda de marisco* (hearty seafood bread soup studded with plenty of shrimp, clams, scallops, and, sometimes, lobster); *frango com piri-piri* (grilled chicken doused with Portugal's incendiary hot sauce); *pastéis de Belém* (luscious custards in crisp pastry cups served warm with a generous sprinkling of confectioners' sugar and cinnamon); and *queijo de Azeitão* (semi-soft cheese with buttery overtones and a slight bite).

What to Drink
Wines from Casa Santos Lima, Caves Velhas, Companhia Agricola do Sanguinhal, DFJ Vinhos, José Maria da Fonseca, Quinta de Chocapalha, Quinta da Cortezia, Quinta de Pancas, and Quinta da Romeira.

RIBATEJO (rib-eh-*tay*-zhoo)

Lying square in the middle of the country, northeast of Lisbon, is the flat, fertile province of the Ribatejo. Its name is a conflation of *riba de Tejo*, meaning "banks of the Tejo," and it spreads out north and south of the river. The Tejo cleaves the region's terrain and agriculture. To the north are low hills that are intensely cultivated with huge swaths of olive groves. The oil produced is so extraordinary it qualifies for *Denominação de Origem Protegida* (DOP) demarcation, guaranteeing it was produced and processed in this region using local traditions and techniques. The northern region boasts vast vegetable farms of beans, corn, tomatoes, and green peppers plus orchards of apples and lemons. To the south, the land opens up into wide fields of bluegrass and *lezírias*, or marshes, where Arabian horses and black bulls graze freely. Farther south grow long rows of irregularly spaced olive and cork trees, looking at first glance like combs with missing teeth. In the spring, the river overflows its banks, creating an alluvial plain, where rice—a staple of the Portuguese diet—is tended.

What to Eat

Sopa de pedra ("stone soup," filled with pork ribs, sausage, beans, root vegetables, and cabbage); *enguias* (eels—stewed, fried, or grilled), *açorda de sável* (here, a bread soup made with shad roe); *ovas de sável à pescador* (grilled shad roe); *arroz de tomate* (tomato rice); *lebrada* (hare stewed in red wine); and *pão-de-ló* (here, an ethereally light sponge cake moistened with flavored syrups).

What to Drink

Wines from Casa Cadaval, Falua Sociedade de Vinhos S.A., João Portugal Ramos, Quinta da Casal Branco, Quinta do Falcão, Quinta da Lagoalva, and Pinhal da Torre.

ALTO ALENTEJO (*ahl*-too ah-len-*tay*-zhoo) and BAIXO ALENTEJO (*buy*-shoo ah-len-*tay*-zhoo)

This immense region regally commands almost a third of the country, and its undulating hills are dotted with gorgeous whitewashed villages that have for centuries attracted admirers from around the world.

The province is a continuum of color because of its agriculture. In spring, the wide plains in the south are caught up in blizzards of almond blossoms, while the long roads that connect the great halves of the region—*alto* (upper) and *baixo* (lower)—are lined with brilliant yellow broom. Beyond, vast fields of wheat, rye, oats, and barley stretch to the horizon, for this is the center of Portugal's grain industry. Here, too, are endless groves of luscious sweet oranges, greengage plums, and apricots.

In the summer, the punishing sun, which can blast well over 100°F at midday, mutes the colors. It's then that the silvery-green olive trees and the much darker cork oaks, which produce two thirds of the world's supply, stand out in stark contrast to the now-straw-colored fields. Into these groves farmers let loose their famous *porco preto*, or black pigs, encouraging them to gorge on the oaks' fallen acorns to fatten them up before the winter *matança*, or slaughter.

What to Eat

Gaspacho (Portuguese version of the cold soup, filled with chopped sweet red or green peppers, garlic, cucumbers, and dense bread softened with a tomato-vinegar broth); *açorda Alentejana* (intensely flavored cilantro and garlic broth, poured over day-old bread and topped with a poached egg); *empadas de galinha* (savory chicken pies); *carne de porco à Alentejana* (pork cubes and clams served over fried potatoes); and *migas* (literally "bread crumbs," moistened day-old bread suffused, for example, with pork drippings or mixed with spinach, molded into ovals, and pan-fried).

What to Drink

Wines from Adega Cooperativa de Borba, Caves Aliança, Cortes de Cima, Eugénio de Almeida, Francisco Nunes Garcia, Herdade da Calada, Herdade da Malhadinha Nova, Herdade do Esporão, João Portugal Ramos, Margarida Cabaço, Monte do Trevo, Paulo Laureano, Quinta Dona Maria (Júlio Tassara Bastos), Quinta do Carmo, Quinta do Mouro, and Tapada de Coelheiros.

ALGARVE (*ahl*-garv)

Nearly one hundred miles of white-sand beaches, secret caves, and year-round mild weather are what draws tourists to the Algarve. Most crowd along the shoreline in the resort towns of Faro, Lagos, and Albufeira, with their world-class golf courses and world-class (read: international) food. But world-class natural beauty refuses to be elbowed out of the way: not far from Faro is the Parque Natural da Ria Formosa lagoon, a barrier-islands system that's a beloved national park. Praia da Marinha, with its ocean-carved cliffs and hidden grottos filled with azure water, has often been named one of the most beautiful and best-preserved beaches in the world.

In the still-pristine and underdeveloped western areas as well as along the lagoons east of Faro, it's easy to find restaurants that staunchly refuse to cave to the whims of the *estrangeiros*, or foreigners. What, then, are the culinary muses of these establishments? Local crops of rice, almonds, oranges, lemons, figs, and, of course, any creature from the sea.

What to Eat

Sardinhas assadas (grilled sardines); *polvo frito* (fried octopus); *lulas recheadas* (squid stuffed with cured meats and cooked in a tomato-onion sauce); *búzios com feijão* (clam, oyster, snail, and bean stew); *amêijoas na cataplana* (clams and spicy sausage cooked in the eponymous *cataplana*—a hinged clam-shaped pan, a kind of spiritual ancestor of the pressure cooker); *caldeirada* (stew brimming with local fish, including fresh tuna, sardines, and scorpion fish, as well as potatoes, onions, and garlic); and *figos cheios* (dried figs stuffed with almonds).

MADEIRA (muh-*thay*-rduh) and THE AZORES (uh-*soar*-ridz)

An entire book could be written about these jaw-droppingly beautiful volcanic islands, strewn across the Atlantic like a handful of green marbles. Madeira, discovered circa 1424, has a subtropical climate, so on the south side, which is favored by warm ocean breezes, everything from bananas and orchids to mangoes and sugarcane grows. Traveling north, into the staggering peaks covered in dense forests (*madeira* means "wood"), the lush volcanic landscape is cut by waterfalls hundreds of feet high. Like the Algarve, the island is a hotbed for tourists, but most stay in and around the capital city of Funchal, named for *funcho*, or fennel, a prolific crop that greeted the early settlers.

The subtropical Azorean islands—Santa Maria, São Miguel, Terceira, São Jorge, Graciosa, Pico, Faial, Flores, and Corvo—are happily stranded halfway between the United States and Europe. Life here is simpler, more rustic. Some towns weren't even hooked up for electricity, gas, and telephone until the 1960s. But the pace of living is changing alarmingly fast. Cell phones and wireless cafés are catching on, much to the consternation of the older generations.

Because the islands are the peaks of ancient volcanoes, the land is impossibly verdant, with soaring summits, huge dormant-craters-turned-lagoons ringed with hydrangeas, and valleys perfect for grazing. Here the prized beast of burden is the cow. The Azores, especially São Jorge, are famous for their cheese. Microclimates are in evidence here, and some of the world's finest pineapples come from a small, protected valley on the south side of São Miguel, while Europe's only commercial tea plantation resides on the sloping northern shore. Nearby, in the town of Furnas, bubbly, sulfurous fissures act as ovens, and locals lower pots filled with all types of meats, sausages, and vegetables into them to cook the dish called *cozido*.

What to Eat

In Madeira, *cebolinhas de escabeche* (pickled onions); *milho frito* (fried cornmeal squares); *espada* (scabbard fish); *carne de vinha d'alhos* (pork cubes in a wine and garlic sauce served over slices of bread and ringed with oranges); *espetada* (beef chunks threaded on bay laurel branches and grilled over an open flame); *bolo de caco* (flat bread rounds made with sweet potato); and *bolo de mel* (molasses cake).

In the Azores, *favas ricas* (stew of fava beans seasoned with a bit of cinnamon); *lapas grelhadas* (grilled limpets in a lemon-butter sauce); *sopa do Espírito Santo* (a soup rife with beef, cabbage, sausages, bacon, wine, mint, and spices, served on the Feast of the Holy Ghost); *sopa de funcho* (fennel soup); *alcatra* (beef rump braised with wine, onions, allspice, bay leaf, and cinnamon); *cozido* (see description above); *massa sovada* (a slightly sweet, eggy bread); *bolos lêvedos* (flat round breads similar to an English muffin); and *malassadas* (literally "badly baked," pockmarked, sugar-covered doughnuts).

What to Drink

Madeira is most well known, of course, for its eponymous fortified wines. You can't go wrong with bottles from Barbeito, Blandy's, Broadbent, Cossart Gordon, D'Oliveira, Henriques & Henriques, Leacock's, Justino Henriques, or Quinta do Serrado.

MADEIRA MADNESS

Ever since the region's fortified wines were accidentally over-heated in holds of ships traveling along hot, tropical trade routes and, to everyone's surprise, vastly improved, the world has had a passion for Madeira. It's been a celebratory tipple for centuries, the most famous toast being the one at the signing of the Declaration of Independence.

No longer set adrift to mature, Madeira is now carefully aged in stifling attics. There are four major types of wine, neatly named after the grape varietals:

MALMSEY (malvasia) is the sweetest, with lovely hints of nuts, caramel, and coffee. Grab a bottle when you're looking for a postprandial sip or a wine to pair with deeply flavored desserts, such as Chocolate Mousse (page 219).

BOAL (aka bual) is the medium-sweet wine of the quartet. It's rich with toffee and caramel flavors and teams beautifully with cheeses, as well as with custard desserts. Pour some when munching on a Baked Custard Tart (page 217).

VERDELHO crosses the line into drier territory. It offers up whispers of fig, spicy orange, and more acidic fruits. Traditionally served with soup and salad courses, it's a pleasant surprise coupled with White Gazpacho with Crab Salad (page 59).

SERCIAL, the driest and sprightliest of the group, has definite insistence of vanilla, almonds, and crisp green apples. It's an excellent match for most lighter hors d'oeuvres.

THE PORTUGUESE PANTRY

In my kitchen, I've stocked sections of my pantry and fridge with ingredients I use to cook Portuguese dishes. Through trial and error, I've discovered American ingredients that are either identical to or successful substitutes for those in Portugal. Nothing is more frustrating than thinking one thing when an author intends something else, so in these entries, I've described the exact variety of onion, the precise kind of bay leaf, and the perfect cultivar of potato to use for making the recipes in the United States, so that we're—literally—on the same page. It's not an exhaustive list; it includes only those ingredients you'll need to cook from this book. For those few harder-to-find items, such as Portuguese sausages and bottled sauces, I've provided a list of stores and online purveyors in the Sources section (page 251).

Without a doubt, though, the biggest contributor to the success of your dishes is to buy the best-quality ingredients you can afford. Gently poke a few tomatoes in the name of comparison shopping, drum up the courage to speak to your fishmonger about salt cod, and ignore the bargain bin and splurge on well-priced port wine you wouldn't mind sipping after an enjoyable evening of cooking.

Oh, and considering Portuguese is tough to wrap your lips around, I've included a handy pronunciation guide. *Boa sorte!*

BACON *toucinho* (tow-*seen*-yoo)

Pork is the undisputed king of meat in Portugal, and nose-to-tail eating is the rule. But for decades, authors and translators of Portuguese recipes have left cooks banging their heads against kitchen cabinets with the indiscriminate use of the word *bacon* to mean *toucinho*. There are three types of *toucinho*, only one of which is similar to bacon as we know it, and each one has a different cooking use.

Toucinho gordo ("fat bacon") is pure pork fat, similar to our fatback, with no striations of meat and with the skin often attached. It's cut from most any part of the animal and, like all *toucinho*, is traditionally salted (*salgado*) rather than smoked, although nowadays it's possible to buy *toucinho fumado* in all three forms. Chunks are added to dishes such as *feijoada* (bean-meat casserole), *cozido* (a one-pot meal of boiled meats and vegetables), and even some desserts.

Toucinho magro ("skinny bacon") has significantly more meat than fat. In the past, this type of *toucinho* was chunked, fried until crisp, and placed in a clay pot until ready to be added to recipes as a flavor booster. I don't call for this type of bacon in these recipes, but if you stumble upon particularly lean farmstead bacon, definitely try it.

Toucinho entremeado is half fat, half meat and is usually preferred smoked rather than salted. This is the closest to our bacon, and it's what I used in developing the recipes for this book. To mimic the taste, pass over packaged sliced bacon and reach for slab bacon or pancetta, even though it's not smoked. Whatever you do, avoid flavored bacons, such as maple or mesquite.

BEANS, DRIED *feijão* (fay-*zhowhn*)

Dried beans have played a long and important role in Portuguese cooking and history. They were used to feed sailors who traveled west to the New World for riches, as well as those who navigated round the Cape of Good Hope on their voyages east for spices. The attraction, obviously, is that dried beans keep a long time and pack a nutritious wallop. Back home, beans carried peasant farmers through fallow growing seasons, bolstered late-winter meals when pantries were bare, and served as barter when pockets were empty.

Walk through any open-air market in Portugal today, and you'll still see rows of woven baskets filled with beans of just about every size, shape, and color. For the recipes in this book, stock up on dried black-eyed peas, Great Northern, navy, and red kidney beans. While you're at it, grab frozen and fresh fava beans when you find them; they're preferable to their dried counterpart.

The best kind of dried beans to buy are fresh, which isn't an oxymoron. In today's jumbo-marts, with their huge inventories, beans can sit indefinitely. But at farmers' markets and stores with high turnover, it's possible to buy dried beans that aren't ancient. Before using beans, rinse them well and sort through them, plucking out any stray pebbles. Keep in mind that cooking times in this book are merely guidelines. Depending on the size and age of your beans, timing can vary dramatically, so always nibble a few beans as you cook to determine doneness.

CHEESE *queijo (kay-zhoo)*

For such a small country, Portugal can rival France or Italy in sheer number of cheeses. But, alas, variety and nuance are limited, as the lion's share of cheeses are made from either sheep's or goat's milk. A few are a mixture of both, with even fewer adding cow's milk to soften and round out the flavor. A handful of cheeses are made from just cow's milk, but only one ranks up there with the best, and that's São Jorge, from the Azorean island of the same name.

However, since Portugal joined the European Economic Community, the precursor to the European Union (EU), in 1986, its cheese production has improved immeasurably, and quite a few varieties now share winners' circles with other world-class cheeses. The finest have been given *Denominação de Origem Protegida* (DOP) status, which guarantees that the cheeses have been produced and processed in a specific area using local traditions and techniques. (Portugal now has more than one hundred foods with protected status.) Of the countless cheeses Portugal produces, most are made in such small quanti-

ties that they never make it beyond the borders for foreigners to enjoy. The ones you're most likely to find online or at gourmet shops in the United States are listed below.

Queijo Serra da Estrela (DOP) (*kay*-zhoo *seh*-ruh duh esh-*trel*-luh)

This is the reigning monarch of Portuguese cheese and has been for more than eight hundred years. Produced from the raw milk of Bordaleira sheep that graze on Beira Alta's soaring Serra da Estrela mountain range, hence the name, queijo da Serra is still a handmade, artisanal cheese. Because of the work involved, each maker can turn out at most three wheels a day, but the EU is pressuring makers to automate the process. The cheese is produced in colder months, primarily from November to March, and it undergoes a four- to six-week maturation process. Initially the cheese is sumptuously, creamily soft, and the linen-wrapped wheels are traditionally served with their tops shorn off and spoons are passed around for scooping. As it ages, the cheese firms up but never hardens.

When I was visiting Quinta do Vallado, a winery in the Douro region, my host told me a queijo da Serra secret that I've taken full advantage of since: after most of the cheese has been scooped and scraped from the wheel, boil up some spaghetti, drain it, and dump it into the hollow wheel. A quick stir and a good dose of freshly ground black pepper is all you need for an exquisite dinner.

To pick a perfect wedge or wheel, definitely poke. The rind should yield under even the slightest pressure. And always serve the cheese at room temperature, taking it out of the fridge up to three hours in advance if necessary. If you're bereft of queijo da Serra in your area, you can order it online (see Sources, page 251) or for these recipes you can substitute Spain's queso de la Serena or an imported Brie or Camembert.

Azeitão (DOP) (ah-zay-*towhn*)

Some Portuguese swear by Azeitão, claiming it's even better than queijo da Serra. This raw sheep's-milk cheese is produced on small *quin-*

tas, or estates, cut into the vertiginous slopes of Estremadura's Arrábida mountains on the Setúbal Peninsula, about twenty-five miles south of Lisbon. As Azeitão ages, it moves elegantly from unctuously soft in its youth to firmer but eminently spreadable in later life, never losing its characteristic earthy tang and sweet floral overtones.

If you come up empty-handed at your cheese monger, ask for a soft or semi-soft sheep's-milk cheese such as Spain's queso de la Serena.

Serpa (DOP) (*sair*-puh)

One of the Alentejo's triumvirate of cheeses (the others are Nisa and Évora), Serpa is a raw sheep's-milk cheese. Traditionally it was made from the milk of merino sheep, but nowadays the milk of the more prolific Lacaune sheep is often used. Serpa, like most of Portugal's great cheeses, isn't coagulated with rennet but rather with the flowers of the cardoon thistle, a popular tradition on the Iberian Peninsula. The resulting paste is a light straw color with a distinctive buttery texture and a complex sweet-pungent taste when young; it matures into a firmer feel and spiky bite when aged.

If you can't find Serpa, ask your cheese monger for a semi-soft sheep's-milk cheese along the lines of a Spanish Torta del Casar.

Nisa (DOP) (*nee*-suh)

The second Alentejan sister is Nisa, a semi-firm raw sheep's-milk cheese that ranges from mild and nutty in its youth to intensely flavorful with tangy, barnyardy overtones in maturity. To mimic the flavor and piquancy of Nisa, substitute a lovely young Spanish Manchego, Malvarosa, or Roncal.

Évora (DOP) (*eh*-vuh-rduh)

Another noteworthy Alentejan cheese is Évora, from the UNESCO city of the same name. In fact, these small, salty wheels were once so coveted they were used as currency. Considered by many to be the best of the Alentejan trio, this old-style raw sheep's-milk cheese is occasionally eaten young, when it's soft and has a creamy, slightly salty edge. But more often it's preferred aged, when it's firmer and can bite back with its characteristic spicy tang. A good stand-in for Évora, both in texture and saltiness, is Pecorino Romano.

São Jorge (DOP) (sowhn *zhorzh*)

Hailing from the impossibly lush volcanic island of São Jorge in the Azorean archipelago, queijo de São Jorge (also commonly known as queijo da Ilha) is a holdover from fifteenth-century Flemish settlers who took cows with them from mainland Europe. Until recently, the cheese was made in the traditional manner, by small farm families; now a cooperative, which includes all but one farm, produces it. Still, by comparison to other countries, the production is extremely small. Aged two, three, or four months (only four-month-old São Jorge is considered DOP-worthy), the cheese ranges from mild and sweet to nutty and mouth-tinglingly piquant. It's also surprisingly versatile: it can be set out as an *acepipe*, or pre-dinner nibble; chunked into salads; or grated on top of gratins. Substitute an assertive English Cheddar or Cantal.

Requeijão (reh-kay-*zhowhn*)

Made from the whey of sheep's milk, Requeijão is similar in texture to Italy's famous ricotta, another whey cheese. The best Requeijão by far is made from the whey of queijo da Serra. In Portugal, you can find Requeijão everywhere, but at farmers' markets and small *mercados*, or markets, the artisan-made cheese is still sold nestled in little baskets. The Portuguese eat Requeijão as both a savory snack, sprinkled with salt and spread on bread, and a dessert, dusted with cinnamon and sugar or drizzled with honey.

If you can't find Requeijão at your local gourmet shop, pick up some excellent-quality ricotta. Before using it, drain it in a cheesecloth-lined colander to remove some of the excess moisture; Requeijão is a bit drier than ricotta. Be careful of Requeijão cremoso, if you see it—it's as soft as yogurt and isn't suited for the recipes in this book.

CLAMS *amêijoas* (uh-*may*-zhoo-izh)

Clams are the great codependent ingredient of Portuguese cuisine. They're found in classic dishes that pair them up with pork, such as the famous Alentejan-Style Pork with Clams (page 135) and the equally well-known Clams in a Cataplana (see page 92). They're also part of *açorda de marisco*, a shellfish and bread soup studded with mussels, shrimp, and sometimes scallops, which are prohibitively expensive in Portugal.

The most commonly eaten clams in the country are in the family that includes the Carpet Shell and Venus varieties. Small, delicate, and deliciously sweet, they also have a unique characteristic: they have two necks! Excellent substitutes are cockles, Manila clams (often marketed as Japanese cockles), and butter clams.

But make sure to buy the smallest you can—about 1¹/₂ inches across. In a pinch, tiny East Coast littlenecks will do, but they'll have to be served the moment they pop open, or they'll quickly turn to rubber.

CURED MEATS *carnes curadas* (kahnizh koo-*rah*-thizh)

If the symbol of working-class prosperity in this country was once, as Herbert Hoover said, a chicken in every pot, then, unquestionably, in Portugal it's a dry-cured smoked sausage in every pan. So ubiquitous are sausages, as well as hams, that until very recently nearly every country household made its own. My family still does here in the States. My uncle even built a smoker the size of a minivan in the middle of Somerville, Massachusetts, so we all could enjoy my grandmother's and aunts' truly incomparable sausages.

If you have the chance to buy Portuguese sausages at the market, make sure they're firm, not squishy. Spongy links mean a lot of fillers, and bloated ones are waterlogged. True artisanal sausages are bumpy with dry skin—sometimes with a harmless white bloom on it—and a deep smoky aroma. If your local specialty store doesn't carry them, see Sources (page 251) for purveyors.

Chouriço (show-*rdee*-soo)

It's my experience that chouriço is the favored link in Portugal. Made from chunks of pork loin with a good amount of added fat—the proportions are always the secret of the maker—plus loads of paprika, garlic, red or white wine, and hot piri-piri sauce, chouriço is first air-dried and then heavily smoked. It's served boiled, grilled, fried, or roasted. One of the showier presentations is firemen's sausage, where a link of sausage is doused with *aguardente*, a powerful distilled spirit, and set ablaze. Amid a great whoosh of flame, and shrieks from the table, the sausage's skin chars and blisters and the meat takes on a sweetness when dipped in the liquor.

Linguiça (leen-*gwee*-suh)

Some Portuguese may have conniptions when they read this, but nonetheless it's true: there's virtually no difference between chouriço and linguiça. They're made from the same basic ingredients in the same exact manner. Still, some Portuguese insist that linguiça is spicier, yet I've had some chouriço so hot it blisters your lips. Others maintain that linguiça is more finely ground or leaner than chouriço. Not necessarily true. After a decade of asking questions on two continents, I've come to the conclusion than any slight difference tends to be the result of the producer as opposed to nationally accepted categorization. The only consistent distinction is that linguiça is smaller in diameter, because it's made from the small intestines of the pig, while chouriço is made from the large. Oh, one other misconception: linguiça is not made from tongue, even though *lingua* is the Portuguese word for tongue.

For both sausages, you can substitute Spanish chorizo, but make sure it's the dry-cured version; Spain also makes a raw product. Be forewarned, though: Spanish links can be much fattier than chouriço or linguiça, so the fat will need to be drained or skimmed during cooking. Regarding the skin, you can leave it on or remove it—your choice.

Presunto (preh-*zoon*-too)

This dry-cured ham of Portugal has few equals. Its supremacy comes from allowing the pigs to gorge themselves for up to sixty days on cork oak acorns before meeting their fate, as well as from the laborious process of quick-salting, rinsing, long-term salting, and natural air-drying. This leaves the sublimely silky meat a deep red purple with superb marbling, ringed by a layer of opalescent ivory fat.

The country's two finest areas for presunto production are the towns of Chaves and Lamego, in the Trás-os-Montes region in the north, which rubs its hams with a coating of sweet paprika and olive oil before smoking; and the Alentejo, in the south, which prefers to keep its hams uncoated and unsmoked. For the Alentejan presunto, the hoof is left on to prove it comes from the famous *porco preto*, or black pig (see page 28). Presunto is served in thin slices on its own, in sandwiches, and alongside fresh fruit. It's also used in cooking to add a depth of flavor and a bit of a salty bite.

Unfortunately, because Portugal is still grappling with the United States over exporting presunto here, you'll have to settle for some excellent domestic versions (see Sources, page 251) or you can substitute Spain's jamón serrano (serrano ham) or Italy's prosciutto di Parma.

Note: If the cured ham you get is too salty, soak it in cold water for 5 minutes. Also, some of these recipes call for a $\frac{1}{8}$- or $\frac{1}{4}$-inch-thick slice of presunto. Depending on what part of the leg it's cut from, and therefore how big the piece, you may not need all of it for the recipe. It'll keep for several weeks in the refrigerator or up to two months in the freezer, tightly wrapped. Add it to cheese platters, omelets, or salads, or cut it into small cubes, fry, and sprinkle on baked potatoes.

GARLIC *alho* (ahl-yoo)

The Portuguese can't put enough garlic cloves, called *dentes*, or teeth, into their dishes. It's even part of *refogado* (see Lightly Sautéed Onions and Garlic, page 240), the foundation for nearly every savory dish in the Portuguese repertoire. Forget buying pre-minced stuff. Buy heads that feel firm and full for their size. If you happen to slice into a clove and see a slender green tendril, called the germ, growing in the middle, pop it out with the tip of the knife. It makes for a bitter bite.

HEAT *calor* (cuh-lord)

Heat is without a doubt the most taken-for-granted, and overlooked, ingredient in cooking. But it's, perhaps, one of the hardest ingredients to deal with. Throughout this book, I've specified precise degrees of burner heat and oven temperatures, as well as cooking times. But nothing's more variable than heat: my medium-high flame or 350°F oven inevitably won't be exactly like yours. Think of my instructions as guidelines. What you need to do is use your five senses. Does the Orange Cake (page 220) look deeply golden brown and spring back when touched? If not, let it stay in until it does, even if it takes 10 minutes longer in your oven. If the onions for the Tuna Spread (page 42) are cooking too quickly, nudge down the heat or take the pan off the burner for a while. Smell, touch, taste, listen, and watch: it's how my grandmother learned to be a great cook. She was illiterate, and she couldn't write a recipe—or even read this cookbook if she had wanted to—yet the memories of her food still haunt my family.

HERBS AND SPICES *ervas e especiarias* (*aird*-vuhz ee eh-shpee-suh-*ree*-izh)

Allspice *pimenta de Jamaica* (pee-*man*-tuh duh zhuh-*may*-kuh)

Because of its complex flavor, allspice is often thought to be a combination of warm aromatics that include cinnamon, clove, and nutmeg. But it's a spice unto itself. Although not often used in mainland Portuguese cooking, allspice, frequently in its whole-berry form, is a staple of Azorean cooking. Make sure to have it on hand for an excellent twist on Alcatra (see page 144), a classic beef braise from the island of Terceira.

Bay leaf *louro* (*low*-rdoo)

Another classic ingredient, bay leaf is found in many Portuguese soups, stews, and braised dishes. But a little bay goes a long way. Make sure to buy Turkish bay leaf if you can, rather than the more pungent and overpowering California variety. If all you have is the latter, use only half a leaf for each whole one called for in the recipe. All the recipes in this book were developed using the more easily found dried leaves, which don't have the bitter bite of the fresh version. Before serving, always remove the leaf from any dish except Amped-Up Red Pepper Paste (page 232), which pulverizes the

herb in a food processor. To order Turkish bay leaves online, see Sources (page 251).

Cinnamon *canela* (ka-*na*-luh)

Although the spice was first taken to Europe from Sri Lanka in the thirteenth century by Arab traders and returning Crusaders, no one has made better use of, or had a more insatiable appetite for cinnamon than the Portuguese. It has insinuated its way into savory dishes as well as countless egg sweets, many of which hark back to the Moors. If you can find "true" cinnamon from Ceylon, pick it up. Sweeter, lighter in color, and floral in scent, it simply trounces the closely related cinnamon stand-in spice, cassia, which is more widely available in the States. Make sure to have both ground cinnamon (*canela em pó*) and cinnamon sticks (*canela em pau*) on hand.

Cilantro *coentro* (koo-*ayn*-troo)

Although it's indigenous to southern Europe, cilantro is almost all but ignored by everyone on the continent except the Portuguese. And that's one of the great differences between Portuguese and Spanish cooking. Traditionally used extensively in the cooking of the southern provinces of the Alentejo and the Algarve, cilantro now takes the prize as the most popular herb nationwide.

When buying cilantro, root out the most tender, most fragrant bunches possible. At home, soak the herb well in a bowl of cold water to remove all traces of grit; lift out, leaving the dirt behind; then roll the bunch in a damp paper towel and store in a plastic bag in the fridge. It should last for at least a week.

Paprika *colorau* (koo-loo-*rahw*) and *páprica* (*pah*-pree-kuh)

Ah, another conundrum. The pepper family has always caused great confusion throughout the world when it comes to nomenclature. Considering that the Portuguese were responsible for distributing the fruit around the rest of the globe, after Christopher Columbus took it back from the New World, you'd think there'd be some sort of a unified naming system for them. Alas, there's not.

It's best to think of paprika on a scale from mild to hot. On the mildest end is *colorau doce*, which is made from ground, dried red bell peppers. Inching toward the hot end is *colorau*. Even closer to the hotter end of the spectrum is what the Portuguese call *páprica*, made from more piquant peppers in the same family. In Portugal, these spices aren't always used interchangeably. Many cooks prefer to use *colorau* for adding a terra-cotta color and just a touch of flavor to dishes. My maternal grandmother, vovó Costa, never let her soups or rice dishes leave her kitchen unless they were blushing with *colorau*. *Páprica* is reached for when more heat is required.

As you flip through these recipes, you'll notice I use Spanish smoked paprika a lot. I do this for two reasons. First, because it's been slowly showing up on spice shelves in Portuguese homes. But more important, because it's a gamble whether domestic smoked chouriço or linguiça will have the requisite brio to make a dish stand out, I call on smoked paprika to do some of the heavy lifting. It mimics that musky smokiness that pervades so many popular Portuguese dishes.

While living in Portugal, I was surprised to discover that *páprica*, and even *colorau*, can vary not just in heat but also in bitterness. Experiment a bit with different brands. For best results, I suggest buying the sweetest, least bitter paprika—both regular and smoked—you can find.

Parsley *salsa* (sahl-suh)

Parsley is second only to cilantro as Portugal's favorite herb. It's steeped in soups, tucked into braises, and sprinkled over entrées. When shopping, look for the flat-leaf variety with lush, tender stems and leaves. Rinse the herb well in water, then roll the bunch in a damp paper towel and store in a plastic bag in the fridge. It'll last for at least a week.

KALE *couve* (kove)

Arguably the leafy vegetable most associated with Portugal, kale is what lends the "green" to Green Soup (page 69), or Caldo Verde, which many consider to be the national dish. While several varieties of kale are grown in Portugal, the most popular, and the only one used in caldo verde, is *couve galega*. The leaves, which grow on tall woody stalks, are broad and flat—perfect for cutting into the whisker-thin shavings for the soup. To this day, cooks can find bags of pre-slivered clippings at markets such as the Bulhão in Porto, filled with bawdy farmers' wives and feisty fishmongers, or the Mercado da Ribeira, in Lisbon.

I find the kale sold in the States to be tougher and less tasty than that in Portugal. I've had greater success using collard greens.

LARD *banha* (bah-nyuh)

Banha is identical to our rendered leaf lard, the fat found around a pig's kidneys. It's pristine white and still widely used when cooking meats. Although it's a saturated fat, it's a far cry from the hydrogenated products loaded with trans fats so often used in this country. In fact, it's sublime. And with the recent studies undemonizing saturated fats, lard, used with a light hand, can add tremendous flavor to your cooking. Resist those commercial bricks lingering on grocery shelves, though. Instead, render your own (see page 247). The taste is infinitely better.

OLIVE OIL *azeite* (uh-zayt)

Until recently, when cooks thought of olive oil, Portugal didn't rush to mind. And for good reason. For quite a long time, many producers would leave heaps of the harvested olives sitting for days before pressing, kicking off anaerobic fermentation deep inside the mounds, a process that gave the oil a fusty odor and taste—something prized by the Portuguese. To add insult to injury, the Portuguese have always loved oils with high acidity (read: rancidity). I don't, nor do, it seems, the European Union and the International Olive Oil Council. The two groups clamped down, and now growers from the Alentejo, Ribatejo, the Beiras, and Trás-os-Montes—the four largest oil-producing regions—are turning out oils that can hold their own on the world market.

But rather than shelling out big bucks for bottles of top-shelf extra-virgin olive oil for the recipes in this book, pick up a bottle of less expensive extra-virgin oil or fine-quality virgin olive oil. Either is perfectly acceptable for the skillet, where its flavor is changed by the heating process and the foods being cooked. High-end olive oil should be reserved for drizzling over salads, vegetables, and soups just before serving so its flavor shines (see Sources, page 251).

OLIVES *azeitonas* (ah-zay-taw-nizh)

The Portuguese have what could be described as a love affair with olives. At parties, I've seen people moan when a bowl is set out and sneak an extra handful when the host or hostess isn't looking.

So in love with their olives are the Portuguese, they have many methods of preparing their favorite ones.

The beloved olive of the Alentejo is the Maçanilha, which gets the spa treatment around the town of Elvas, a stone's throw from the Spanish border. There the olives are washed daily in water for two weeks, then nestled in salt along with marjoram and plenty of fresh bay leaves. In the same region, the Cordovil and, sometimes, the Maçanilha olives are pitted and stuffed with almonds, garlic, red bell pepper, or capers. In Vila de Rei, in the dead center of the country, they're fond of stuffing their brined olives with bits of salt cod, cheese, or leftover pork, and they happily gild the lily by coating and deep frying them (see page 36). The folks in Vila Real and Bragança, in the north, prefer their olives, the black DOP Negrinha de Freixo, straight up—with nothing but a bowl for the pits.

In the sunny Algarve, in the south, the Maçanilha is used to create the delicacy *azeitonas britadas* (cracked olives). For this the green olives are split using stones and rinsed each morning in water for several weeks before being submerged in brine and flavored with lemon zest, garlic, and whatever herbs please the cook.

I've had good success substituting Spanish manzanilla for Portuguese green olives and Greek kalamata, Italian gaeta, and French niçoise for Portuguese black olives.

ONIONS *cebolas* (seh-*bow*-lizh)

Hands-down, the most popular onion in Portugal is the familiar yellow onion with its brown papery skin. Walking down the hill near my apartment in Lisbon in the morning, I'd see bags of them slumped against the doors of all the restaurants in the Alfama section.

Yellow onions have a more pungent kick than the seasonal sweet varieties such as Vidalia and Maui, which are better for eating raw. When cooked, though, yellow onions become marvelously sweet and add texture and layers of flavor to a dish. They're so important to Portuguese cooking that they're the base of countless dishes. Nearly every savory recipe begins with "*Faz* (make) *um refogado.*" *Refogado* is onion, and sometimes a bit of garlic, slowly cooked in olive oil until meltingly tender. I always have a jar on hand (see page 240) so I can plop a few tablespoons of the golden mixture into a pan and be on my way. Saves a lot of time during the week.

Considering that many supermarkets don't distinguish between yellow onions and the gigantic softball-size Spanish onions, here are the general diameters of onions called for in this book: small are 2 inches, medium are 3 inches, and large are 3¾ inches. When buying onions, pick those that are firm, feel heavy for their size, and have no soft spots. Store them in a basket in a cool, dry, dark place. Whatever you do, avoid the crisper of your fridge, which will cause them to spoil.

PEPPERS *piri-piri* (*pee*-rdee *pee*-rdee)

Piri-piri are fiery-hot little bird peppers from Mozambique, a former colony, that made their way to Portugal aboard the ships returning from the African coast and points farther east. Immigrants from Mozambique and Angola, another former colony, with their insatiable appetites for the pepper, sparked an interest in all things piri-piri on the mainland. Dishes from the classic repertoire include Grilled Chicken Slathered in Hot Sauce (page 118) and Grilled Shrimp with Piri-Piri Sauce (page 97).

Because fresh piri-piri peppers are impossible to find in North America, choosing the right chile to substitute can be a challenge. Chileheads will automatically reach for the hottest of the hot, but hold off: piri-piri peppers vary enormously. The ones used in Portuguese cooking clock in at about the 40,000- to 60,000-unit mark on the Scoville scale, developed to measure the heat in chiles. While piri-piri peppers are most definitely hot, they won't blow off the top of your head. Substitute fresh or dried red cayenne, tabasco, pequín, or santaka peppers. In your supermarket, look for those that rank a heat rating of 7 or 8 (on a scale of 1 to 10).

The greatest difference between Portugal's pigs—both black and not—and our own is that we've bred every last ounce of flavor and fat out of ours. The "other white meat" may be lean, but it can't stand up to the dishes in this book. I've made appropriate substitutions in the recipes by, for example, opting for pork tenderloin or even pork shoulder instead of hockey-puck-dry loin. In Portugal, pork loin is exceptionally tender and juicy. To get the most out of the pork recipes in this book, I suggest talking with your butcher. He may sell heritage pork, from free-roaming breeds of pigs that root out their own food and, as a result, produce better meat. You can also order excellent cuts of pork from online suppliers; see Sources (page 251).

POTATOES *batatas* (buh-*tah*-tizh)

What would Portuguese cooking be without potatoes? They're served everywhere in just about every form—boiled, puréed, fried, sautéed, and "punched." And while I risk making enemies by saying this, I happen to find the potatoes of the mainland superior in taste to those of Madeira and the Azores. Those of the continent are deep yellow with an incomparable earthy, nutty flavor. According to my friend, gentleman farmer Luís Vasconcellos e Souza, the most highly prized is the Dutch cultivar Mona Lisa, and, when planted in the rich soil of the Ribatejo region, it's the one reached for when making Punched Potatoes (see page 173).

To simplify things, there are two major types of potatoes in Portugal: "red" and "white," which refer to their skin color (a misnomer because the white potato actually has a yellowish skin) and correspond more or less in texture and taste to our Red Bliss and Yukon Gold, respectively. If you can't find Red Bliss, any round red boiling potato will do, as will any all-purpose yellow potato for the Yukon Gold. Floury potatoes, such as our Idaho spuds, are rarely seen in Portugal.

PORK *porco* (*poor*-koo)

From the Minho in the north to the Algarve in the south, as well as in Madeira and the Azores, pork rules. It's the national meat, and only in the Azores does pork have a rival, for there the beef is so exceptional it holds DOP status.

At the top of the pork pyramid is the Alentejan *porco preto*, or black pig, officially designated in Portugal as Porco de Raça Alentejana. It's an ancient, dark-skinned breed descended from wild boars, and the pigs are distinctive because they're allowed to forage for food, most notably acorns from the area's cork trees. The result is dark flesh full of sweet flavor and striated with succulent fat.

RICE *arroz* (uh-*rawsh*)

A staple of the Portuguese table, rice is the country's favorite starch. The average Portuguese eats thirty-six pounds of rice a year—versus thirteen pounds for other Europeans. In fact, it's so adored it's not unusual to have rice *and* potatoes on the same plate. My grandmother often made her soups with both, and my aunt Irena still serves creamy Tomato Rice (page 185) with roasted pork and potatoes.

What comes as a surprise to many people is that Portugal has been a large producer of rice for close to four centuries. The Ribatejo region and the area near Figueira da Foz, in Beira Litoral, are renowned for their rice paddies. One of Portugal's most common rices is the short-grained Carolino, a product of the Lezírias Ribatejanas area just north and south of the Tagus River. The rice, which sops up flavors and liquid superbly and is called for in many classic dishes, now carries the Indicação Geográfica Protegida (IGP) designation, meaning only rice from this region that undergoes a particular process can be called Carolino. Arroz Agulha is long-grained, and some Portuguese prefer it for use in side dishes.

With the exception of the Rice Pudding Redux (page 214) and the risottos, which call for Carolino, Carnaroli, or Arborio rice, any high-quality long-grain rice works well in these recipes.

SALT *sal* (sahl)

The most important thing I can say about salt isn't what kind to buy but rather how to use it. Too many cooks hold off salting—and peppering—their food until it's minutes away from being served. The results: negligible. You have to salt as you go. And don't forget to taste! Salt is so important because it brings out the flavors of food. Correctly salted food will never taste salty; it will taste only of the other ingredients.

I use coarse kosher salt in cooking because it's widely available and because I can control

exactly how much I'm using when I pinch some between my fingertips. There are excellent salts in central Portugal, but I find the best are in the Algarve. One of the finest is Belmandil (see Sources, page 251). The company has salt pans in the Parque Natural da Ria Formosa, a protected national park filled with marshes and lagoons that stretches from Faro almost to the Spanish border. The salt is still hand-harvested in the same backbreaking way it always has been, using salt rakes. Belmandil's two most sought-after products are *flor de sal*, a finest-grade sea salt for topping food at the table, and *sal marinho tradicional*, a coarser salt perfect for cooking and grilling.

SALT COD *bacalhau* (buh-kul-*yow*)

Because salt cod is one of Portugal's iconic foods, many think the Portuguese were instrumental in its discovery, which, alas, they weren't. Nearly five hundred years before the Portuguese began fishing for cod in the Grand Banks off the coast of Newfoundland, the Vikings had stumbled upon one of the world's largest caches of cod and figured out how to air-dry the fish. Not long after, the wily Basques cornered the cod market because not only did they have an uncanny ability to keep mum about where they were getting such top-shelf stock, they also figured out that salting the fish before drying it made it last even longer. Of course, they had a global (and unwitting) partner: the Catholic church, whose laws demanding a staggering number of meatless days practically lined Basque pockets with gold. Nonetheless, once the Portuguese, excellent seamen themselves, discovered the secrets, they wasted no time in catching up.

But salt cod today isn't like the cod of centuries ago—or even several decades ago. I remember when I was six years old walking into the local grocery, the floor strewn with sawdust, and watching my grandfather flip through big boxes of *bacalhau*, turning over massive hard planks of the stuff, trying to find the right cut, the right thickness. He'd thwack his hands together every once in a while to clean them, so thickly encrusted with salt were the pieces. Nowadays, the cod is mildly salted and in some cases, such as pieces that are sold in plastic bags, isn't even entirely dry. While it took two, sometimes three, days to desalt and rehydrate a loin of cod when I was a kid, it can now be done in as little as a day, depending on the piece and supplier.

The reason why salt cod is so prized in the Portuguese community, besides being a cheap and shelf-stable staple, is because the drying and salting gives a superior taste and texture to

an otherwise characterless fish. When a meaty slab of *bacalhau* is properly desalted and cooked, it will flake perfectly and have just the slightest toothsomeness.

But what exactly *is* properly desalted cod? To some, it's cod without any trace of salt. To others, like my father, it still has a bit of a salty bite. I prefer to remove almost all of the salt, so I'm left with something resembling a well-seasoned piece of fish.

Look for salt cod, preferably from Norway, in Portuguese, Italian, Greek, Spanish, or Latin markets. I've also had very good luck with several online purveyors (see Sources, page 251). Buy the thickest, firmest pieces possible; they'll make for a more substantial meal and a prettier presentation.

To reconstitute the fish, rinse well under running water to remove surface salt. Place the pieces in a large bowl and cover with cold water by 2 inches. Stretch plastic wrap over the top and refrigerate, changing the water several times, until the fish is sufficiently desalted for you. Take a nibble—it's perfectly safe to eat. If it's too salty, change the water again, and let it sit for a few more hours. The process can take anywhere from 12 to 48 hours, depending on the size of the fillet. Above all, bear this in mind: you can always add more salt, but you can't remove it from a finished dish.

To cook *bacalhau*, bring a saucepan filled with water—or, if you prefer, milk—to a boil. Reduce the heat to low, add the soaked cod, and simmer gently until it flakes easily when poked with a fork, 15 to 20 minutes, depending on the thickness. Drain in a colander and let cool. Remove any bits of skin, bones, and spongy ends, and the cod is ready to use.

TOMATO *tomate* (toh-*maht*)

Since the Spanish and Portuguese voyages to the Americas, tomatoes, a New World fruit, have been worshipped in the Iberian kitchen. They're pressed into service in an enormous number of dishes, from hors d'oeuvres to desserts. My personal favorite sweet treatment is Tomato Jam (see page 225). But the Portuguese draw very particular—and peculiar—lines when it comes to their tomatoes. For cooking, they prefer the drop-dead ripe *chucha* (sometimes spelled *xuxa*) variety, which is similar to our plum tomato. But for salads, sandwiches, and eating out of hand, they reach for firm globe fruit with a goodly amount of green tinge to them. One day when walking through the Mercado 31 de Janeiro in the Saldanha district of Lisbon, I asked my friend Teresa why the odd preference. She said simply, "We like the sweet and sour flavor and the firmness." For the recipes in this book, use the ripest, juiciest plum tomatoes you can find. If they're out of season, canned San Marzano are an ideal substitute.

Also you may notice I call for double-concentrate tomato paste in some recipes. And that's exactly what it is—a stronger, more flavorful paste. I find it lends a dish the kind of depth of flavor that Portuguese tomatoes do.

TURNIP GREENS *nabiças* (nuh-*bee*-sizh) and *grelos* (*greh*-loosh)

Many authors and cooks have stated incorrectly that *grelos* is the Portuguese term for turnip greens, sending generations of American cooks on disappointing trips through the supermarket. After speaking to many farmers and *engenheiros agrónomos* (agricultural engineers) and digging though countless produce cartons in markets, I discovered there are three major forms of *grelos* used in Portuguese cooking—and none is identical to our greens.

First are *nabiças*, the shoots of young turnips that are harvested for their leaves; the turnip isn't given a chance to develop. If a recipe requires them, you can safely reach for plain old American turnip greens. While not the same, they offer up a similar flavor and texture.

Next are *grelos de nabo*, by far the most popular *grelos*, which are formed when the turnip matures and its energy is sent into the stalks, causing them to start to bud with tiny yellow flowers. If a recipe calls for *grelos de nabo*, grab a bunch of broccoli rabe, which is more closely related to the turnip family than to the broccoli clan. It has the same mini heads, pleasant crunch, and slight bitterness of the Portuguese green.

Last are *grelos de couve*. Grown in a few regions in Portugal, they're the green shoots of particular cultivars of kale. Young collard greens are a suitable substitute.

LITTLE BITES

ACEPIPES

Spicy Pumpkin Seeds · *Fried Stuffed Olives* ·
Salt Cod and Shrimp Fritters · *Potato Skin Curls with Herbs* ·
Tuna Spread · *Sausage Spread* · *Green Olive Dip* ·
Mini Chicken Pies · *Goat Cheese, Walnut, and Honey Triangles* ·
Beef Turnovers · *Shrimp Turnovers*

SPICY PUMPKIN SEEDS

pevides de abóbora picantes

MAKES 2 CUPS

When I was a kid, this was a treat I'd look forward to every autumn. My father has always had a huge garden in the backyard, and squash is one of his favorite crops. After he harvested them, we pulled the seeds right from the guts of the gourds, washed them, and tossed them in spices before popping them in the oven. Because we had a limited supply, we ate them sparingly on cold Sunday morning walks. He's fond of calling them "Portuguese popcorn."

ATENÇÃO ✦ *For a more elegant take, I use shelled pumpkin seeds, which you can find in Latin or health food stores. You can use whole seeds for a more rustic crunch, as my dad does, if you wish. What I like about this recipe is that you can tinker with it, adding more or less of each spice to suit your taste. It's a perfect accompaniment to a crisp, effervescent* vinho verde, *nicely chilled.*

Humidity is the archenemy of these seeds. If they get a bit sticky after storing, reheat them in a 325°F oven for about 5 minutes.

NONSTICK COOKING SPRAY	$1^{1}/_{4}$ TEASPOONS SWEET SMOKED PAPRIKA
1 LARGE EGG WHITE	
2 TABLESPOONS PLUS 1 TEASPOON SUGAR	$^{3}/_{4}$ TEASPOON CAYENNE PEPPER
	SCANT $^{1}/_{4}$ TEASPOON GROUND CINNAMON
$1^{1}/_{4}$ TEASPOONS KOSHER SALT	
	2 CUPS SHELLED RAW PUMPKIN SEEDS

1. Heat the oven to 300°F. Line a baking sheet with a nonstick mat or parchment paper and coat with the cooking spray.

2. Whisk the egg white in a medium bowl until very foamy. Add the sugar, salt, paprika, cayenne, and cinnamon and whisk well. Stir in the seeds to coat, then lift them up with a slotted spoon, allowing them to drain, and spread in a single layer on the baking sheet. Discard any liquid left in the bowl.

3. Roast the seeds, tossing them several times with a spatula, until puffed and edged with brown, about 25 minutes. Transfer the baking sheet to a wire rack to cool completely.

4. Gently pry the seeds from the sheet and break up any large clumps into smaller shards. The seeds will last for 2 weeks in an airtight container.

FRIED STUFFED OLIVES

azeitonas fritas recheadas

MAKES 40 OLIVES

Fried olives are a favorite bite in Vila de Rei, a tiny town near Castelo Branco in the central region of Portugal. The fillings, or *recheios*, are endless, and, in fact, I use any extra tidbits that happen to be lying around the kitchen when I'm making them.

ATENÇÃO ✦ *Pop an olive in your mouth before coating them. If it's particularly salty, give the rest a quick rinse under cold water. You can stuff, crumb, and refrigerate these* acepipes, *covered with plastic, for up to 4 hours. Just before guests arrive, heat up the oil and fry. It'll take all of 15 minutes.*

FOR THE OLIVES

½ CUP ALL-PURPOSE FLOUR

2 LARGE EGGS, BEATEN

¾ CUP DRIED BREAD CRUMBS

40 GREEN OR BLACK BRINED OLIVES, SUCH AS MANZANILLA, KALAMATA, GAETA, OR NIÇOISE, DRAINED AND PITTED

VEGETABLE OIL, FOR DEEP-FRYING

LEMON WEDGES

FOR THE STUFFING—YOUR CHOICE OF

SHARDS OF COOKED SALT COD (SEE PAGE 30), DRAINED CANNED TUNA IN OIL, PRESUNTO, SERRANO HAM, OR PROSCIUTTO

MINCED HARD-BOILED EGG

FIRM SHEEP'S-MILK CHEESE, SUCH AS NISA, ÉVORA, OR PECORINO TOSCANO

ROASTED ALMONDS

ANCHOVIES

1. Fill three bowls, from left to right, with the flour, eggs, and bread crumbs. Stuff the olives with your choice of fillings.

2. Spear an olive with a toothpick and twirl it in the flour to coat evenly, swirl it in the egg, and then roll it in the bread crumbs. Use a fork to pop it off the toothpick onto a plate. Repeat until all the olives are crumbed. Those who like to get their hands dirty can eschew the toothpick.

3. Heat 1½ inches of oil in a medium saucepan until it reaches 350°F on a deep-fat or candy thermometer (see "Small Fry," page 39). Place a few of the olives at a time in the bowl of a slotted metal spoon and lower them into the oil. Fry in batches until golden brown, less than 1 minute. Fish out the olives with the spoon and transfer them to paper towels. Spritz them with lemon while still sizzling, if you like. Serve hot.

SALT COD AND SHRIMP FRITTERS

pastéis de bacalhau e camarões

MAKES ABOUT 36 FRITTERS

Pastéis de bacalhau, salt cod fritters, are a staple in just about every restaurant, *tasca* (small family-run eatery), and home in Portugal. When I lived in Lisbon, I'd spend afternoons at different cafés in the Baixa and Chiado districts, and there were always platters heaped high with the fritters pressed up against the front windows.

This version adds another Portuguese favorite to the mix: shrimp. It gives the fritters a sweetness and lighter flavor, ideal for those still acquiring a taste for salt cod. And, unlike many of the fritters I've eaten all over Portugal, some of which can be veritable belly bombs, these are exceptionally light, a result accomplished by separating the egg, whipping the white, and then gingerly folding it into the mixture.

ATENÇÃO *The fritters can be made up to 4 hours in advance and reheated, uncovered, in a 300°F oven for 20 minutes.*

1 POUND YUKON GOLD POTATOES, PEELED AND CUT INTO 1-INCH CUBES

KOSHER SALT

3 TABLESPOONS OLIVE OIL

1 MEDIUM YELLOW ONION, MINCED

1/2 POUND MEDIUM SHRIMP, SHELLED AND FINELY CHOPPED

3 GARLIC CLOVES, MINCED

10 OUNCES SALT COD, RINSED, SOAKED, COOKED, AND FLAKED (SEE PAGE 30)

1 TEASPOON PIRI-PIRI SAUCE (PAGE 233) OR STORE-BOUGHT HOT SAUCE, OR TO TASTE

3 TABLESPOONS FINELY MINCED FRESH CILANTRO OR FLAT-LEAF PARSLEY LEAVES

1 LARGE EGG, SEPARATED

VEGETABLE OIL, FOR FRYING

MILK "MAYONNAISE" (PAGE 237) OF YOUR CHOICE, FOR SERVING (OPTIONAL)

1. Plonk the potatoes into a large pot and cover with cold water by 2 inches. Add 1 tablespoon salt, cover, and bring to a boil over high heat. Cook until tender, 10 to 15 minutes. Drain, dump the potatoes into a medium bowl, and mash them well. Set aside.

2. Heat the oil in a small skillet over medium heat until it shimmers. Add the onion and cook, stirring often, until golden brown, about 10 minutes. Turn up the heat to medium-high and add the shrimp. Sear, stirring constantly, until just opaque, about 3 minutes. Add the garlic and cook for a minute more. Scoop the mixture into the bowl with the potatoes.

(recipe continues)

3. Drop the cooked cod into a food processor and pulse until finely shredded. Add the cod to the bowl, along with the piri-piri sauce and cilantro. Mix well and taste. Depending how salty the cod is, you may not need to season the mixture. If it tastes flat, add a healthy pinch or two of salt. Stir in the egg yolk.

4. Whisk the egg white to soft peaks in a small bowl, and gently fold it into the cod mixture.

5. Heat 1½ inches of oil in a medium saucepan until it reaches 350°F on a deep-fat or candy thermometer (see "Small Fry," below). Meanwhile, pinch off walnut-sized pieces of the cod mixture, roll them into balls, and set them on a large plate. Alternatively, you can use a 1-inch ice cream or meatball scoop.

6. Place a few of the balls in a slotted metal spoon and carefully lower them into the oil. Fry, in batches of 4 or 5, until golden brown, about 2 minutes. Fish out the fritters with the slotted spoon and transfer them to paper towels. Sprinkle with salt while they're still sizzling. Serve warm or at room temperature, with your favorite version of milk mayonnaise.

CLÁSSICO ❧ **SALT COD FRITTERS** *pastéis de bacalhau*

To make the original version of these fritters, omit the shrimp, increase the salt cod to 1 pound, and add the whole egg to the mixture (without whipping the white).

VARIAÇÃO ❧ **SALT COD AND SHRIMP FRITTERS WITH SALMON ROE**
pastéis de bacalhau e camarões recheados com ovas de salmão

Tuck ½ teaspoon salmon roe inside each fritter when forming it.

SMALL FRY

Whenever you deep-fry in small batches, there are a few things to keep in mind:

- It's best to use a thermometer, so you can maintain consistent heat.

- Keep the oil's temperature between 350° and 365°F.

- To add the food, place it in a slotted metal spoon with a heatproof handle, and lower it slowly into the oil.

- Always add the food a few pieces at a time, and turn them often. That way you can control the cooking, and the temperature of the oil won't drop drastically.

- Always let the oil return to the proper temperature between batches.

- Use a pan with high sides. It prevents splattering and is safer.

POTATO SKIN CURLS WITH HERBS

batatas com ervas finas

MAKES ABOUT 2 CUPS

I flipped over these addictive curls while sitting at Spot LX in the Casino Lisboa. When I asked the restaurant manager, my friend Nuno Faria, how they were made, he let me in on a little secret: Portuguese frugality made it difficult for the chefs, who were making potatoes for other dishes, to toss out the skins. So they peeled the skins thick enough to be fried up as a bar snack. The flavor comes from frying the curls in an herb-infused oil. The result? Every bite is full of crunchy potato and crisp flecks of herbs.

ATENÇÃO ❧ *You can use more or fewer peelings by simply adjusting the amount of the other ingredients. For every cup of skins, use about 1½ cups oil and ½ cup chopped fresh herbs.*

HERBED OIL

1 CUP ROUGHLY CHOPPED MIX OF FRESH HERBS, SUCH AS THYME, ROSEMARY, SAGE, FLAT-LEAF PARSLEY, CILANTRO, OR MARJORAM LEAVES

3 CUPS VEGETABLE OIL

2 CUPS THICK YUKON GOLD POTATO PEELINGS (FROM ABOUT 2 TO 3 LARGE POTATOES), DRIED WELL

KOSHER SALT AND FRESHLY GROUND BLACK PEPPER

1. Dump half the herbs in a medium saucepan and pour in the oil. Heat the mixture over very low heat until the herbs begin to sizzle, about 8 minutes. Remove from the heat and let cool completely.

2. Strain the oil through a fine sieve and discard the herbs.

3. Return the oil to the pan and heat over medium-high heat until it reaches 350°F on a deep-fat or candy thermometer (see "Small Fry," page 39). Carefully lower the potato peels into the oil and fry until golden and crispy, 5 to 7 minutes. Stir frequently and adjust the heat so they don't burn. Just before the potatoes are done, dump the rest of the herbs into the oil and fry for a mere 30 seconds to crisp them.

4. With a slotted spoon, transfer the skins and herbs to paper towels; toss to drain well. Season with salt and pepper to taste. Serve hot.

TUNA SPREAD

pasta de atum

MAKES ABOUT 2 CUPS

When you go to a restaurant in Portugal, you're usually served a few small plastic packets of *pasta de atum*—a forgettable tuna spread—along with other items that can include olives, marvelous bread, and aged or freshly made cheese as part of your table charge. Those pathetic little packets pale by comparison to this classier and tastier version. Smear it on bread, toast points, or plain crackers, or dip into it with a spoon when no one's looking.

ATENÇÃO ❧ *I prefer to use imported solid light tuna labeled "tonno." It gives the smoothest texture, short of using a mortar and pestle.*

2 TABLESPOONS OLIVE OIL

1 MEDIUM YELLOW ONION, MINCED

2 GARLIC CLOVES, MINCED

TWO 6-OUNCE CANS IMPORTED SOLID LIGHT TUNA IN OIL, DRAINED

8 TABLESPOONS (1 STICK) UNSALTED BUTTER, CUT INTO 8 PIECES, AT ROOM TEMPERATURE

3 TABLESPOONS TAWNY PORT

1 TABLESPOON FRESH LEMON JUICE

PIRI-PIRI SAUCE (PAGE 233) OR STORE-BOUGHT HOT SAUCE

KOSHER SALT AND FRESHLY GROUND WHITE PEPPER

1 TEASPOON MINCED FRESH FLAT-LEAF PARSLEY LEAVES, FOR GARNISH

1. Heat the olive oil in a small skillet over medium heat until it shimmers. Drop in the onion and cook, stirring often, until slick and deeply golden brown, about 20 minutes.

2. Add the garlic and cook for 2 minutes more. Remove from the heat and let cool to room temperature.

3. Combine the onion mixture, tuna, butter, port, and lemon juice in a food processor and buzz until a smooth paste is formed. Season with piri-piri sauce and salt and pepper to taste.

4. Scoop the spread into a serving dish and swirl the top with a spatula. Cover with plastic wrap and refrigerate for at least 1 hour for the flavors to marry. The spread will last for 1 week, tightly covered, in the fridge. Let return to room temperature before serving, garnished with the parsley.

VARIAÇÃO ❧ SMOKED TUNA SPREAD *pasta de atum fumado*

Substitute two 6-ounce cans solid light smoked tuna for the regular tuna.

SAUSAGE SPREAD

mousse de chouriço

MAKES ABOUT 2 CUPS

The Portuguese are just mad about their sausages and press them into service in just about every course. I've had many versions of this starter. Some contain a mixture of chouriço, *morcela* (blood sausage), and soft *farinheira* (sausage stuffed with flour and pork drippings). Others, like this one, rely solely on the flavor of the chouriço to carry the dish—so choosing an excellent sausage is imperative (see page 22).

Spread this on crackers or crisp bread thins freshly toasted in the oven. A dollop onto creamy scrambled eggs isn't out of the question.

ONE 10-INCH PIECE OF CHOURIÇO, LINGUIÇA, OR DRY-CURED SMOKED SPANISH CHORIZO

$2/3$ CUP MILK "MAYONNAISE" (PAGE 237) OR STORE-BOUGHT MAYONNAISE, OR MORE TO TASTE

5 TABLESPOONS UNSALTED BUTTER, CUT INTO 1-INCH PIECES, AT ROOM TEMPERATURE

3 OR 4 FRESH MINT LEAVES

RUBY PORT

CAYENNE PEPPER

KOSHER SALT

MINCED FRESH FLAT-LEAF PARSLEY LEAVES, FOR GARNISH

1. Cut the chouriço into 1-inch chunks. Drop them into a food processor and pulse until the pieces are finely chopped. Plop in the mayonnaise and butter, add the mint, and buzz until the mixture is as smooth as possible.

2. Take a taste. If the chouriço is lean, the mixture might be a bit dry. If so, add a tablespoon or two more mayonnaise. Add any combination of drops of port, sprinkles of cayenne pepper, and pinches of salt to suit your taste. If necessary, refrigerate the spread to allow it to firm up a bit; 15 minutes should do it. This will keep for up to a week in the fridge. Serve, garnished with the parsley.

GREEN OLIVE DIP

patê de azeitonas verdes

MAKES ABOUT 1½ CUPS

When I visited A Bolota, a lovely restaurant perched on the sweeping plains of the eastern Alentejo, this dip was brought to our table. As I nattered away with friends, I dipped, spread, and nibbled, until I realized I alone had eaten all of it. Later, when I became friendly with the cook, Ilda Vinagre, I watched her make it and was flummoxed when she whipped up its silky base: Milk "Mayonnaise" (page 237)—whole milk whirred into a smooth consistency with the addition of vegetable oil. I serve this as a dip with a platter of crudités, alongside crackers or bread, or, sometimes, as a topping for grilled fish.

ATENÇÃO ❧ *Don't make this in a food processor. The bowls of most processors are too large to allow the scant amount of ingredients to whip up to the right consistency. A small narrow blender, or a mini chop or handheld blender, works best.*

⅓ CUP WHOLE MILK

6 OIL-PACKED ANCHOVY FILLETS

1 SMALL GARLIC CLOVE, SMASHED

LEAVES AND TENDER STEMS OF
  6 FRESH CILANTRO SPRIGS

PINCH OF FRESHLY GROUND WHITE
  PEPPER

¾ CUP VEGETABLE OIL

⅔ CUP PITTED GREEN OLIVES SUCH AS
  MANZANILLA, RINSED QUICKLY IF
  PARTICULARLY SALTY, ROUGHLY
  CHOPPED

1. Add the milk, anchovies, garlic, two thirds of the cilantro, and the pepper to a blender and pulse to combine. With the motor running, pour the oil in what the Portuguese call a *fio*, or fine thread. Keep whirring until the oil is incorporated and the mixture thickens, 30 to 40 seconds.

2. Scrape the dip into a serving bowl and stir in the olives. Mince the remaining cilantro, sprinkle on top, and serve.

MINI CHICKEN PIES

empadinhas de galinha

MAKES SIXTEEN 2-INCH PASTRIES

In the quaint walled city of Estremoz, I happened upon a small bakeshop facing the town square. It was almost noon, and I was famished. Inside, in the glass case, were piles of chicken pies—an anomaly in this pork-rich region. Just out of the oven, they filled the shop with a rich, herby smell. I bought a few and sat in the park—just in time, too, as the townsfolk, probably called by the aroma, descended upon the place.

2 TABLESPOONS LARD OR OLIVE OIL

1/4 POUND CHOURIÇO, LINGUIÇA, OR DRY-CURED SMOKED SPANISH CHORIZO, MINCED

1 MEDIUM YELLOW ONION, FINELY CHOPPED

2 GARLIC CLOVES, MINCED

1/4 CUP DRY WHITE WINE

1/4 CUP CHICKEN STOCK (PAGE 243) OR STORE-BOUGHT LOW-SODIUM BROTH

1 TABLESPOON ALL-PURPOSE FLOUR, PLUS MORE FOR DUSTING

1/2 POUND DARK MEAT (THIGHS AND LEGS) FROM A ROTISSERIE CHICKEN, SKINNED AND SHREDDED (ABOUT 2 CUPS)

2 TEASPOONS FRESH MARJORAM LEAVES, MINCED

1/8 TEASPOON GROUND NUTMEG

PINCH OF GROUND CLOVES

KOSHER SALT AND FRESHLY GROUND BLACK PEPPER

ONE 17 1/4-OUNCE PACKAGE FROZEN PUFF PASTY, THAWED

1 LARGE EGG, BEATEN WITH 1 TABLESPOON WATER

1. Heat the lard in a medium skillet over medium-high heat until it shimmers. Fry the chouriço, stirring occasionally, until crispy, 5 to 6 minutes. Using a slotted spoon, transfer to paper towels.

2. Dump the onion into the pan and cook, stirring often, until softened, about 5 minutes. Add the garlic and cook for 1 minute more.

3. Turn the heat to high, splash in the wine, and cook until it has almost evaporated. Add the stock, sprinkle with the flour, and cook, stirring continuously, until the liquid thickens, about 2 minutes. Remove from the heat and fold in the chouriço, chicken, marjoram, nutmeg, and cloves. Season well with salt and plenty of pepper. Let cool completely.

4. Position a rack in the center of the oven and crank up the heat to 400°F.

5. Lighty dust a work surface and rolling pin with flour. Roll out one pastry sheet into an 11-by-15-inch rectangle, lifting it several times to prevent sticking. Prick it very well with a fork. Using biscuit cutters or drinking glasses, cut eight 3 1/2-inch circles and eight 2 1/4-inch circles. Tuck the larger

disks into a mini-muffin tin, with 2-by-1-inch wells, pressing the dough against the bottom and up the sides of each well to make a small, even lip around the top. Divide half the filling among the pastries. Brush the lips with the egg mixture, cap with the smaller disks of dough, and press together. Repeat with the remaining dough and filling.

6. Crimp the edges of each pie together with a fork, then place the 2¼-inch biscuit cutter over it and press down to remove the excess dough and make a clean edge. Brush the tops with the egg mixture.

7. Bake the pies until golden brown and puffed, about 15 minutes. Transfer the tins to racks to cool for 5 minutes, then remove the pies and let cool on the racks until slightly warm before serving.

GOAT CHEESE, WALNUT, AND HONEY TRIANGLES

triângulos de queijo de cabra, nozes, e mel

MAKES 24 PASTRIES

To celebrate my friend Alan Dunkelberger's visit to Portugal, I planned a colossal dinner for eight in his honor. It was to be my first dinner party abroad, so everything had to be perfect. I agonized over the menu, drove purveyors crazy with questions in bad Portuguese, and assembled a respectable batterie de cuisine. The afternoon of the dinner, though, disaster struck. My American food processor went up in flames. I'd miscalculated the metric conversions, so I had food for only six people. And, worst of all, the ingredients, which cost a bundle thanks to the sagging dollar, didn't behave as they do here.

My friend José Vilela rescued us by hosting us at his house. The only dish of mine that made it to the table was this fail-safe *acepipe* adapted from a tidbit at Oliver Café in Lisbon. It was the undeniable hit of the evening.

$^1/_3$ CUP CHOPPED WALNUTS	$^1/_4$ TEASPOON FRESHLY GROUND BLACK PEPPER
6 OUNCES FRESH GOAT CHEESE	ALL-PURPOSE FLOUR, FOR DUSTING
$1^1/_2$ TEASPOONS MINCED FRESH THYME LEAVES	ONE $17^1/_4$-OUNCE PACKAGE FROZEN PUFF PASTY, THAWED
$1^1/_2$ TEASPOONS MINCED FRESH ROSEMARY LEAVES	1 LARGE EGG, BEATEN WITH 1 TABLESPOON WATER
$^3/_4$ TEASPOON GRATED LEMON ZEST	HONEY
1 TO 3 TABLESPOONS WHOLE MILK	*FLOR DE SAL* (SEE PAGE 29)
KOSHER SALT	

1. Toast the walnuts in a dry small skillet over medium heat, tossing often, until golden brown, about 5 minutes. Turn out onto a plate to cool.

2. Mix the walnuts, goat cheese, thyme, rosemary, and lemon zest in a small bowl with just enough milk to make the filling creamy. Season with a pinch of salt and the pepper.

3. Lightly dust a work surface and a rolling pin with flour. Roll out one sheet of dough into a 15-by-13-inch rectangle, lifting it several times to prevent sticking. Prick very well with a fork. Cut twelve $3^1/_2$-inch squares, using a ruler and a pizza cutter or sharp knife.

4. Dollop 1 rounded teaspoon of the cheese mixture onto each square. Wet the edge of two adjacent sides with the egg mixture, fold in half to make a triangle, and seal very well with a fork. Place the pastries on a parchment-

lined baking sheet, cover with plastic, and refrigerate. Roll, cut, fill, and fold the second sheet of pastry. Let the triangles rest in the fridge for 30 minutes. Reserve the remaining egg mixture.

5. Position a rack in the center of the oven and crank up the heat to 400°F.

6. Brush the triangles with the egg mixture and bake until golden and well puffed, about 15 minutes. Transfer to a wire rack and cool until warm.

7. To serve, arrange the pastries on a decorative platter, drizzle with a little honey, and sprinkle lightly with *flor de sal.*

VARIAÇÃO ❧ Substitute pine nuts for the walnuts.

BEEF TURNOVERS

rissóis de carne

MAKES ABOUT 36 TURNOVERS

I got the recipe for these turnovers from two feisty elderly sisters who were selling them from a jerry-rigged stall during the Festa do Senhor Santo Cristo dos Milagres, Portugal's largest religious feast, on the island of São Miguel in the Azores. Traditionally, the meat is *picada*, or minced, by hand—as one sister was doing while the other was handing out turnovers to customers as fast as they came out of the oil—and I highly recommend undertaking the task. It's good for the meat's texture, and it's good for your soul.

I played with the recipe a bit and got rid of the egg-and-bread-crumb coating, which can make the turnovers heavy. Now there's nothing but a light crunch.

FOR THE TURNOVER DOUGH

2 CUPS WHOLE MILK

4 TABLESPOONS UNSALTED BUTTER, CUT INTO 3 PIECES

1½ TEASPOONS KOSHER SALT

2 CUPS ALL-PURPOSE FLOUR, PLUS MORE FOR DUSTING

FOR THE FILLING

2 TABLESPOONS OLIVE OIL

¾ POUND BONELESS BEEF CHUCK OR ROUND, MINCED BY HAND, OR ¾ POUND GROUND BEEF

1 SMALL YELLOW ONION, MINCED

2 GARLIC CLOVES, MINCED

1½ TABLESPOONS AMPED-UP RED PEPPER PASTE (PAGE 232)

1 TABLESPOON DOUBLE-CONCENTRATE TOMATO PASTE

½ TEASPOON GROUND ALLSPICE

PINCH OF GROUND CLOVES

¼ CUP DRY RED WINE

PIRI-PIRI SAUCE (PAGE 233) OR STORE-BOUGHT HOT SAUCE

KOSHER SALT AND FRESHLY GROUND BLACK PEPPER

1 TABLESPOON MINCED FRESH FLAT-LEAF PARSLEY LEAVES

VEGETABLE OIL, FOR DEEP-FRYING

1. Heat the milk, butter, and salt in a medium saucepan over medium-high heat until wisps of steam curl up. Lower the heat to medium-low, dump in the flour all at once, and immediately beat the mixture with a handheld mixer set to low, stopping occasionally to scrape the beaters clean, or with a wooden spoon—this takes some muscle—until the dough is cooked through and pulls away from the pan, 2 to 3 minutes. Transfer to a lightly floured work surface and flatten it into a large circle about ¾ inch thick. Cover tightly with a clean tea towel and let cool completely.

2. Heat the olive oil in a large skillet over medium-high heat until hot. Crumble in the beef and cook, breaking up the chunks with a wooden

(recipe continues)

spoon, until it's no longer pink, about 3 minutes. Using a slotted spoon, transfer the beef to paper towels to drain.

3. Lower the heat to medium, add the onion to the skillet, and cook, stirring frequently, until golden brown, about 6 minutes. Scrape in the garlic and cook for 1 minute more. Stir in the red pepper paste, tomato paste, allspice, and cloves. Add the beef and mix well. Splash in the wine and cook until it evaporates almost completely, so no alcohol taste remains. Season with piri-piri sauce and salt and pepper to taste. Stir in the parsley. Remove from the heat and let cool completely.

4. To assemble and fry the turnovers, set a small glass of water nearby. Lightly dust a work surface and a rolling pin with flour. Divide the dough in half, keeping the rest covered. Roll out the one half until $1/16$ inch thick. Cut out $3^1/2$-inch circles using a biscuit cutter or drinking glass. Dollop 2 level teaspoons of filling on each disk. Wet half the edge of each circle with your finger, fold the turnover in half, and crimp the edges closed with a fork. Repeat with the remaining dough and filling. Gather the scraps, reroll, and cut out more circles, if you have extra filling. The turnovers can be refrigerated for several hours or frozen for up to 2 months.

5. Heat 2 inches of vegetable oil in a medium saucepan until it reaches 350°F on a deep-fat or candy thermometer (see "Small Fry," page 39). Place 2 or 3 turnovers in the bowl of a slotted metal spoon and lower them into the oil. Fry, turning often, until golden brown, 2 to 3 minutes. Transfer to paper towels and sprinkle with salt while still sizzling. Repeat with the remaining pastries. In Portugal, these are often served at room temperature, but I've never met a guest who doesn't prefer them warm.

SHRIMP TURNOVERS

rissóis de camarão

These turnovers are a specialty of the Estremadura region, which straddles the Tagus River and includes Lisbon. Walk around Rossio, the city's grandest square, and you'll see trays of them in the windows of just about every café. Naturally, every customer has his preference and every cook has her version. This is mine. I prefer to make the filling with a quick stock made from the shrimp shells instead of the customary milk, for a more intense flavor.

$\frac{1}{2}$ POUND MEDIUM SHRIMP, PEELED AND DEVEINED, SHELLS RESERVED

2 TABLESPOONS UNSALTED BUTTER

1 SMALL YELLOW ONION, MINCED

1 GARLIC CLOVE, MINCED

$2\frac{1}{2}$ TABLESPOONS ALL-PURPOSE FLOUR

2 TABLESPOONS HEAVY CREAM

2 TEASPOONS MINCED FRESH CILANTRO LEAVES

PIRI-PIRI SAUCE (PAGE 233) OR STORE-BOUGHT HOT SAUCE

KOSHER SALT AND FRESHLY GROUND WHITE PEPPER

TURNOVER DOUGH (PAGE 51)

VEGETABLE OIL, FOR DEEP-FRYING

1. Pour $1\frac{1}{2}$ cups of water into a medium saucepan and bring to a boil over high heat. Turn the heat to low, add the shrimp, and simmer until just cooked through, about 3 minutes. Remove the shrimp with a slotted spoon and transfer them to paper towels to drain.

2. Add the reserved shells to the water, return the heat to high, and boil, partially covered, for 15 minutes. Meanwhile, finely chop the shrimp. Strain the cooking liquid into a measuring cup and discard the shells. You should have 1 cup of shrimp broth.

3. Melt the butter in a medium skillet over medium heat. Add the onion and cook until deeply golden, 7 to 10 minutes. Add the garlic and cook for 1 minute more. Sprinkle in the flour and stir until incorporated. Remove the skillet from the heat and slowly add the shrimp broth, whisking the whole time.

4. Return the pan to the heat and cook, stirring constantly, until the mixture thickens and loses its floury taste, about 3 minutes. Whisk in the cream, then add the shrimp and cilantro. Season with piri-piri sauce, salt, and pepper to taste. Remove from the heat and let cool completely.

5. Roll and cut the dough as in step 4 for Beef Turnovers (opposite). Fill each turnover with 1 teaspoon of the filling and then fry as directed in step 5.

SOUPS

SOPAS

Chilled Fava Bean Soup with Apples

White Gazpacho with Crab Salad   Gazpacho with Garnishes

Cilantro Bread Soup with Poached Eggs

Rich Fish Soup with Corn Bread Croutons   Purslane and Cheese Soup

Lemon–Mint Chicken Soup   Green Soup

Azorean Kale, Sausage, and Bean Soup   Stone Soup

Pumpkin Soup with Spicy Seeds

CHILLED FAVA BEAN SOUP WITH APPLES

sopa de favas com maçãs

SERVES 6

One spring evening, I was sitting in the restaurant at the Hotel Albatroz, in Cascais, with a magnificent sunset fading outside. But I barely saw it. What was stealing my attention was the soup. Until then, my fava experience—which I believed to be considerable—had consisted of enjoying them stewed, pickled, deep-fried, or tossed in a pepper-cinnamon sauce. But I had never encountered Portugal's favorite bean in a chilled soup. This dish, with its bright-green color, refreshing taste, and cool, smooth texture, forever changed my concept of that humble, hard-working bean.

ATENÇÃO ❧ *Fresh fava beans are notoriously seasonal, appearing for only several weeks in spring, but many Middle Eastern and Mediterranean grocery stores sell frozen fava beans. If you use them, there's no need for blanching, because the skins pop right off. Frozen baby lima beans can work in a pinch and require neither blanching nor peeling.*

3½ POUNDS FRESH FAVA BEANS, SHELLED, 1½ POUNDS FROZEN FAVAS, PEELED, OR 1 POUND FROZEN BABY LIMA BEANS

3 TABLESPOONS EXTRA-VIRGIN OLIVE OIL, PLUS MORE FOR DRIZZLING IF DESIRED

1 LARGE YELLOW ONION, DICED

1 MEDIUM YUKON GOLD POTATO, PEELED AND DICED

6 CUPS CHICKEN STOCK (PAGE 243) OR STORE-BOUGHT LOW-SODIUM BROTH

KOSHER SALT AND FRESHLY GROUND WHITE PEPPER

1 TABLESPOON UNSALTED BUTTER

1 SMALL SHALLOT, HALVED AND CUT THROUGH THE ROOT END INTO ½-INCH-WIDE HALF-MOONS

½ MEDIUM GRANNY SMITH APPLE, CORED AND CUT INTO THIN HALF-MOONS

---

1. If using fresh fava beans, bring a large pot of water to a boil. (If using frozen fava or lima beans, skip to step 2.) Add the fava beans, return the water to a boil, and blanch for 1 minute. Dump the beans into a colander and rinse with cold water. Nick each bean with a paring knife or your fingernail and squeeze to pop the bean out of its tough skin.

2. Heat the oil in a large pot over medium heat until it shimmers. Add the onion and cook, stirring often, until softened, about 7 minutes. Add the potato and cook, stirring, for 5 minutes. Pour in the chicken stock, bring to a boil, and cook until the potato is tender, about 5 minutes.

3. Reserve 18 of the smallest beans in the fridge for garnish. Add the blanched beans (or frozen fava or lima beans) and cook until tender, 3 to 5 minutes more.

4. Meanwhile, fill a large bowl with ice water and set aside. Using a handheld blender, or working in batches in a food processor, buzz the soup until puréed. For a smooth texture, pass it through a fine-mesh sieve into a medium bowl, pressing down with the back of a ladle. Place the bowl in the ice water until the soup is cool, then refrigerate for at least 1 hour, or up to 24 hours.

5. Just before serving, season the soup with salt and pepper to taste. Heat the butter in a small skillet over medium-high heat, add the shallot half-moons, and cook, turning several times with the tip of a knife, until edged with brown, 1 to 2 minutes. Remove from the heat.

6. Ladle the soup into six shallow bowls. Top each with several slices of apple and shallots and 3 of the reserved fava beans. Drizzle with olive oil, if desired.

WHITE GAZPACHO WITH CRAB SALAD

gaspacho branco com salada de caranguejo

SERVES 4 TO 6

One of Portugal's most famous shellfish dishes is *santola no carro*—a creamy crab salad served in the shell. This recipe, from my friend chef Fausto Airoldi, takes many of those ingredients—crab, mayonnaise, celery, brandy—and plunks them into the middle of this utterly refreshing, non-tomato gazpacho.

FOR THE GAZPACHO

- 1½ CUPS ¾-INCH CUBES OF DAY-OLD RUSTIC WHITE BREAD, CRUST REMOVED
- ⅔ CUP BLANCHED WHOLE ALMONDS
- 1 SMALL FENNEL BULB (ABOUT 6 OUNCES), STALKS REMOVED, CORED AND CHOPPED (RESERVE A FEW OF THE FRILLY FRONDS FOR GARNISH)
- ½ CUP CHOPPED SWEET ONION
- ½ SEEDLESS ENGLISH CUCUMBER, PEELED AND CHOPPED
- LEAVES FROM 4 SPRIGS FRESH OREGANO
- ¼ CUP PLUS 2 TABLESPOONS EXTRA-VIRGIN OLIVE OIL
- 3 TABLESPOONS WHITE WINE VINEGAR
- KOSHER SALT AND FRESHLY GROUND BLACK PEPPER

FOR THE CRAB SALAD

- 1½ CUPS JUMBO LUMP CRABMEAT, PICKED OVER AND DRAINED WELL
- ½ SMALL CARROT, PEELED AND MINCED
- ½ STALK CELERY, MINCED
- 1 TABLESPOON BRANDY
- 1 TEASPOON PIRI-PIRI SAUCE (PAGE 233) OR STORE-BOUGHT HOT SAUCE, OR TO TASTE
- ⅓ CUP MILK "MAYONNAISE" (PAGE 237), OR MORE IF NEEDED
- KOSHER SALT AND FRESHLY GROUND BLACK PEPPER
- 2 CUPS BABY SALAD GREENS (OPTIONAL)

1. Soak the bread in cold water until softened, about 5 minutes. Squeeze dry.

2. Toss the almonds into a blender and pulse into a fine powder. Drop in the fennel, onion, cucumber, oregano, and 1½ cups of water and buzz on high until liquefied. Add the wet bread, oil, and vinegar and whir again until the mixture is as smooth as possible. Put the blender canister, covered, in the fridge for 3 hours, or up to 6 hours.

3. Meanwhile, toss together the crab, carrot, celery, brandy, and piri-piri sauce in a small bowl. Cover with plastic and refrigerate.

4. When ready to serve, fold the mayonnaise into the crab mixture and season with salt and pepper. If you want it a bit creamier, plop in more mayonnaise.

5. Whir the gazpacho in the blender for a few seconds to froth it again. Season with salt and pepper to taste, and pour it into a pitcher. Make a small bed of greens, if using, in the center of each chilled bowl, top with the crab, and poke in a bit of the reserved fennel fronds. Place the bowls in front of your guests and pour the gazpacho around the crab.

GAZPACHO WITH GARNISHES

gaspacho com guarnições

SERVES 4 TO 6

This soup is from the south of Portugal, where the temperature can hover well over 100 degrees in summer. My friend, chef Ilda Vinagre, whose recipe this is, does something a bit heretical for a Portuguese cook: she prefers to *liquefazer*, or purée, this in the Spanish manner for a creamier texture. She also likes the taste of red bell pepper instead of the more plebeian green variety. She does maintain one tradition: she slips an ice cube into each bowl to stave off the punishing heat of the day. For something a bit different, I often add cubes of frozen tomato juice or frozen cucumber slices.

FOR THE SOUP

2½ CUPS ¾-INCH CUBES OF DAY-OLD RUSTIC BREAD, CRUST REMOVED

2½ POUNDS VERY RIPE TOMATOES, CORED, SEEDED, AND CHOPPED, OR ONE 35-OUNCE CAN WHOLE PEELED TOMATOES, PREFERABLY SAN MARZANO, WITH THEIR JUICE

1 LARGE RED BELL PEPPER, STEMMED, SEEDED, AND CHOPPED

½ MEDIUM SEEDLESS ENGLISH CUCUMBER, PEELED AND CHOPPED

1 GARLIC CLOVE, CRUSHED

LEAVES FROM 4 SPRIGS FRESH OREGANO

¼ CUP EXTRA-VIRGIN OLIVE OIL

1 TABLESPOON PLUS 1 TEASPOON WHITE WINE VINEGAR

KOSHER SALT AND FRESHLY GROUND BLACK PEPPER

FOR THE GARNISHES

1 MEDIUM TOMATO, CORED, SEEDED, AND CHOPPED INTO ¼-INCH CUBES

ONE ¼-INCH-THICK SLICE PRESUNTO, SERRANO HAM, OR PROSCIUTTO, TRIMMED OF EXCESS FAT AND CUT INTO ¼-INCH CUBES

½ MEDIUM SEEDLESS ENGLISH CUCUMBER, PEELED AND CUT INTO ¼-INCH CUBES

1 CUP ¼-INCH CROUTONS CUT FROM SOME OF THE REMAINING RUSTIC BREAD, TOASTED IN A DRY SKILLET IF YOU WISH

1. Soak the bread in cold water until softened, about 5 minutes. Squeeze dry.

2. Working in batches, dump the wet bread, tomatoes, red pepper, cucumber, garlic, and oregano into a blender and buzz until smooth. Add the oil, vinegar, and ¾ cup of water and whir again. Pass the soup through a fine-mesh sieve, grinding the solids with the back of a ladle to push through as much of the liquid as possible. Pour the soup into a large bowl, cover with plastic, and refrigerate for at least 2 hours, or up to 24 hours. When ready to serve, taste and season with salt and pepper.

3. Fill four small ramekins with the diced tomato, presunto, cucumber, and croutons. Ladle the soup into chilled bowls and encourage your guests to help themselves to the garnishes.

CILANTRO BREAD SOUP WITH POACHED EGGS

açorda alentejana

SERVES 6

This is an iconic soup of the Alentejo region, which cuts a huge swath through the middle of Portugal from Spain to the Atlantic. Like many old dishes, it's a paean to frugality. Traditionally the soup was made by loading a tureen of boiling water with fresh cilantro and hunks of day-old bread. Plenty of eggs were cracked in to poach—an inexpensive way of filling peasant bellies. This elegant take on the classic is made with toasted bread cubes on which the requisite eggs perch, and the broth is a blend of water and chicken stock for a richer taste.

10 CUPS (ABOUT 13 OUNCES) ³/₄-INCH CUBES OF DAY-OLD RUSTIC BREAD

¹/₂ CUP EXTRA-VIRGIN OLIVE OIL, PLUS MORE FOR DRIZZLING

KOSHER SALT AND FRESHLY GROUND WHITE PEPPER

7 GARLIC CLOVES

4 CUPS CHICKEN STOCK (PAGE 243) OR STORE-BOUGHT LOW-SODIUM BROTH

7 CUPS LIGHTLY PACKED FRESH CILANTRO LEAVES, PLUS 2 TABLE-SPOONS MINCED FRESH CILANTRO LEAVES (ABOUT 3 LARGE BUNCHES)

1 TABLESPOON WHITE VINEGAR

6 LARGE EGGS

1. Position a rack in the center of the oven and crank up the heat to 350°F.

2. Toss the bread cubes with ¹/₄ cup of the oil, salt and pepper to taste, and scatter them on a baking sheet. Toast them, tossing occasionally, until golden and crisp, about 20 minutes. Transfer the sheet to a wire rack to cool.

3. Meanwhile, bring a small saucepan of water to a boil, drop in the garlic, and blanch for 1 minute—this will mellow the garlic's bite.

4. Bring the stock and 4 cups of water to a roiling boil in a medium pot over high heat. Combine the 7 cups of cilantro, the garlic, the remaining ¹/₄ cup of oil, and 1 cup of the hot stock mixture in a blender and whir until lique-fied. Pour the mixture back into the pot and stir to combine. Take a taste, and season with salt and pepper. Cover the pot and keep the soup warm.

5. Fill a deep skillet with 3 inches of water, add the vinegar, and bring almost to a boil over medium heat. Reduce the heat so the water barely simmers. One at a time, break the eggs into a ¹/₄-cup measure and gently tip each one into the skillet. Poach for 3 minutes, or a bit longer if you prefer firmer yolks.

6. Meanwhile, make a small island of bread cubes in each bowl. Scoop the eggs from the skillet with a slotted spoon, trim any straggly bits, and place one on top of each mound of bread. Ladle the soup around the cubes, then sprinkle with the minced cilantro. Pass the remaining bread cubes for those who want a heartier dish.

RICH FISH SOUP
WITH CORN BREAD CROUTONS

sopa rica de peixe com broa

SERVES 4 AS A MAIN COURSE, 6 AS A STARTER

With such a delicate broth, this soup's name seems like a misnomer. But according to the chef at Arcadas da Capela at the magisterial hotel Quinta das Lágrimas, in Coimbra, *rica*, or *rich*, refers not to any heavy spicing or over-the-top fat content but rather to the jumble of succulent ingredients. At the hotel, the soup is served with oversized croutons made from *broa*, a hearty, jaw-exercising corn bread (see page 188). I discovered that American-style corn bread works better: its sweetness beautifully balances the slight heat of the chile.

ATENÇÃO ❧ *The success of this soup lives or dies on using a very light fish stock. A salty or fishy stock will overpower the delicate notes of the shrimp.*

FOR THE SOUP

1 POUND EXTRA-LARGE SHRIMP, SHELLED AND DEVEINED, SHELLS RESERVED

KOSHER SALT

2 TABLESPOONS OLIVE OIL

1 SMALL YELLOW ONION, DICED

1 MEDIUM LEEK, WHITE AND PALE GREEN PARTS ONLY, HALVED LENGTHWISE, THINLY SLICED, AND WELL RINSED

2 GARLIC CLOVES, MINCED

2 MEDIUM RIPE TOMATOES, HALVED, SEEDED, AND DICED

3 CUPS FISH STOCK (PAGE 245) OR STORE-BOUGHT LOW-SODIUM CHICKEN BROTH

2 TABLESPOONS DOUBLE-CONCENTRATE TOMATO PASTE

$1/2$ TO 1 SMALL MEDIUM-HOT RED CHILE, SUCH AS CAYENNE, TABASCO, PEQUÍN, OR SANTAKA (SEE PAGE 27), TO TASTE, STEMMED, SEEDED, AND MINCED

1 TEASPOON SWEET PAPRIKA

$1/2$ POUND WHITE FISH FILLET(S), SUCH AS TURBOT, RED SNAPPER, OR COD, CUT INTO 1-INCH CHUNKS

FRESHLY GROUND BLACK PEPPER

FOR THE GARNISH

2 TABLESPOONS UNSALTED BUTTER

FOUR OR SIX $1/2$-INCH-THICK SLICES STORE-BOUGHT CORN BREAD

12 FRESH CILANTRO LEAVES

1. Bring 2 cups of water, the reserved shrimp shells, and $1/4$ teaspoon salt to a boil in a small saucepan over high heat. Reduce the heat to low, cover, and simmer for 15 minutes. Strain through a sieve, and discard the shrimp shells. Set the shrimp stock aside.

2. Heat the oil in a large saucepan over medium heat until it shimmers. Add the onion and cook, stirring occasionally, until golden, 5 to 7 minutes. Add

(recipe continues)

the leek and cook, stirring often, until tender, about 5 minutes. Toss in the garlic and cook for 1 minute more, then stir in the tomatoes. Add the shrimp stock, fish stock, and tomato paste. Bring to a boil over high heat, turn the heat to low, and simmer, covered, for 10 minutes.

3. Add the chile and paprika and let burble for 5 minutes. Turn off the heat, add the shrimp and fish, and let sit, covered, for 20 to 30 minutes; the residual heat will cook the fish perfectly. Just before serving, season with salt and pepper.

4. Meanwhile, heat the butter in a nonstick skillet over medium heat until the foaming subsides. Add the corn bread and fry, turning once or twice with a spatula, until lightly toasted on both sides, 3 to 4 minutes total. Adjust the heat to avoid burning the bread. Transfer to paper towels.

5. To serve, ladle the soup into bowls, perch the croutons on the rims, and garnish with the cilantro leaves.

PURSLANE AND CHEESE SOUP

sopa de beldroegas

SERVES 8 TO 10

Purslane is a succulent summer herb that grows wild in Portugal, which is why this is a forager's soup. Traditionally, farmers in the Alentejo, from where this soup originates, have scoured the countryside, looking for edible plants for their dishes. The addition of slices of sheep's-milk cheese is my twist. Originally, hollowed-out dried cheese rinds were tossed in for extra flavor. I've further tweaked the recipe by adding presunto for bass notes and lemon juice for a spark of brightness, but at heart, it's still a homey dish.

For a nod to tradition, ladle the soup over a slice of toasted rustic bread and top it with a poached egg.

ATENÇÃO ❀ *Purslane can be bought in the summer at gourmet shops; you can also find it as* verdolagas *in Spanish markets.*

1/4 CUP OLIVE OIL

2 LARGE YELLOW ONIONS, CUT LENGTHWISE IN HALF AND SLICED INTO THIN HALF-MOONS

1/4 CUP MINCED PRESUNTO, SERRANO HAM, OR PROSCIUTTO

4 GARLIC CLOVES, MINCED

3 BUNCHES (ABOUT 1 1/2 POUNDS) PURSLANE OR 10 OUNCES WATERCRESS, THICK STEMS REMOVED, LEAVES WASHED WELL, AND ROUGHLY CHOPPED

2 POUNDS RED POTATOES, PEELED AND CUT INTO 1/2-INCH CUBES

8 CUPS CHICKEN STOCK (PAGE 243) OR LOW-SODIUM STORE-BOUGHT BROTH

1 TABLESPOON MINCED FRESH OREGANO LEAVES

1 TO 2 TABLESPOONS FRESH LEMON JUICE, TO TASTE

KOSHER SALT AND FRESHLY GROUND BLACK PEPPER

EIGHT TO TEN 1/8-INCH-THICK SLICES FIRM SHEEP'S-MILK CHEESE, SUCH AS NISA, ÉVORA, OR MANCHEGO

1. Heat the oil in a large pot over medium heat until it shimmers. Drop in the onions and presunto and cook, stirring occasionally, until lightly golden, about 10 minutes. Add the garlic and purslane and sauté until the garlic is fragrant and the leaves have lost some of their moisture, about 5 minutes. (If using watercress, cook the garlic for just 1 minute, and stir the watercress into the pot when the potatoes are finished cooking in step 2.)

2. Plonk the potatoes into the pot, pour in the chicken stock, cover, and bring to a boil over high heat. Reduce the heat to medium-low and simmer, covered, until the potatoes are just tender, 10 to 15 minutes. Add the oregano and lemon juice and season with salt and pepper to taste.

3. Ladle the soup into warm bowls and top each with a cheese slice and a grinding of pepper.

LEMON-MINT CHICKEN SOUP

canja de galinha

SERVES 6

José Maria de Eça de Queiroz, the great nineteenth-century Portuguese novelist and gourmand, immortalized some of the country's favorite dishes in his works. *Queijadas de Sintra*, sweet cheese tarts, were celebrated in his masterwork *Os Maias*, while *arroz com favas*, rice with fava beans, and *canja de galinha* were lionized in *A Cidade e as Serras*.

Despite what some cookbooks say, *canja* isn't synonymous with chicken soup spiked with lemon juice and laced with mint. There are also *canja de bacalhau* (salt cod soup) and *canja de conquilhas* (cockle soup), among others. And the *canja de galinha* Queiroz wrote about had nary a whisper of lemon or hint of mint. That being said, both are popular additions. This version goes one step further and adds tiny cubes of carrots for color and crunch.

ATENÇÃO ❧ *Don't even think of using store-bought chicken broth for this recipe. It'll never lend the right depth of flavor.*

8 CUPS CHICKEN STOCK (PAGE 243), OR MORE IF NEEDED

$1^{1}/_{2}$ POUNDS BONE-IN CHICKEN BREASTS, LEGS, OR THIGHS, SKIN AND ANY VISIBLE FAT REMOVED

$^{1}/_{2}$ LEMON

$^{2}/_{3}$ CUP RICE-SHAPED PASTA, SUCH AS RISO OR ORZO

$^{1}/_{2}$ MEDIUM CARROT, PEELED AND CUT INTO $^{1}/_{8}$-INCH DICE

3 TABLESPOONS FRESH LEMON JUICE

KOSHER SALT AND FRESHLY GROUND BLACK PEPPER

10 FRESH MINT LEAVES, STACKED, ROLLED UP LENGTHWISE, AND SLICED RAZOR-THIN

1. Bring the stock to a boil in a large saucepan over high heat. Turn the heat to low and add the chicken. If the pieces poke out of the stock, weigh them down with a plate. Gently simmer, covered, for 20 minutes. Remove the pot from the heat and let sit until the chicken is cooked through, 15 to 20 minutes.

2. Transfer the chicken to a plate to cool. Remove 1 strip of lemon zest with a vegetable peeler and add it to the pot along with the riso. Grate the rest of the zest and set aside. Bring the pot to a boil over high heat and cook, covered, until the riso is tender, about 10 minutes.

3. Meanwhile, shred the chicken into bite-sized pieces.

4. When the riso is cooked, remove the zest strip, add the shredded chicken and the carrot to the pot, and simmer for several minutes to warm. Turn off the heat, pour in the lemon juice, and stir. Season with salt and pepper to taste.

5. Ladle the soup into bowls, scatter with the mint and reserved grated zest, and serve immediately, before the lemon loses its zing.

GREEN SOUP

caldo verde

SERVES 6 TO 8

This is such a beloved recipe, it's called the national dish of Portugal. And it has been the cause of plenty of fisticuffs over the years, at least in my neck of the woods. Growing up, every Portuguese kid I knew defended his mother's *caldo verde*, insisting it was the best, lest blood be drawn.

Traditionally, the soup, from the Minho region, is made with just water, and the onion and potato are dropped in raw to cook as the broth simmers. Adding chicken stock and sautéing the vegetables along with garlic gives the soup more layers of flavor. Also, rather than drizzling olive oil on top, I use the pan drippings from the chouriço to lend smokiness and a bit of color.

Custom dictates the soup be served with one—and just one—slice of sausage. Big deal. I'd rather fight than stint on the tasty chouriço.

ATENÇÃO ❧ Caldo verde *has a tendency to thicken after being refrigerated, so add a bit of stock or water to leftover soup when reheating.*

---

7 TABLESPOONS OLIVE OIL

1 LARGE YELLOW ONION, CHOPPED

1 POUND YUKON GOLD POTATOES, PEELED AND DICED

2 GARLIC CLOVES, MINCED

4 CUPS CHICKEN STOCK (PAGE 243) OR STORE-BOUGHT LOW-SODIUM BROTH

1 BUNCH COLLARD GREENS OR KALE (ABOUT 1 POUND), THICK CENTER STEMS AND FIBROUS VEINS REMOVED

1 TABLESPOON CIDER VINEGAR (OPTIONAL)

KOSHER SALT AND FRESHLY GROUND WHITE PEPPER

EIGHTEEN OR TWENTY-FOUR $\frac{1}{4}$-INCH-THICK SLICES CHOURIÇO, LINGUIÇA, OR DRY-CURED SMOKED SPANISH CHORIZO

---

1. Heat 2 tablespoons of the oil in a large pot over medium heat until it shimmers. Dump in the onion and cook, stirring frequently, until light golden, about 10 minutes. Drop in the potatoes and cook, stirring often, until they start to spot with color, about 7 minutes. Add the garlic and cook for 1 minute more.

2. Pour in the chicken stock and 3 cups of water and bring to a boil over high heat. Reduce the heat to medium-low, cover, and simmer until the potatoes are falling-apart tender, 20 to 25 minutes.

3. Meanwhile, stack several collard leaves, roll them lengthwise into a tight cigar shape, and cut crosswise into whisker-thin slices. Repeat with the rest

(recipe continues)

of the greens. If the strands are so long they're unwieldy, cut them in half to avoid having wisps of collards dangling from your lips while eating.

4. Purée the soup using a handheld blender, or liquefy in batches in a food processor. Return it to the pot, and bring it back to a boil. Turn the heat to low, stir in the greens, and simmer, uncovered, until just tender, 5 to 10 minutes. Swirl in the vinegar, if using. Season well with salt and pepper.

5. Meanwhile, heat the remaining 5 tablespoons of olive oil in a small skillet over medium heat until it shimmers. Add the chouriço and cook until crispy, 3 to 5 minutes. Transfer to paper towels. Let the chouriço oil cool a bit.

6. To serve, ladle the soup into warm bowls, crown each with 3 slices of chouriço, and drizzle some of the flavored oil from the skillet over the top.

CLÁSSICO ❧ Plonk the potatoes, onion, and garlic into the pot, pour in 7 cups of water, and bring to a boil over high heat. Reduce the heat to medium-low, cover, and simmer until the potatoes are tender, as in step 2. Purée the mixture, as in step 4. Use only 6 or 8 slices of chouriço, and, instead of browning them in oil, add them to the broth when you add the collard clippings. To serve, ladle the soup into the bowls, fishing out a slice of chouriço for each. Finish the dish by drizzling each bowl with a swirl of a grassy extra-virgin olive oil.

AZOREAN KALE, SAUSAGE, AND BEAN SOUP

sopa de couve

SERVES 8 TO 10

If the mainland's Green Soup (page 69) is an uptown kale soup, this Azorean version is definitely its downtown and more rugged cousin. This is my mom's recipe, which she's been making for almost fifty years. What I like about it, and what my mother always insists on, is that it has a sizable amount of chouriço—not the miserly single slice of a bowl of classic *caldo verde*. As odd as it may sound, try reheating a few ladlefuls for breakfast on a cold morning, as my dad does. It'll hold you better than oatmeal.

$1\frac{1}{4}$ CUPS DRIED RED KIDNEY BEANS, PICKED OVER, RINSED, AND SOAKED OVERNIGHT IN WATER TO COVER BY 3 INCHES

2 TABLESPOONS OLIVE OIL, OR MORE IF NEEDED

12 OUNCES CHOURIÇO, LINGUIÇA, OR DRY-CURED SMOKED SPANISH CHORIZO, CUT INTO $\frac{1}{4}$-INCH COINS

2 LARGE YELLOW ONIONS, CHOPPED

1 TURKISH BAY LEAF

3 GARLIC CLOVES, MINCED

$\frac{1}{2}$ TEASPOON CRUSHED RED PEPPER FLAKES

4 CUPS BEEF STOCK (PAGE 244) OR LOW-SODIUM STORE-BOUGHT BROTH

$1\frac{1}{2}$ POUNDS RED POTATOES, PEELED AND CUT INTO $\frac{1}{2}$-INCH CUBES

$\frac{1}{2}$ POUND COLLARD GREENS OR KALE, THICK CENTER STEMS AND FIBROUS VEINS REMOVED, ROUGHLY CHOPPED

KOSHER SALT AND FRESHLY GROUND BLACK PEPPER

1. Drain the beans, dump them into a medium saucepan, and cover with water. Bring to a boil, then reduce the heat to low and simmer, partially covered, until the beans are tender but still hold their shape, about 45 minutes. Drain and set aside.

2. Meanwhile, heat the olive oil in a large pot over medium heat until it shimmers. Toss in the chouriço and cook until browned, 7 to 10 minutes. Fish out the slices with a slotted spoon and transfer to paper towels. Pour off all but 3 tablespoons of fat from the pot, or, if the pot is dry, drizzle in more oil so you have 3 tablespoons. Add the onions and bay leaf and cook, stirring often, until the onions are deeply golden brown, 20 to 25 minutes. Adjust the heat as necessary to prevent the onions from burning.

3. Add the garlic and red pepper flakes and cook for 1 minute. Pour in the beef stock and 5 cups of water, add the potatoes, and bring to a boil over high heat. Reduce the heat to low and simmer, covered, until the potatoes are just tender, 10 to 12 minutes.

(recipe continues)

4. While the soup is simmering, spoon a third of the beans and a bit of the soup broth into a food processor. Pulse to make a loose paste, then, if desired, pass the paste through a sieve. Straining the paste gives the dish extra body without errant bean skins floating in your soup. It's entirely optional but, I think, preferable.

5. When the potatoes are cooked, stir in the collards, chouriço, bean paste, and beans. Turn off the heat and let the soup sit for 10 minutes to marry the flavors.

6. Remove the bay leaf, season the soup with salt and pepper to taste, and ladle into warm bowls.

VARIAÇÃO ❧ A HEARTIER AZOREAN KALE, SAUSAGE, AND BEAN SOUP
sopa de couve com mais substância

For a more substantial dish, in step 5 add leftover, falling-apart-tender meat from the Braised Beef Shanks (page 144) or shredded bits from a cooked ham hock or two. For more vegetables, cut carrots, turnips, or parsnips into ½-inch cubes and add them to the soup in step 3, after adding the stock and water. Cook them until firm-tender then add the potatoes and continue with the recipe.

STONE SOUP

sopa de pedra

SERVES 8 TO 10

This soup is famous as much for the enduring folktale attached to it (see "The Fable of Stone Soup," opposite) as for its hearty, soul-satisfying taste. Any combination of vegetables will do, but those included here are some of the classics. The dish is vastly improved when left to mellow in the fridge overnight.

5 CUPS BEEF STOCK (PAGE 244) OR LOW-SODIUM STORE-BOUGHT BROTH

1½ POUNDS BABY BACK (PORK LOIN) RIBS, SILVERY MEMBRANE ON THE BONE SIDE REMOVED, CUT INTO INDIVIDUAL RIBS

3 GARLIC CLOVES, SMASHED

1 TURKISH BAY LEAF

1½ CUPS DRIED RED KIDNEY BEANS, PICKED OVER, RINSED, AND SOAKED OVERNIGHT IN ENOUGH WATER TO COVER BY 3 INCHES

2 LARGE CARROTS, PEELED AND SLICED INTO ¼-INCH COINS

2 MEDIUM YELLOW ONIONS, CUT IN HALF LENGTHWISE AND SLICED INTO VERY THIN HALF-MOONS

1¼ POUNDS MEDIUM RED POTATOES, PEELED AND CUT INTO ½-INCH CUBES

1 MEDIUM TURNIP, PEELED AND CUT INTO ½-INCH CUBES

¾ POUND CHOURIÇO, LINGUIÇA, OR DRY-CURED SMOKED SPANISH CHORIZO, CUT INTO ¼-INCH COINS

½ MEDIUM HEAD OF CABBAGE, CUT IN HALF, CORED, AND THINLY SLICED

KOSHER SALT AND FRESHLY GROUND BLACK PEPPER

1. Bring the stock and 5 cups of water to a boil in a large pot over high heat. Add the ribs, garlic, and bay leaf, reduce the heat to medium-low, and simmer, partially covered, skimming any unsightly gray scum from the top, until the meat is tender and pulls easily from the bone, 45 minutes to 1 hour. Transfer the ribs to a plate to cool.

2. Meanwhile, drain the beans, dump them into a medium saucepan, and cover with water. Bring to a boil, then reduce the heat to low and simmer, partially covered, until the beans are tender but still hold their shape, about 45 minutes. Drain and set aside.

3. Drop the carrots and onions into the pot and continue simmering, partially covered, for 15 minutes. Stir in the potatoes and turnip and simmer until tender, 10 to 15 minutes more.

4. Meanwhile, once the ribs are cool, shred the meat and toss it back into the pot, discarding the bones.

5. Scoop the cooked beans, chouriço, and cabbage into the soup and turn the heat to high to warm them, about 5 minutes. Remove the bay leaf and season the soup generously with salt and pepper. Serve in warm bowls.

THE FABLE OF STONE SOUP

One winter's day, a tired, hungry stranger came into a tiny village near the town of Almeirim in the province of Ribatejo and knocked on a door. A woman with a face like leathery smoked ham cracked it open and peered out.

"Please, *minha senhora*," said the old stranger, holding his hat, "would you have any food to share?"

The ham-faced woman heaved her huge body against the door, closing it firmly. "No, we're all poor here, with barely enough for ourselves," she shouted. "Go away." Dejected, the stranger went to another house, where, through a window, he saw a sad young man eating a small biscuit. He rapped on the glass.

"Excuse me, *senhor*, would you happen to have another biscuit for a hungry traveler?"

The man simply shook his head and walked away from the window. The stranger went from house to house and met the same fate. Finally, exhausted, he built a fire in the square and pulled a soup kettle from his wagon. Doors began opening, and the townsfolk slowly gathered. Only when he knew all were near did the man reach into his pocket and pull out a stone, which he ceremoniously placed in the kettle.

"What are you doing?" asked the youngest villager.

"Making stone soup," he replied, pouring in a bucket of water from the town well. Some sniggered, thinking the old man a fool. "But it would certainly taste better with a bit of cabbage," he said.

An old woman, entranced by his work, hobbled to her house and returned, thrusting a small head of cabbage at him. "Here," she said, "will this do?"

"Perfectly," he said, smiling.

As he ran down his wish list of ingredients—sausages, pork ribs, potatoes, carrots, onions, garlic, bay leaf—the townsfolk, now spellbound, brought them all to him. Slack-jawed, they watched as he ladled out some soup for himself and then filled bowl after bowl held out to him.

When the kettle was empty, he grabbed his stone, cleaned it off, and dropped it back into his pocket. While the normally taciturn villagers were enjoying each other's company, the stranger slipped away, only the youngest villager noticing.

PUMPKIN SOUP WITH SPICY SEEDS

sopa de abóbora com pevides picantes

SERVES 8

The gourd family is a favorite of the frugal Portuguese, as the fruit can be picked and then kept for months. A curious storage technique, which I discovered during an autumn trip through the vertiginous rural side of the island of Madeira, is to line up the colorful globes on a house's tiled roof.

This is an adaptation of the soup I thoroughly enjoyed while dining with Dirk Niepoort, scion of the Niepoort wine and port family, at his *quinta*, or estate, in the Alto Douro. It calls for butternut squash, the closest in taste to a Portuguese pumpkin. The spicy seeds are my father's doing.

4 POUNDS BUTTERNUT SQUASH, PEELED, SEEDED, AND CUT INTO 1-INCH CHUNKS

2 MEDIUM YELLOW ONIONS, QUARTERED

3 GARLIC CLOVES, CRUSHED

4 FRESH SAGE LEAVES

3 TABLESPOONS OLIVE OIL

KOSHER SALT AND FRESHLY GROUND BLACK PEPPER

5 CUPS CHICKEN STOCK (PAGE 243) OR LOW-SODIUM STORE-BOUGHT BROTH

$3/4$ TEASPOON GROUND CUMIN

$1^1/_2$ TABLESPOONS WHITE WINE VINEGAR

$1/2$ CUP SPICY PUMPKIN SEEDS (PAGE 34), FOR SERVING

1. Position a rack in the center of the oven and crank up the heat to 400°F.

2. Toss the squash, onions, garlic, and sage leaves with the oil on a large rimmed baking sheet. Season well with salt and pepper, toss again, and jiggle into an even layer. Roast the vegetables, flipping them occasionally with a spatula, until the squash is very tender, the onions are edged with brown, and the sage has shriveled but not burned, 50 to 70 minutes, depending on how firm the squash is.

3. Working in batches, scoop the vegetables into a blender or food processor, tip in a ladleful or two of the stock, and whirl until smooth. Scrape the soup into a large bowl. Stir in the rest of the stock and 3 cups of water.

4. Pour the soup through a fine-mesh sieve into a large saucepan, grinding the solids with the back of a ladle to get every bit of squash. Don't cheat here—it takes time, but, I assure you, the velvety texture is worth it. Discard the little bit of solids you can't force through. Bring the soup to a gentle simmer over medium-low heat, sprinkle in the cumin, and let burble until hot, about 10 minutes. Season with salt and pepper if needed, and stir in the vinegar.

5. To serve, ladle the soup into warm bowls and garnish with the spicy pumpkin seeds. Rush to the table.

FISH AND SHELLFISH

PEIXES E MARISCOS

Sea Bass with Fennel and Orange ❧ Trout and Presunto Napoleons ❧

Olive Oil–Poached Fresh Cod with Roasted Tomato Sauce ❧

Skate with Leeks in Saffron Broth ❧ Seared Skate in Garlic-Pepper Oil ❧

Kettle of Fish ❧ Clams in a Cataplana ❧ Stuffed Squid ❧

Grilled Shrimp with Piri-Piri Sauce ❧ Curried Mussels ❧

Warm Baby Octopus and Potato Salad ❧

Salt Cod of My Youth ❧ Mini Salt Cod Sandwiches ❧

Salt Cod in a Potato Jacket

SEA BASS WITH FENNEL AND ORANGE

robalo com funcho e laranja

SERVES 4

This is an adaptation of a recipe from Miguel Castro e Silva, chef at Bull & Bear in Porto—one of the most acclaimed restaurants in Portugal. It's what good fish cookery is all about: simplicity. I love the intense, fresh flavors and the fact that I'm in and out of the kitchen in less half an hour with a company-quality meal worth blogging (and bragging) about.

3 ORANGES

$\frac{1}{2}$ SMALL FENNEL BULB, STALKS REMOVED, CORED AND THINLY SLICED (RESERVE A FEW OF THE FRILLY FRONDS FOR GARNISH)

$1\frac{1}{4}$ CUPS CHICKEN STOCK (PAGE 243) OR STORE-BOUGHT LOW-SODIUM BROTH

$1\frac{1}{2}$ TEASPOONS CORNSTARCH, MIXED WITH 3 TABLESPOONS COLD WATER

KOSHER SALT AND FRESHLY GROUND BLACK PEPPER

FOUR 6-OUNCE SEA BASS FILLETS (ABOUT 1 INCH THICK), SKIN ON

2 TABLESPOONS OLIVE OIL

1 SMALL TOMATO, PEELED, CORED, SEEDED, AND CUT INTO $\frac{1}{4}$-INCH CUBES (SEE PAGE 91)

1. Juice 2 of the oranges; you should have $\frac{1}{2}$ cup. Set aside. Cut off the top and bottom of the remaining orange and set it on a work surface. Using a paring knife, start at the top of the orange and follow the curve of the fruit to remove the peel and white pith in wide strips. Slice between the membranes of the orange sections to release them. Set aside. Chop the fennel fronds and set aside as well.

2. Pour the chicken stock and orange juice into a small saucepan, bring to a boil, and cook until reduced to about 1 cup. Add the cornstarch mixture and fennel slices and boil, stirring constantly, for 1 minute more. Remove from the heat, and season the sauce with salt and pepper to taste.

3. Pat the fillets dry and season with salt and pepper. Heat the oil in a large nonstick skillet over medium-high heat until hot. Sear the fish, skin side down, pressing lightly with a spatula to prevent curling, until crispy, about 4 minutes. Flip and cook until just opaque in the center, about 4 minutes more.

4. Just before serving, drop the tomato and the orange sections into the warm sauce. To serve, arrange the fillets on four warm plates, spoon the sauce around and on top, and shower with some chopped fennel fronds. Waste no time getting the fish to the table.

TROUT AND PRESUNTO NAPOLEONS

trutas à moda moderna de bragança

SERVES 6

Traditionalists from the town of Bragança, in Trás-os-Montes, from where this dish hails, insist that whole trout be wrapped in a few slices of presunto and seared in a skillet. I freshened up the recipe, to make a quick, elegant meal with all the same flavors plus the added texture of crisp skin and without the problem of any fish eyes staring up at you condemningly.

SIX 6-OUNCE TROUT FILLETS, SKIN ON

KOSHER SALT AND FRESHLY GROUND
   BLACK PEPPER

ALL-PURPOSE FLOUR, FOR DREDGING

5 TABLESPOONS UNSALTED BUTTER,
   PLUS MORE IF NEEDED

6 WAFER-THIN SLICES PRESUNTO,
   SERRANO HAM, OR PROSCIUTTO, CUT
   FROM THE LARGE END OF THE HAM

OLIVE OIL

SIX $^{1}/_{2}$-INCH-THICK LEMON SLICES,
   PLUS MORE LEMON FOR SPRITZING

$^{2}/_{3}$ CUP DRY WHITE WINE

$^{1}/_{2}$ TEASPOON GRATED LEMON ZEST

1 TABLESPOON MINCED FRESH
   FLAT-LEAF PARSLEY LEAVES

1. Heat the oven to warm, and slip in a wire rack set on a baking sheet.

2. Pat the fillets dry, season well with salt and pepper, and coat them with flour, shaking off the excess. Heat 3 tablespoons of the butter in a large nonstick skillet over medium-high heat until the foaming subsides. When the pan is hot, sear the trout in batches until browned, 2 to 3 minutes per side. Transfer the sautéed fillets to the rack in the oven to keep warm as you continue cooking, adding more butter to the pan if needed.

3. Reduce the heat under the skillet to medium, lay in the presunto slices, a few at a time, and cook until they're firm, fragile sheets, about 1 minute. Transfer to the rack in the oven.

4. Heat a thin film of oil in a small skillet over high heat until it shimmers and sauté the lemon slices until charred on both sides, about 3 minutes total. Transfer the slices to a plate.

5. Crank up the heat under the skillet the fish was cooked in to high, pour in the wine, and boil to reduce a bit, 1 to 2 minutes. Remove from the heat, swirl in the remaining 2 tablespoons of butter and the zest, and season with a bit of salt if needed and pepper.

6. With a sharp knife, cut the fillets into thirds. Trim the presunto slices into 3 pieces each to match the fillets. Stack 3 pieces of fish, each topped with a piece of presunto, per plate. Drizzle with the sauce, spritz with lemon, sprinkle with the parsley, and serve with a seared lemon slice.

OLIVE OIL–POACHED FRESH COD WITH ROASTED TOMATO SAUCE

confitado de bacalhau fresco com tomatada assada

SERVES 4

After a centuries-long love affair with salt cod, the Portuguese are beginning to flirt with the fresh version. And, to me, no preparation is better than this. If you've never had the pleasure of tucking into oil-poached fish, you're in for a treat. The oil, infused with lemon, slowly cooks the fish until it's unctuous and amazingly supple.

ATENÇÃO ⟡ *Yes, 2 to 3 cups of olive oil is a lot, but the good thing is you can use it again to poach more fish. To reuse the oil, let it cool, filter it through several layers of cheesecloth, and store in a glass jar in the fridge for up to 2 weeks.*

FOR THE TOMATO SAUCE

1½ POUNDS PLUM TOMATOES, CORED, QUARTERED LENGTHWISE, AND SEEDED

1 MEDIUM YELLOW ONION, CUT LENGTHWISE IN HALF AND SLICED INTO VERY THIN HALF-MOONS

3 GARLIC CLOVES, MINCED

ZEST OF ½ LEMON, REMOVED WITH A VEGETABLE PEELER

3 TABLESPOONS OLIVE OIL

KOSHER SALT AND FRESHLY GROUND BLACK PEPPER

1 TABLESPOON WHITE WINE VINEGAR

FOR THE COD

FOUR 6-OUNCE COD FILLETS, SKIN ON, AT ROOM TEMPERATURE

KOSHER SALT AND FRESHLY GROUND BLACK PEPPER

2 TO 3 CUPS OLIVE OIL

GRATED ZEST OF 3 LEMONS

1 TEASPOON CHOPPED FRESH OREGANO LEAVES

LEMON WEDGES, FOR SERVING

1. Position a rack in the center of the oven and crank up the heat to 450°F.

2. Toss the tomatoes, onion, garlic, and zest with the oil on a rimmed baking sheet, then flip all the tomatoes cut side up. Season generously with salt and pepper. Roast until the tomatoes soften and a few stray onions begin to color, 15 to 20 minutes.

3. While the tomatoes are roasting, generously season the cod fillets on both sides with salt and pepper. Fit them snugly in one layer into a small baking dish. Add just enough oil to cover completely, then pour off the oil into a small saucepan, add the zest, and warm over low heat for 10 minutes. The bits of lemon will sizzle as the oil infuses, which is a sign the mixture is at the perfect temperature. Remove from the heat and allow to steep for 10 minutes.

4. Remove the tomatoes and onions from the oven, and reduce the oven temperature to 225°F. Opening the oven door will help hasten things; it's crucial to wait until the proper temperature is reached. Too high a temperature will cause the cod to lose it suppleness. Meanwhile, toss out the strips of lemon zest from the tomatoes and scoop the contents of the baking sheet into a small saucepan. Stir in the vinegar, season with salt and pepper to taste, and cover to keep warm.

5. Pour the infused oil over the cod, transfer to the oven, and poach until just opaque in the center, 20 to 30 minutes.

6. Just before serving, warm the tomato sauce over low heat. Carefully remove the cod fillets from the oil with a spatula, blot with paper towels, and slide onto four warmed plates. Spoon the tomato sauce on top, sprinkle with the oregano, and spritz with lemon juice.

SKATE WITH LEEKS IN SAFFRON BROTH

raia com alho francês e caldo de açafrão

SERVES 6

This is a perfect counterpoint to the skate recipe on page 88—new versus old, modern versus classic. It's a riff on a dish served at the super-sleek Restaurante Eleven in Lisbon. It takes two Portuguese favorites, skate and saffron, and pairs them with leeks, shallots, and the yellow sister of the more tradition-ally Portuguese red bell pepper. This dish is as delicate as the other is strong.

ATENÇÃO ❧ *Reducing most commercial broths can make them taste salty. If you don't have homemade stock, make the saffron broth this way: Bring 1 cup store-bought low-sodium chicken broth, ½ cup heavy cream, and ¼ teaspoon crushed saffron threads to a boil. Mix together 2 teaspoons cornstarch and 1 tablespoon cold water, and stir it into the broth-cream mixture. Boil, stirring constantly, for 2 minutes more. Season to taste with salt if needed and pepper.*

FOR THE SAFFRON BROTH

2 CUPS FISH STOCK (PAGE 245) OR CHICKEN STOCK (PAGE 243); SEE ATENÇÃO

1 CUP HEAVY CREAM

¼ TEASPOON SAFFRON THREADS, CRUSHED

KOSHER SALT AND FRESHLY GROUND WHITE PEPPER

2 TABLESPOONS UNSALTED BUTTER

6 MEDIUM LEEKS, WHITE AND PALE GREEN PARTS ONLY, HALVED LENGTHWISE, SLICED INTO ¼-INCH HALF-MOONS, AND RINSED WELL

1 MEDIUM SHALLOT, MINCED

1 YELLOW BELL PEPPER, STEMMED, SEEDED, AND CUT INTO ¼-INCH SQUARES

KOSHER SALT AND FRESHLY GROUND WHITE PEPPER

2½ POUNDS SKATE, CARTILAGE AND SKIN REMOVED, CUT INTO 12 PIECES (ASK YOUR FISHMONGER TO DO THIS)

ALL-PURPOSE FLOUR, FOR DREDGING

2 TABLESPOONS VEGETABLE OIL, OR MORE IF NEEDED

FRESH CHIVES OR CHOPPED FRESH FLAT-LEAF PARSLEY LEAVES, FOR GARNISH

1. Add the fish stock, cream, and saffron to a small saucepan and bring almost to a boil. Turn the heat to low and simmer until reduced to 1½ cups, about 10 minutes. Season to taste with salt if needed and pepper. Keep warm.

2. Heat the oven to warm, and slip in a wire rack set on a baking sheet.

3. Heat the butter in a medium skillet over medium heat until the foaming subsides. Add the leeks and shallot and cook, stirring often, until just soft-ened, about 8 minutes. Stir in the yellow pepper and cook for 1 minute more. Season to taste with salt and pepper. Scrape into a small bowl and cover to keep warm.

4. Pat the skate dry, season lightly with salt and pepper, and dredge them in flour, shaking off the excess. Heat the oil in a large nonstick skillet over medium-high heat until hot. Sear the fish in batches until golden and just opaque in the center, 2 to 3 minutes per side. Transfer the sautéed fillets to the rack in the oven to keep warm as you continue cooking, adding more oil to the pan if needed.

5. To serve, pile the vegetables into six bowls. Pour the saffron broth around, top with the skate, and decorate each bowl with a few long blades of chives.

SEARED SKATE IN GARLIC-PEPPER OIL

raia com molho de pitau

SERVES 6

The Portuguese are a generous people. While living in Lisbon, I told a restaurateur friend I was mourning my life because I wasn't able to ingratiate my way into home kitchens to uncover secrets and gather recipes, as I had hoped. A few days later, I got a call from Maria Emilia Ferreira Pinto, known to all as Mani, inviting me to a party—in my honor.

This is just one of the many dishes she made that night. It's a classic from Beira Litoral, which she served with the requisite sliced boiled potatoes.

FOR THE GARLIC-PEPPER OIL

3/4 CUP OLIVE OIL

3 GARLIC CLOVES, CRUSHED

1 TABLESPOON GREEN, PINK, AND WHITE PEPPERCORNS, CRACKED

6 SPRIGS FRESH OREGANO

3/4 TEASPOON SWEET PAPRIKA

1/4 CUP CIDER VINEGAR

KOSHER SALT

FOR THE SKATE

2 1/2 POUNDS SKATE, CARTILAGE AND SKIN REMOVED, CUT INTO 12 PIECES (ASK YOUR FISHMONGER TO DO THIS)

KOSHER SALT AND FRESHLY GROUND BLACK PEPPER

ALL-PURPOSE FLOUR, FOR DREDGING

2 TABLESPOONS OLIVE OIL, OR MORE IF NEEDED

2 TABLESPOONS CHOPPED FRESH CILANTRO LEAVES

1. Pour the oil into a small saucepan, dump in the garlic, peppercorns, oregano, and paprika, and warm over medium-low heat. As soon as the garlic starts to sizzle, reduce the heat to very low. When the garlic has softened and turned a nutty golden brown, after about 30 minutes, strain the oil through a sieve into a small bowl. Strip the fried oregano leaves from their stems and return them to the oil along with the garlic nuggets; toss out the stems and peppercorns. Whisk in the vinegar and season with salt to taste. Set the oil aside and keep warm.

2. Heat the oven to warm, and slip in a wire cooling rack set on a baking sheet.

3. Pat the skate dry, season lightly with salt and pepper, and coat them with flour, shaking off the excess. Heat the oil in a large nonstick skillet over medium-high heat. When the pan is hot, sear the fish in batches until golden brown, 2 to 3 minutes per side. Transfer the sautéed fillets to the rack in the oven to keep warm as you continue cooking, adding more oil to the pan if needed.

4. Arrange the skate on a platter. Whisk the garlic-pepper oil with a fork, drizzle it over the fish, and sprinkle with the cilantro.

KETTLE OF FISH

cataplana de peixe

SERVES 6

Acataplana, a fixture in the Algarve, is kind of a spiritual cousin to the pressure cooker. Shaped like a giant clam, the copper-hinged pan is clamped together for cooking, locking in the juices of its contents. When Teresa Paiva, whose recipe this is, carried hers to the table and popped it open, the room filled with steam redolent of the sea. If you're bereft of a cataplana, a Dutch oven with a tight-fitting lid works perfectly, even if it's less striking.

ATENÇÃO ❧ *Because this dish has such pure flavors, and it's cooked for such a short time, seasoning is absolutely crucial to make the flavors shine. Carefully salt and pepper throughout the cooking process. (See "Salt," page 29.)*

---

3 TABLESPOONS OLIVE OIL

$^1/_2$ MEDIUM FENNEL BULB, STALKS REMOVED, CORED AND CUT INTO $^1/_4$-INCH SLICES (RESERVE A FEW OF THE FRILLY FRONDS FOR GARNISH)

2 MEDIUM LEEKS, WHITE AND PALE GREEN PARTS ONLY, HALVED LENGTHWISE, SLICED INTO $^1/_4$-INCH HALF-MOONS, AND RINSED WELL

1 LARGE YELLOW BELL PEPPER, STEMMED, SEEDED, AND CUT INTO $^1/_4$-INCH-WIDE SLICES

A 1-INCH THUMB OF GINGER, PEELED AND GRATED

$^1/_2$ GARLIC CLOVE, MINCED

KOSHER SALT AND FRESHLY GROUND BLACK PEPPER

$^1/_3$ CUP FISH STOCK (PAGE 245), STORE-BOUGHT LOW-SODIUM CHICKEN BROTH, OR WATER

1 POUND SKINLESS MONKFISH, RED SNAPPER, OR OTHER MILD FIRM-FLESHED FISH FILLETS, CUT INTO 1-INCH CHUNKS

1 POUND SKINLESS BLACK SEA BASS, GROUPER, SEA BREAM, OR PORGY FILLETS, CUT INTO 1-INCH CHUNKS

$^1/_2$ TEASPOON PINK PEPPERCORNS, CRACKED

5 SMALL RIPE TOMATOES, PEELED, CORED, SEEDED, AND CHOPPED (SEE PAGE 91)

$^2/_3$ CUP DRY WHITE WINE

$^1/_2$ POUND MEDIUM SHRIMP, SHELLED AND DEVEINED

LEMON WEDGES, FOR SERVING

$1^1/_2$ TABLESPOONS MINCED FRESH FLAT-LEAF PARSLEY LEAVES

$1^1/_2$ TABLESPOONS MINCED FRESH CILANTRO LEAVES

---

1. Heat the oil in a large cataplana or pot over medium heat until it shimmers. Layer in the fennel, leeks, and yellow pepper, and sprinkle with the ginger and garlic. Season with salt and pepper. Pour in the stock, seal the cataplana or cover the pot, and cook, stirring occasionally, until the vegetables begin to soften, about 5 minutes.

2. Push the vegetables to one side and add the monkfish, sea bass, and peppercorns, then cover with the vegetables. Scatter the tomatoes over the top and

(recipe continues)

splash in the wine. If using a cataplana, lock it and cook for 4 to 5 minutes on one side, then flip carefully to minimize spilling the cooking liquid and cook for 4 to 5 minutes more. If using a pot, cover and cook until the fish is opaque, 7 to 10 minutes.

3. Add the shrimp, cover, and cook just until they turn pink, 2 to 3 minutes more. Take a taste and season with salt and pepper if needed. Ladle into bowls, spritz with lemon, sprinkle with the parsley and cilantro, and decorate with the reserved fennel fronds.

TOMATOES: TAKING IT ALL OFF

Peeled fresh tomatoes are used a lot in Portuguese cooking. And they're easy to prep. Have a bowl filled with ice water at the ready. Bring a medium pot of water to a boil over high heat. Make a small X in the bottom of each tomato with the tip of a knife. Using a slotted spoon, lower them, one at a time, into the pot for 5 to 10 seconds, depending upon how ripe they are. Fish them out and dunk them into the ice water to cool for about 1 minute. Peel the tomatoes by starting from the X mark on the bottom and pulling back the curled skin. If the recipe calls for seeded tomatoes, slice them through the equator and scoop out the seeds.

CLAMS IN A CATAPLANA

amêijoas na cataplana

SERVES 4 AS A MAIN COURSE, 6 AS A STARTER

This is a meaty counterpart to the delicate fish cataplana on page 89. Interestingly, I first had it twelve years ago in Bridgewater, Connecticut, of all places, at the home of my friends Manny Almeida and Kevin Bagley. Manny, who's from the same Azorean island as my family, just whipped it up one summer evening. I've since had it many times in Portugal, most memorably at an ocean-side joint in the town of Sagres, just east of the vertiginous promontory where legend has it that Henry the Navigator built a school and shipyard for his sailors.

3 TABLESPOONS OLIVE OIL

8 OUNCES CHOURIÇO, LINGUIÇA, OR DRY-CURED SMOKED SPANISH CHORIZO, CUT INTO ¼-INCH COINS

ONE ¼-INCH-THICK SLICE PRESUNTO, SERRANO HAM, OR PROSCIUTTO, TRIMMED OF EXCESS FAT AND CUT INTO ¼-INCH CUBES

2 MEDIUM YELLOW ONIONS, CUT LENGTHWISE IN HALF AND SLICED INTO THIN HALF-MOONS

1 TURKISH BAY LEAF

4 GARLIC CLOVES, MINCED

ONE 28-OUNCE CAN WHOLE PEELED TOMATOES, PREFERABLY SAN MARZANO, DRAINED AND CHOPPED

¼ CUP DRY WHITE WINE

½ TEASPOON SWEET PAPRIKA

4 POUNDS SMALL CLAMS, SUCH AS COCKLES, MANILA, BUTTER, OR LITTLENECKS, SCRUBBED AND RINSED

FRESHLY GROUND BLACK PEPPER

3 TABLESPOONS MINCED FRESH FLAT-LEAF PARSLEY LEAVES

1. Heat the oil in a large cataplana or a pot with a tight-fitting lid over medium-high heat until it shimmers. Dump in the chouriço and presunto and cook, stirring occasionally, until touched with brown, 6 to 8 minutes.

2. Lower the heat to medium, drop in the onions and bay leaf, and cook, stirring occasionally, until the onions are soft, 5 to 7 minutes. Add the garlic and cook for 1 minute more. Stir in the tomatoes and any accumulated juice, the wine, and paprika. Discard any clams that feel heavy (which means they're full of sand), have broken shells, or don't close when tapped. Plonk the clams into the pot and turn the heat to high. If using a cataplana, lock it and cook for 6 minutes on one side, then flip carefully to minimize spilling the cooking liquid, and cook until the clams open, 4 to 6 minutes more. If using a pot, cook, covered, until the clams pop open, 7 to 12 minutes.

3. Carry the cataplana triumphantly to the table, making sure everyone's watching, then release the lid. Bask in the applause. Discard the bay leaf and toss out any clams that refuse to pop open. Season with a few grinds of pepper, shower with parsley, and ladle the stew into wide shallow bowls. Oh, and have a big bowl on hand for the shells.

STUFFED SQUID

lulas recheadas

SERVES 4 TO 6 AS A MAIN COURSE, 6 TO 8 AS A STARTER

With Portugal's nearly six hundred miles of coastline, it's no surprise that blindingly fresh fish is sold at markets all over the country. But there's absolutely no better way to eat any of it than right there on the *esplanada*, in full view of the boats unloading their catch. The Portuguese are mad for just about any seafood, and squid is no exception. They like it stewed, grilled, fried, or baked. I've even seen it stuffed and poached in seawater. This recipe is a classic, and it brings together many traditional flavors: tomato, onion, garlic, presunto, and bay leaf.

FOR THE SQUID

2 TABLESPOONS OLIVE OIL

1 MEDIUM YELLOW ONION, MINCED

ONE 1/4-INCH-THICK SLICE PRESUNTO, SERRANO HAM, OR PROSCIUTTO, TRIMMED OF EXCESS FAT AND MINCED

2 GARLIC CLOVES, MINCED

THIRTY-TWO 4- TO 5-INCH SQUID (ABOUT 3 POUNDS), CLEANED (HAVE YOUR FISHMONGER DO THIS), TENTACLES MINCED

1 LARGE EGG PLUS 1 LARGE YOLK, BEATEN

2 TABLESPOONS FRESH LEMON JUICE

3 TABLESPOONS MINCED FRESH FLAT-LEAF PARSLEY LEAVES

KOSHER SALT AND FRESHLY GROUND BLACK PEPPER

FOR THE SAUCE

3 TABLESPOONS OLIVE OIL

1 LARGE YELLOW ONION, CHOPPED

3 GARLIC CLOVES, MINCED

2 TABLESPOONS DOUBLE-CONCENTRATE TOMATO PASTE

ONE 28-OUNCE CAN WHOLE PEELED TOMATOES, PREFERABLY SAN MARZANO, SEEDED AND CHOPPED, WITH THEIR JUICE

1/2 CUP DRY RED WINE

1 TURKISH BAY LEAF

KOSHER SALT AND FRESHLY GROUND BLACK PEPPER

1. To make the stuffing, heat the oil in a medium skillet over medium heat until it shimmers. Add the onion and cook, stirring occasionally, until golden, about 10 minutes. Dump in the presunto and garlic and cook for 1 minute more. Add the squid tentacles and cook until any excess liquid evaporates, 1 to 2 minutes.

2. Remove the pan from the heat and stir in the egg and the yolk. Return to very low heat and cook, stirring continually, until the mixture thickens, 2 to 3 minutes. Stir in the lemon juice and parsley, and season with salt and pepper if needed. Set the stuffing aside.

3. Position a rack in the center of the oven and crank up the heat to 350°F.

4. To make the sauce, heat the oil in a large skillet over medium heat until it shimmers. Add the onion and cook, stirring occasionally, until golden, 7 to 10 minutes. Add the garlic and cook for 1 minute more. Stir in the tomato paste, tomatoes and their juice, wine, and bay leaf. Season with salt and pepper, remove the skillet from the heat, discard the bay leaf, and set sauce aside.

5. Fill a small plastic freezer bag with the stuffing, seal the bag, and snip off one corner. Stuff each squid body a scant two-thirds full. Loosely skewer each one with a toothpick and lay the squid in a single layer in a 9-by-13-inch baking dish. Pour the sauce over the top and bake until the sauce is bubbly and the squid is tender, about 40 minutes.

VARIAÇÃO ❧ GRILLED STUFFED SQUID *lulas recheadas grelhadas*

Skip the sauce. Heat a gas or charcoal grill to medium-high. Lightly brush the stuffed squid with olive oil and grill them until the filling firms up and is cooked through and the squid are lined with grill marks, 2 to 4 minutes per side. Sprinkle with minced fresh parsley or cilantro, spritz them with lemon juice, and drizzle with Smoked Paprika Oil (page 242), if you wish.

GRILLED SHRIMP WITH PIRI-PIRI SAUCE

camarões grelhados com piri-piri

SERVES 4 TO 6

Hit most any seaside joint in Portugal, and you'll find these grilled shrimp on the menu. Heck, you'll find them in many backyards and even in some swank city eateries. But I like them best on the beach, sitting under a huge Sagres umbrella—Sagres is a brand of Portuguese beer—with a hunk of bread and a cool drink to kill the fire.

2½ POUNDS EXTRA-LARGE SHRIMP, SHELLED AND DEVEINED

1 CUP PIRI-PIRI SAUCE (PAGE 233) OR STORE-BOUGHT HOT SAUCE, PLUS MORE FOR SERVING

2 LEMONS, CUT INTO WEDGES

KOSHER SALT

1. Combine the shrimp and piri-piri sauce in a large sealable freezer bag and toss to coat. Place the bag in a shallow dish and marinate in the fridge, turning a few times, for at least several hours, or, preferably, overnight.

2. Heat a gas or charcoal grill to medium.

3. Thread the shrimp and lemon wedges on skewers and season with salt. Grill the shrimp over indirect heat, turning several times, until just opaque, 5 to 6 minutes. For an extra spike of flavor, brush the skewers with fresh piri-piri sauce just before serving.

CURRIED MUSSELS

mexilhões com caril

SERVES 6 AS A MAIN COURSE, 8 TO 10 AS A STARTER

The Portuguese passion for curry harks back to the Age of Discovery, when Vasco da Gama and his sailors made their way to the East, opening a new trade route, which Portugal dominated for almost a century. Traditionally used in small amounts, perhaps due to cost, curry is now sprinkled in by the tablespoon in modern recipes. Shrimp is the classic curried shellfish, but I had some lovely mussels in a tiny coastal restaurant. This is my *tributo*, or homage.

3 TABLESPOONS OLIVE OIL

2 LARGE YELLOW ONIONS, CHOPPED

3 GARLIC CLOVES, MINCED

3 MEDIUM TOMATOES, PEELED, CORED, SEEDED, AND CHOPPED (SEE PAGE 91)

2 TO 3 TABLESPOONS CURRY POWDER, TO TASTE

1/2 TEASPOON GROUND GINGER

PINCH OF GROUND CINNAMON

6 POUNDS MUSSELS, SCRUBBED, DEBEARDED, AND RINSED

1 1/2 CUPS DRY WHITE WINE

2/3 CUP HEAVY CREAM

PIRI-PIRI SAUCE (PAGE 233) OR STORE-BOUGHT HOT SAUCE

KOSHER SALT AND FRESHLY GROUND BLACK PEPPER

5 CUPS COOKED WHITE RICE

2 TABLESPOONS CHOPPED FRESH CILANTRO LEAVES

1. Heat the oil in a large skillet over medium heat until it shimmers. Drop in the onions and cook, stirring occasionally, until golden brown, about 15 minutes. Add the garlic and cook for 1 minute more. Stir in two thirds of the tomatoes and cook for 2 minutes. Sprinkle in the curry powder, ginger, and cinnamon and cook, stirring constantly, until fragrant, about 1 minute. Set aside.

2. Discard any mussels that feel heavy (which means they're full of sand), have broken shells, or don't close when tapped. Pour the wine into a roomy pot. Clatter in the mussels, cover tightly, and cook over high heat, shaking the pan occasionally, until the shells pop open, 7 to 10 minutes. Toss out any mussels that refuse to open, then pluck all but 18 from their shells. Strain the mussel liquid.

3. Add 1 1/2 cups of the mussel liquid to the skillet with the tomato mixture, then add the cream and bring to a boil over high heat to thicken slightly. If you prefer a brothy curry, add more mussel liquid; if it's a creamy curry you're after, reduce the mixture more. Season with piri-piri sauce, salt, and pepper to taste. Take the pan off the heat and stir in the shelled mussels.

4. Spoon the rice into six bowls and top with the mussels. Garnish each with mussels in their shells, and shower with the remaining tomatoes and the cilantro. Pass the piri-piri sauce at the table.

WARM BABY OCTOPUS AND POTATO SALAD

salada quente de polvo e batatas

SERVES 6

My father tells stories of catching octopus off the coast of Maia, his hometown on the island of São Miguel. He and my grandfather had an ingenious way of snagging them: they'd pierce the end of bamboo rods with a bit of pig fat. Cephalopods hunt by stealth, hiding in underwater grottoes, waiting for unsuspecting prey to swim by. My father and grandfather would dangle the bamboo sticks in the water, luring the octopuses from their lairs, then pluck them out with their hands. Legend has it my father was the youngest in the town to catch an octopus by himself—at all of six years old.

Aptly, this recipe is an adaptation of a salad I had at Largo da Matriz, a stylish new spot in Ponta Delgada, São Miguel's capital, situated just across from the church where my parents were married in 1958.

FOR THE OCTOPUS

2 CUPS CHICKEN STOCK (PAGE 243) OR STORE-BOUGHT LOW-SODIUM BROTH

2 CUPS DRY WHITE WINE

KOSHER SALT

2 TURKISH BAY LEAVES

1 TEASPOON CRUSHED RED PEPPER FLAKES

2 POUNDS CLEANED BABY OCTOPUS, DEFROSTED IF FROZEN, RINSED WELL, ESPECIALLY INSIDE THE HEADS

FOR THE SALAD

1 TABLESPOON DIJON MUSTARD

1 TABLESPOON DOUBLE-CONCENTRATE TOMATO PASTE

3 TABLESPOONS SHERRY VINEGAR

1 TABLESPOON FRESH LEMON JUICE

3 GARLIC CLOVES, FINELY MINCED

3/4 CUP OLIVE OIL

KOSHER SALT AND FRESHLY GROUND BLACK PEPPER

1 POUND BABY YUKON GOLD POTATOES

8 CUPS MESCLUN GREENS

3 TABLESPOONS MINCED FRESH CILANTRO LEAVES

1. Pour the chicken stock, wine, and 2 cups of water into a medium pot. Take a taste, and season with just enough salt to bring out the flavors. Drop in the bay leaves and pepper flakes and bring to a boil over high heat.

2. Meanwhile, with your fingers, press the area where the head and tentacles of one octopus meet to check for what feels like a bead. If you feel one, cut the octopus apart just above and below the bead and discard that piece. If not, cut the octopus in half below the head. Repeat with the rest.

3. Lower the heat under the pot so the liquid barely simmers, and drop in the octopus pieces. Cover and simmer until tender, about 45 minutes. Check often to make sure the water remains at the merest simmer; otherwise, you'll end up with a pot full of rubbery bits.

4. While the octopus pieces cook, combine the mustard, tomato paste, vinegar, lemon juice, and garlic in a large bowl. Slowly dribble in the olive oil, whisking until luscious and gleaming. Season well with salt and pepper to taste. Set the dressing aside.

5. Using a slotted spoon, lift the octopus pieces out of the pot and drop them into a colander to drain. Add the potatoes to the poaching liquid, turn the heat to medium–high, and cook until just tender, 18 to 20 minutes.

6. Meanwhile, cut the octopus tentacles in half—4 legs per piece. Slice the heads into ¼-inch rings. Scoop the pieces into a bowl and cover with a plate to keep warm.

7. Drain the potatoes in the colander. When cool enough to handle, slice them lengthwise into quarters, then add them to the octopus. Toss it all with ⅓ cup of the dressing. Take a nibble and season with salt and pepper if necessary. In another bowl, toss the greens with ⅓ cup of the dressing.

8. Divide the salad among six plates, crown with the octopus–potato mixture, and sprinkle with the cilantro. Serve immediately, with the remaining dressing on the side for drizzling.

SALT COD OF MY YOUTH

bacalhau da minha infância

SERVES 6

If you don't like salt cod, this is the recipe for you. Think of it as bacalhau 1.0. It's actually similar to the dish I cut my teeth on. I hated salt cod as a kid, but my mother and grandmother were always foisting *bacalhau à Gomes de Sá* on me (see the Clássico, opposite). I've since come to love the dish, but back then the only way I could eat it was by mashing it all up with butter and milk. I thought I was so clever, but I discovered that my Portuguese teacher, Cristina Vasconcelos, makes a similar dish for her son, Bernardo. In fact, it's a common home dish in Portugal. It has no official name, so I gave it my own.

3 TABLESPOONS OLIVE OIL

6 MEDIUM YELLOW ONIONS (ABOUT 2 POUNDS), CUT LENGTHWISE IN HALF AND SLICED INTO THIN HALF-MOONS

1 TURKISH BAY LEAF

6 GARLIC CLOVES, MINCED

2 POUNDS YUKON GOLD POTATOES, PEELED AND CUT INTO 1-INCH CUBES

KOSHER SALT

6 TABLESPOONS UNSALTED BUTTER

2 CUPS WHOLE MILK, PLUS MORE IF NEEDED, WARMED

3 TABLESPOONS CHOPPED FRESH FLAT-LEAF PARSLEY LEAVES

FRESHLY GROUND WHITE PEPPER

2 TABLESPOONS ALL-PURPOSE FLOUR

PINCH OF GROUND NUTMEG

1½ POUNDS SALT COD, RINSED, SOAKED, COOKED, AND FLAKED (SEE PAGE 30)

3 OUNCES SHEEP'S-MILK CHEESE, SUCH AS NISA, ÉVORA, MANCHEGO, ZAMORANO, OR PECORINO TOSCANO, SHREDDED

1. Heat the oil in a large skillet over medium heat until it shimmers. Add the onions and bay leaf, reduce the heat to medium-low, and cook, covered, stirring often, for 15 minutes; adjust the heat as necessary so the onions don't burn. Uncover and continue cooking and stirring until the onions are golden brown, about 25 minutes more. Add the garlic and cook for 5 minutes. Scoop the mixture into a bowl, toss out the bay leaf, and set aside. Set the skillet aside, as well.

2. Plonk the potatoes into a large pot and cover with cold water by 2 inches. Add 1 tablespoon salt, cover, bring to a boil, and cook over high heat until tender, 10 to 15 minutes.

3. Drain the potatoes in a colander and return them to the pot. Add 4 tablespoons of the butter and ½ cup of the milk. Mash until smooth, adding more milk if necessary. Stir in the parsley and season with salt and pepper. Set aside.

4. Position a rack in the center of the oven and crank up the heat to 425°F.

5. Add the remaining 2 tablespoons of butter to the skillet the onions were cooked in, and melt over medium-low heat. Add the flour and cook, stirring continually, for 1 to 2 minutes. Whisk in the remaining 1½ cups of milk, making sure to catch all the lumps. Bring the sauce to a boil over medium heat, then reduce the heat to low and simmer, whisking constantly, until it's the consistency of a creamy bisque, 3 to 4 minutes. Add the nutmeg and season with salt and pepper. Remove the skillet from the heat and fold in the cooked cod.

6. Scoop the cod mixture into six 1-cup gratin dishes. Cover with the onions, swirl the potatoes on top, and sprinkle with the cheese. Bake until bronzed, about 25 minutes. Let stand for 15 minute before serving.

CLÁSSICO ❧ SALT COD, POTATO, AND ONION CASSEROLE *bacalhau à gomes de sá*

Position a rack in the center of the oven and crank up the heat to 350°F. The ingredients for this classic differ slightly, as does the preparation, from my version. Tradition has it that the onions should be limp and light golden, but Momma Leite, whose recipe this is, can't abide that: she likes her onions dark and sweet. In step 1, use 3 pounds onions, sliced into rings. Cook them, along with the bay leaf, covered, stirring often, for 15 minutes, then uncover and cook until deeply golden brown, about 35 minutes more. Adjust the heat as necessary so the onions don't burn. Add the garlic and cook for 5 minutes more. Toss out the bay leaf. In step 2, bring 2 pounds small boiling potatoes in their skins to a boil, and cook until just tender, about 10 minutes. Drain, peel, and cut them into ¼-inch slices. Skip steps 3 through 6. Instead, working in batches, heat several tablespoons of olive oil in a nonstick skillet over medium heat and brown the potato slices, 5 to 7 minutes. Wipe the pan and add more oil between batches when needed.

To assemble and bake the casserole, line the bottom of an oiled shallow 2-quart baking dish with half the potato slices, cover with half the cooked cod, and top with half the sautéed onions, a sprinkle of the parsley, and a few grinds of white pepper. Repeat layering the rest of the potatoes, cod, and onions, and drizzle with ¼ cup olive oil. Bake until spitting hot and tipped with brown, 35 to 40 minutes. Let cool a bit, then top with 2 sliced hard-boiled eggs, 10 sliced black olives, and the rest of the parsley.

MINI SALT COD SANDWICHES

o mcsilva

MAKES 10 SANDWICHES

When I first had one of these sandwiches, the brainchild of Luís Baena, I was enthralled. The man has a sense of whimsy matched by few chefs I've met. His concept: Portuguese-ize McDonald's Filet-O-Fish. So he came up with the moniker McSilva—Silva is a common name in Portugal—and swapped out the fried fillet for a savory salt cod patty, a *patanisca*. He also created a red pepper jam for a condiment. The whole thing was served in a McDonald's-style container, with the name emblazoned across the top, which Luís happily popped open for each diner.

1 CUP ALL-PURPOSE FLOUR

3 TABLESPOONS OLIVE OIL, PLUS MORE FOR PAN FRYING THE PATTIES

1 LARGE EGG

1 GARLIC CLOVE, MINCED

2 TABLESPOONS MINCED FRESH CILANTRO LEAVES

3 TABLESPOONS MINCED SHALLOTS

1/2 POUND SALT COD, RINSED, SOAKED, COOKED, AND FINELY SHREDDED (SEE PAGE 30); 1/2 CUP OF THE COOKING WATER RESERVED

1 LARGE EGG WHITE

1/2 CUP MAYONNAISE

3 TABLESPOONS SWEET PICKLE RELISH

10 MINI HAMBURGER BUNS

10 SMALL LETTUCE LEAVES

2 SMALL TOMATOES, EACH CUT INTO 5 SLICES

SWEET RED PEPPER JAM (PAGE 226) OR KETCHUP

1. Whisk the flour, oil, whole egg, garlic, cilantro, shallots, and the reserved cod water in a medium bowl until smooth. If the batter seems thick, add an extra tablespoon or two of water. Stir in the cooked cod.

2. Heat 2 tablespoons of olive oil in a medium nonstick skillet over medium heat. Meanwhile, whisk the egg white to soft peaks and fold it into the cod mixture. Working in batches, drop the cod batter by scant 1/4-cupfuls into the hot oil and fry until golden brown and cooked through, 2 to 4 minutes per side. Take a nibble. You want to make sure there's no floury taste. Transfer to paper towels to drain, and add more oil to the pan as needed. Mix the mayonnaise and relish in a small bowl.

3. Spread the bottoms of the buns with some of the mayonnaise mixture, and layer each with a lettuce leaf, a tomato slice, and a patty. Dollop with a bit of the red pepper jam and crown with the top of the bun.

SALT COD IN A POTATO JACKET

bacalhau numa casca de batata

SERVES 4

I first enjoyed this dish at Herdade do Esporão, a vineyard in the western Alentejo. Legend has it the Portuguese have a thousand ways of preparing salt cod, and I thought I'd eaten just about all of them. This, though, was new to me. I was immediately taken by the creamy, garlicky cod-potato mixture studded with the sweetness of chestnuts. Once I perfected the recipe, I couldn't resist creating a variation for tiny stuffed potatoes; see the second Variação. These go particularly well with a sharp-dressed salad.

ATENÇÃO ❧ *To be entirely gluttonous, you can deep-fry the hollowed-out potato skins in 350°F vegetable oil until golden brown before stuffing them.*

---

2 LARGE YUKON GOLD POTATOES (ABOUT 10 OUNCES EACH)

6 OUNCES BABY SPINACH (ABOUT 4 CUPS, WELL PACKED)

10 OUNCES SALT COD, RINSED, SOAKED, COOKED, AND FLAKED INTO SMALL PIECES (SEE PAGE 30)

1 CUP CHOPPED JARRED ROASTED CHESTNUTS WITHOUT SUGAR (SEE SOURCES, PAGE 251) OR ³/₄ CUP CHOPPED WALNUTS

1 LARGE GARLIC CLOVE, FINELY MINCED

1 CUP MILK "MAYONNAISE" (PAGE 237), OR STORE-BOUGHT MAYONNAISE

KOSHER SALT AND FRESHLY GROUND BLACK PEPPER

¹/₂ CUP DRIED BREAD CRUMBS

---

1. Position a rack in the center of the oven and crank up the heat to 450°F.

2. Stab the potatoes a few times with a knife, wrap them in foil, and roast on a baking sheet until soft, 1 to 1 ¹/₄ hours. Remove and let cool until easy to handle. Bump up the oven temperature to 475°F.

3. Meanwhile, fit a pot with a steamer insert and fill with ¹/₂ inch of water. Bring to a boil over high heat, drop in the spinach, cover tightly, and steam for 3 minutes. Using tongs, transfer the spinach to a colander to drain and cool.

4. Wrap the spinach in cheesecloth and squeeze out the excess water.

5. Cut the potatoes lengthwise in half and scoop out their guts into a bowl, leaving a ¹/₈-inch lining of potato inside the skins. Mash the potato flesh well.

6. Transfer three quarters of the mashed potatoes to a large bowl (reserve the rest for another use), stir in the cooked cod, spinach, chestnuts, garlic, and ³/₄ cup of the mayonnaise. Season with salt and pepper to taste. Mound the mixture into the potato skins, and slather the tops with the remaining ¹/₄ cup of mayonnaise. Sprinkle with the bread crumbs, place on a baking sheet, and roast until golden brown, 12 to 15 minutes. Serve hot.

VARIAÇÃO ❧ Substitute an equal amount of chopped freshly cooked lobster or shrimp for the salt cod for a more delicate flavor.

VARIAÇÃO ❧ For hors d'oeuvres, roast twelve individually foil-wrapped baby Yukon Gold potatoes (about 1¼ pounds) until tender, 45 to 50 minutes. Split, hollow, stuff, and brown as above.

VARIAÇÃO ❧ If I have leftover filling, I form it into 3-inch *croquetes*, roll them in dried bread crumbs, and deep-fry them in 350°F vegetable oil until golden brown, 2 to 3 minutes.

POULTRY

AVES

Quick Weekday Roast Chicken with Potatoes ❧ Chicken in a Pot ❧

Chicken out of a Pot and onto the Grill ❧

Grilled Chicken Breasts with Spicy Coconut Sauce ❧

Grilled Chicken Slathered in Hot Sauce ❧ Roast Turkey with Two Dressings ❧

Partridge in a Fragrant Vinegar Sauce ❧

Duck Risotto with Ham and Sausage ❧ Duck Breasts with Black Olives

QUICK WEEKDAY ROAST CHICKEN
WITH POTATOES

frango assado com batatas

SERVES 4

I always have my Amped-Up Red Pepper Paste (page 232), a pungent paste of
paprika, garlic, wine, olive oil, and herbs, on hand because it makes for an
incredibly fast and flavorful dinner when I have no time to cook. For this recipe,
simply rub the paste on the chicken and pop it in the oven. To *really* save time
and maximize flavor, prepare the bird and potatoes the night before, refrigerate
them, and then roast them when you get home from work the next day.

ONE 3½- TO 4-POUND CHICKEN

¾ CUP AMPED-UP RED PEPPER PASTE
(PAGE 232)

KOSHER SALT AND FRESHLY GROUND
BLACK PEPPER

2 POUNDS YUKON GOLD POTATOES,
CUT INTO 1-INCH CUBES

1 TABLESPOON OLIVE OIL

1. Position a rack in the center of the oven and crank up the heat to 425°F.

2. Remove the excess fat from inside the chicken and reserve the giblets for
   another use. Pat the bird dry, then carefully wiggle your fingers under the
   skin to release it from the meat—the breast, legs, and back—being mindful
   not to rip it. Spoon 5 tablespoons of the red pepper paste into a cup and,
   using your fingers, smear 4 tablespoons under the skin of the chicken and
   inside the cavity. Smear the remaining tablespoon over the entire bird. Tie
   the legs together with twine and tuck the wing tips under. Place the chicken
   breast side down on a V-rack in a foil-lined roasting pan (or cover with
   plastic and refrigerate overnight to roast tomorrow). Sprinkle with salt and
   pepper.

3. Toss the potatoes with ¼ cup of the red pepper paste and the oil and scatter
   them in the pan under the chicken. Season with salt and pepper. Roast the
   bird for 35 minutes, then, using tongs, turn breast side up. Toss the potatoes
   well to coat with the drippings. Brush the breast lightly with a bit more of
   the paste. Lower the heat to 350°F and continue cooking until an instant-
   read thermometer inserted in the thickest part of the thigh reads 165°F,
   50 minutes to 1 hour more (longer if the chicken came from the refrigerator).

4. Remove the bird, tent with foil, and let sit for 10 to 15 minutes. If the potatoes aren't tender, toss again, bump up the oven to 450°F, and finish roasting them while the bird rests.

5. To serve, place the chicken on a platter and scoop the potatoes into a bowl.

CHICKEN IN A POT

frango na púcara

SERVES 6

A *púcara* is a clay pot whose tall, bulbous shape—similar to an urn—makes it superb for cooking chicken. *Púcaras* can be bought all over Portugal, but I found excellent, beautifully decorated ones in São Pedro do Corval, near Reguengos de Monsaraz in the Alentejo.

Traditionally this dish is made by tossing a whole chicken and the other ingredients into the *púcara* and then roasting. The result is a juicy bird, but one with pale, flabby skin. I use chicken pieces and cook them on the stove in a heavy pot with a tight-fitting lid—the way my mom taught me. Not only can I mix and match dark and light meat to suit my guests' preferences, but the dish cooks faster and the pieces brown nicely. Serve the *frango* with roasted potatoes or rice to sop up the delicious sauce.

ATENÇÃO ❈❈ *Aguardente is a potent distilled spirit made from the skins and seeds of pressed grapes. Brandy can be substituted. Don't worry, though: even with three types of alcohol, this isn't a boozy dish.*

10 OUNCES PEARL ONIONS, A SCANT 1 INCH IN DIAMETER

3 TABLESPOONS OLIVE OIL, OR MORE IF NEEDED

4½ POUNDS BONE-IN CHICKEN PIECES (BREASTS, THIGHS, AND LEGS), PATTED DRY

KOSHER SALT AND FRESHLY GROUND BLACK PEPPER

4 GARLIC CLOVES, MINCED

ONE 28-OUNCE CAN WHOLE PEELED TOMATOES, PREFERABLY SAN MARZANO, DRAINED, HALF THE JUICE RESERVED, AND CHOPPED

TWO ¼-INCH-THICK SLICES PRESUNTO, SERRANO HAM, OR PROSCIUTTO, TRIMMED OF EXCESS FAT AND CUT INTO ¼-INCH CUBES

⅓ CUP RAISINS

2 TURKISH BAY LEAVES

3 SPRIGS FRESH FLAT-LEAF PARSLEY

1 CUP TAWNY PORT

½ CUP DRY WHITE WINE

¼ CUP AGUARDENTE OR BRANDY

1 TABLESPOON DIJON MUSTARD

1. Have a bowl of ice water at the ready. Bring a medium saucepan of water to a boil, drop in the onions, and blanch for 30 seconds. Scoop them out with a slotted spoon and plop them into the ice water. To peel, snip off the tips and remove the papery outer layers. Set the onions aside.

2. Heat the oil in a large pot with a tight-fitting lid over high heat until very hot. Season the chicken generously with salt and pepper. Working in batches, sear the pieces, skin side down, until golden brown, about 7 minutes. Flip and sear 2 minutes more. Transfer the pieces to a bowl.

(recipe continues)

3. Drain off all but a thin film of oil from the pot. If the pot is dry, drizzle in more oil. Lower the heat to medium and plonk in the onions. Cook, stirring often, until well spotted with brown, about 5 minutes. Sprinkle in the garlic and cook for 1 minute more. Nestle in the chicken and add the tomatoes and their juice, the presunto, raisins, bay leaves, and parsley.

4. Whisk together the port, wine, aguardente, and mustard in a small bowl and pour over the chicken. Bring to a boil, reduce the heat to medium-low, and simmer, covered, turning the pieces to keep them submerged, until the chicken is cooked through, about 30 minutes.

5. Heat the broiler. Lift the chicken from the pot using tongs and lay the pieces on a foil-lined baking sheet. Set aside. With a slotted spoon, scoop the tomatoes, presunto, and raisins into a small bowl. Toss out the parsley and bay leaves. Turn the heat under the pot to high and boil to reduce the liquid to 1½ cups, 3 to 5 minutes. Skim any fat from the top.

6. Meanwhile, zap the chicken under the broiler to crisp the skin, 1 to 2 minutes—watch closely so the pieces don't burn or dry out.

7. To serve, arrange the chicken in the middle of a large platter and ring with the onions, presunto, and raisins. Pour a bit of the sauce over the top to moisten, and serve the rest on the side.

CHICKEN OUT OF A POT AND ONTO THE GRILL

frango fora da púcara e na brasa

SERVES 4

One night in Madeira, I was having grilled beef kebabs (see page 143) at Adega da Quinta. I got to talking with the chef, a quiet, self-effacing man, as he was flipping some chicken on the grill. I asked him the name of the dish. "*Frango na púcara*," he said. Flummoxed, I looked around: there wasn't a clay pot in sight, just a bucket full of marinating chicken. It was nothing like the mainland version on page 113. "Is it an island specialty?" I asked. He shook his head. "It's my own creation." It took a lot of trial and error to recreate his marinade, but everyone who crowds around my grill thinks it was worth it.

8 GARLIC CLOVES, CRUSHED

²/₃ CUP DRY WHITE WINE

3 TABLESPOONS OLIVE OIL

3 TABLESPOONS KETCHUP

1 TABLESPOON DIJON MUSTARD

1 TEASPOON PIRI-PIRI SAUCE (PAGE 233) OR STORE-BOUGHT HOT SAUCE, OR TO TASTE

1 TABLESPOON BRANDY

1 TABLESPOON HONEY

1 TABLESPOON CHOPPED FRESH ROSEMARY LEAVES

1 TABLESPOON CHOPPED FRESH OREGANO LEAVES

1 TABLESPOON CHOPPED FRESH SAVORY LEAVES

1 TEASPOON GROUND CUMIN

8 WHOLE CLOVES

KOSHER SALT AND FRESHLY GROUND BLACK PEPPER

ONE 3¹/₂- TO 4-POUND WHOLE CHICKEN, QUARTERED

1. Combine the garlic, wine, oil, ketchup, mustard, piri-piri sauce, brandy, honey, rosemary, oregano, savory, cumin, cloves, 1 teaspoon salt, and ¹/₂ teaspoon pepper in a large sealable freezer bag. Add the chicken and jiggle to coat. Place the bag in a shallow dish and marinate overnight in the fridge, turning several times.

2. Remove the bag from the fridge, drain the chicken, reserving the marinade, and transfer to a platter. Let the chicken come to room temperature. Pour the marinade into a small saucepan, and boil for 2 minutes. Set aside.

3. Meanwhile, heat a gas or charcoal grill to medium-high.

4. Season the chicken with salt and pepper and place the pieces, skin side down, on the grill. Close the cover and grill, basting occasionally with the hot marinade, until the skin is crisp and shows grill marks, 8 to 10 minutes. Flip, baste, and grill, covered, until the chicken is cooked through, about 15 minutes more. Toss out any excess marinade. Arrange the chicken on a platter and serve immediately.

GRILLED CHICKEN BREASTS
WITH SPICY COCONUT SAUCE

frango naufragado

SERVES 4

This recipe began life as *frango à cafreal*, a Mozambican dish filled with fiery-hot piri-piri peppers. When Mozambique won its independence from Portugal in 1975, many locals traveled with their recipes to other Portuguese colonies, including Macau, in China, where the dish picked up an Asian accent. While chef Luís Caseiro, a native of Figueira da Foz in Portugal's Beira Litoral region and former chef at Alfama Restaurant in New York City, was working in Macau, he tweaked the dish. He also changed the name to *frango naufragado*, or "shipwrecked chicken," because its travel route was similar to that of the famous Portuguese poet Luís Camões, who was shipwrecked near Goa in 1558 on his way back home from Macau.

FOR THE CHICKEN

1 SMALL YELLOW ONION, CHOPPED

4 GARLIC CLOVES

A 3-INCH THUMB OF GINGER, PEELED

1 CUP CANNED COCONUT MILK

2 TABLESPOONS FRESH LEMON JUICE

2 1/2 TEASPOONS KOSHER SALT

1/2 TEASPOON FRESHLY GROUND
 BLACK PEPPER

2 TEASPOONS CRUSHED RED PEPPER
 FLAKES, PLUS MORE FOR SERVING

4 MEDIUM BONELESS, SKINLESS
 CHICKEN BREAST HALVES

FOR THE COCONUT SAUCE

2 TABLESPOONS OLIVE OIL

1/2 SMALL YELLOW ONION, MINCED

1 TEASPOON GRATED LEMON ZEST

A 1-INCH THUMB OF GINGER, PEELED
 AND GRATED

1 TEASPOON CRUSHED RED PEPPER
 FLAKES

2 TEASPOONS DOUBLE-CONCENTRATE
 TOMATO PASTE

3 GARLIC CLOVES, MINCED

ONE 13 1/2-OUNCE CAN COCONUT MILK

1/4 CUP HEAVY CREAM

KOSHER SALT AND FRESHLY GROUND
 BLACK PEPPER

OLIVE OIL, FOR THE GRILL

4 TO 6 CUPS COOKED WHITE RICE

CHOPPED CHIVES, FOR GARNISH

CRUSHED RED PEPPER FLAKES
 (OPTIONAL)

PIRI-PIRI SAUCE (PAGE 233) OR
 STORE-BOUGHT HOT SAUCE

1. To make the chicken, buzz the onion, garlic, ginger, coconut milk, lemon juice, salt, black pepper, and red pepper flakes in a food processor until smooth. Drop the chicken into a large sealable freezer bag, pour in the marinade, and toss to coat. Place the bag in a shallow dish and marinate in the fridge for at least 4 hours, or, preferably, overnight, turning several times.

2. To make the sauce, heat the oil in a large skillet over medium heat. Add the onion and cook, stirring often, until golden brown, about 7 minutes. Reduce the heat to low, add the lemon zest, ginger, red pepper flakes, and tomato paste, and cook, stirring often, until the colors deepen and the mixture is very fragrant, 8 to 10 minutes. Toss in the garlic and cook for 1 minute more.

3. Pour in the coconut milk and cream and bring to a boil, then turn the heat to low and simmer, uncovered, until the liquid has reduced by one quarter, about 10 minutes. Season to taste with salt and pepper. Cover and keep warm.

4. Meanwhile, heat a gas or charcoal grill to high. Remove the chicken from the fridge and let it sit out for 30 minutes.

5. Lower the heat of the grill to medium and lightly brush the grill rack with oil. Remove the chicken from the marinade and grill until well marked and cooked through, 5 to 6 minutes per side.

6. To serve, slice each breast into 3 pieces on the bias. Dollop the cooked rice onto the plates, top with the chicken slices, and spoon the sauce on top. Sprinkle with chives and, if desired, some red pepper flakes. Definitely pass the piri-piri sauce.

GRILLED CHICKEN SLATHERED IN HOT SAUCE

frango com piri-piri

SERVES 4

Eaten all over Portugal, the crispy grilled chicken known as *frango no chur-rasco* is unbeatable. In the Algarve, younger, utterly tender chickens called *frango de Guia*, named for the town that made them famous, are the bird of choice. And there's something about the heat, the beaches, the crowds, and the wafting smoke from the grills in Guia that has to be experienced. No matter what type of grilled chicken you order, though, a waiter will pose the question, "*Com ou sem?*" With or without?—piri-piri sauce, that is. Do yourself a favor and go with "*com.*"

ATENÇÃO ❧ *We Portuguese can be somewhat cavalier when it comes to fire. This recipe requires that the food be basted with piri-piri sauce while grilling. Flare-ups are inevitable. To avoid charring your food beyond recognition, turn it often, and move it to a cooler corner of the grill or adjust the heat as needed. I also open and close the grill's cover to control the cooking.*

¾ CUP PIRI-PIRI SAUCE (PAGE 233) OR STORE-BOUGHT HOT SAUCE, PLUS MORE FOR SERVING	2 GARLIC CLOVES, MINCED
	½ TEASPOON KOSHER SALT
1 TEASPOON SWEET SMOKED PAPRIKA	ONE 3½- TO 4-POUND CHICKEN
	COARSE SEA SALT

1. Mix together the piri-piri sauce, paprika, garlic, and kosher salt in a large sealable freezer bag. Set aside.

2. Place the chicken breast side down on a cutting board. Using poultry shears, cut down along one side of the backbone, and then the other; discard the bone. Turn the chicken breast side up, open it out, and press down firmly with your palms to flatten it. Place it in the freezer bag, seal, and flip several times to coat. Lay the bag in a shallow dish and marinate in the fridge for at least several hours, or, preferably, overnight, turning a few more times.

3. Heat a gas or charcoal grill to medium. Remove the chicken from the bag, reserving the marinade, and let it sit out for 30 minutes.

4. Baste the bird all over with the marinade, season with sea salt, and place it breast side down on the grill. Grill until the skin is a deep brown and shows grill marks, 12 to 15 minutes. Flip, baste, and grill for about 15 minutes more. The chicken is cooked when the juices run clear if the thigh is pierced or when an instant-read thermometer inserted in the thickest part of the thigh reads 165°F. Just before serving, brush the chicken with fresh piri-piri sauce for an extra kick of heat.

ROAST TURKEY WITH TWO DRESSINGS

peru assado com dois recheios

SERVES 8

When I was growing up, my family often made a simple roast turkey: rubbed with butter and sprinkled with paprika and a dusting of salt and pepper. But for holidays, my grandmother whipped up her bread-based dressing (see page 198) and my godmother, who was half-Portuguese, made a potato-based dressing. When we all ate together, the two versions were happily passed around the table.

While researching turkey in Portugal, I discovered that the classic way to serve it is stuffed with—what else?—both potato and bread dressing. For years my family performed certain rituals without really knowing why. When I stumbled upon this centuries-old tradition of dual dressings, a bit of my identity jiggered into place.

ATENÇÃO ❧ *My grandmother Costa always rubbed her poultry with salt and let it sit in the fridge for several hours. She believed it pulled out impurities. Her ritual is similar to the koshering process, in which poultry is coated with salt and washed several times. The benefit is it leaves the bird juicy and flavorful. That's why I must insist you buy a kosher turkey.*

FOR THE TURKEY

ONE 12- TO 14-POUND KOSHER
   TURKEY, LIVER RESERVED FOR THE
   DRESSING

1 SMALL ORANGE, CUT INTO WEDGES

1 SMALL LEMON, CUT INTO WEDGES

KOSHER SALT AND FRESHLY GROUND
   BLACK PEPPER

4 TURKISH BAY LEAVES

6 TABLESPOONS UNSALTED BUTTER,
   MELTED

2 TEASPOONS SWEET PAPRIKA

FOR THE POTATO DRESSING

$1\frac{1}{2}$ POUNDS YUKON GOLD POTATOES,
   PEELED AND CUT INTO 1-INCH CUBES

KOSHER SALT

2 TABLESPOONS UNSALTED BUTTER,
   PLUS MORE IF NEEDED

$\frac{3}{4}$ POUND GROUND SWEET ITALIAN
   PORK SAUSAGE

1 LARGE YELLOW ONION, CHOPPED

2 GARLIC CLOVES, MINCED

RESERVED TURKEY LIVER, CHOPPED

2 LARGE EGG YOLKS, BEATEN

$\frac{1}{2}$ CUP WHOLE MILK, PLUS MORE IF
   NEEDED

HEALTHY PINCH OF GROUND NUTMEG

2 TABLESPOONS CHOPPED FRESH
   FLAT-LEAF PARSLEY LEAVES

FRESHLY GROUND BLACK PEPPER

GRANDMA COSTA'S DRESSING (PAGE 198)

1. Position a rack in the bottom of the oven and crank up the heat to 425°F.

2. Remove any pin feathers from the turkey and pat the bird dry with paper towels. Rub the cavity with a wedge of orange and of lemon, season well with salt and pepper, and stuff with the remaining wedges and the bay leaves. Tuck the wing tips under the bird and tie the legs together. Mix

together the melted butter, paprika, 1½ teaspoons salt, and 1 teaspoon pepper and brush about half of it over the turkey. Place the bird breast side down on a V-rack set in a roasting pan.

3. Slip the turkey into the oven, pour 2 cups of water into the pan, and roast for 30 minutes. Lower the heat to 350°F, flip the bird breast side up, and brush with some of the remaining butter-paprika mixture.

4. Continue roasting and brushing the turkey every 30 minutes, until an instant-read thermometer inserted into the thickest part of the thigh registers 165°F, 1½ to 2 hours more. Tent the bird with foil if browning too quickly. Transfer the turkey to a serving platter and let stand, tented, for 20 minutes. Although it's not the custom in Portugal, you can make gravy (see Variação).

5. Meanwhile, plonk the potatoes into a large pot of cold water. Add 1 tablespoon salt, cover, and bring to a boil over high heat. Cook until tender, 10 to 15 minutes. Drain the potatoes in a colander, return half to the pot, and mash well. Set the rest aside and keep warm.

6. Heat the butter in a medium skillet over medium-high heat until the foaming subsides. Crumble in the ground sausage and cook, breaking up the clumps, until well browned, 10 to 12 minutes. Using a slotted spoon, scoop the sausage into the pot with the mashed potatoes. Lower the heat to medium and, if the skillet is dry, add a bit more butter. Drop in the onion and cook, stirring occasionally, until golden, about 12 minutes. Scrape in the garlic and cook for 1 minute more. Add the chopped reserved liver and sauté until browned, about 3 minutes. Scoop the mixture into the pot with the mashed potatoes.

7. Whisk the yolks and milk into the potatoes until smooth; if the dressing is too thick, whisk in more milk. Place the pot over medium heat and stir to cook the yolks, about 3 minutes. Fold in the reserved potatoes, sprinkle in the nutmeg and parsley, and season well with salt and pepper to taste. Keep warm.

8. To serve, plate the turkey, scoop the dressings into decorative bowls, and take everything to the table pronto.

VARIAÇÃO ❈ To make gravy, spoon the fat from the roasting pan. Set the pan over two burners and pour in enough Chicken Stock (page 243) or store-bought low-sodium broth to the pan juices to equal 3 cups. Bring the liquid to a boil over medium-high heat, scraping the bottom to loosen any browned bits. Blend together ¼ cup softened unsalted butter and ¼ cup all-purpose flour in a small bowl to form a smooth paste. Scoop the paste into the stock, whisking constantly, until the gravy thickens and no floury taste remains, 5 to 10 minutes. Strain and season with salt and pepper to taste.

PARTRIDGE IN A FRAGRANT VINEGAR SAUCE

escabeche de perdiz

SERVES 4 TO 6

My friend José Vilela is a culinary iconoclast. If there's a cherished dish to be cooked, he's the first to balk. This classic, for example, is usually made with approximately equal parts of oil and vinegar, seasoned with nothing but salt and pepper, and is served cold. José snubs his nose at tradition by concocting his own oil and vinegar ratio, adding a cabinet-load of spices—giving it an unmistakable aroma and flavor—and serving it warm. Ladle this over rice, Puréed Potatoes (page 174), or a bowl of softly oozing cornmeal to sop up the escabeche sauce.

ATENÇÃO *For a less acidic bite, use 1 cup white wine vinegar and ½ cup dry white wine.*

18 PEARL ONIONS, A SCANT 1 INCH IN DIAMETER

4 PARTRIDGES, CORNISH GAME HENS, OR SQUAB (ABOUT 1 POUND EACH)

KOSHER SALT AND FRESHLY GROUND BLACK PEPPER

1 CUP PLUS 2 TABLESPOONS OLIVE OIL

24 LARGE UNPEELED GARLIC CLOVES

3 TURKISH BAY LEAVES

1 TABLESPOON CORIANDER SEEDS, CRACKED

1 TABLESPOON CURRY POWDER

A ½-INCH THUMB OF GINGER, PEELED

1 TEASPOON GROUND CUMIN

TWO 3-INCH CINNAMON STICKS

2 CUPS CHICKEN STOCK (PAGE 243) OR STORE-BOUGHT LOW-SODIUM BROTH

1½ CUPS WHITE WINE VINEGAR

1. Have a bowl of ice water at the ready. Bring a medium saucepan of water to a boil. Drop in the onions and blanch for 30 seconds. Scoop them out with a slotted spoon and plop them into the ice water to cool. To peel the onions, snip off the tips and remove the papery outer layers. Set the onions aside.

2. Place the birds breast side down on a cutting board. Using poultry shears, cut down along one side of each backbone, and then the other; discard the bones. Flip the birds over and cut them in half down the breastbone. Snip off the first joint of each wing and separate the legs and thighs from the breast. (Have your butcher do this if it's too much for you.) Pat the birds dry with paper towels. Season well with salt and pepper.

3. Heat the 2 tablespoons of oil in a Dutch oven over medium-high heat until hot. Working in batches, add the partridge pieces skin side down and sear

(recipe continues)

until golden brown, about 8 minutes. Flip and sear for 2 minutes more. Transfer to a platter.

4. Reduce the heat to medium-low, drop in the onions and garlic, and cook, stirring often, until the onions are spotted with brown, about 10 minutes. Add the bay leaves, coriander seeds, curry powder, ginger, cumin, cinnamon, 2 teaspoons salt, and 1 teaspoon pepper and cook for 30 seconds, stirring constantly. Nestle in the partridge pieces and add any accumulated juices. Pour in the 1 cup of oil, the stock, and vinegar, and add just enough water to almost cover the birds. Bring to a boil, then reduce to the lowest heat and let burble, covered, for 45 minutes.

5. Remove the pot from the stove and let cool for 1 hour, and then refrigerate for 24 to 48 hours.

6. The chilled marinade will have gelled. To serve, toss out the bay leaves and cinnamon, then remove the partridge pieces from the pot and wipe them clean. Heat the marinade over low heat until liquefied but not warm. Arrange the partridge pieces, as well as the onions and garlic cloves, on a platter and spoon some of the marinade on top. Or do as José does and heat the marinade and pieces until both are warmed through, and take the pot to the table. This is a messy dish, so instruct your guests to feel free to use their hands and to squeeze the garlic cloves right from their skins.

DUCK RISOTTO WITH HAM AND SAUSAGE

risoto de pato

SERVES 4 TO 6 AS A MAIN COURSE, 6 TO 8 AS A STARTER

Arroz de pato, or duck with rice, is a specialty of the Minho region. Traditionally it's made by first boiling the duck to cook it and make a stock, then later roasting shredded bits of the meat along with the rice. But I find this technique leaves the duck flavorless and dry. Plus, to degrease the stock, it takes another day. This riff, which is inspired by my friend, chef Vitor Veloso, calls for braising the legs in chicken stock, then shredding the meat and stirring it into a creamy risotto, along with the de rigueur ingredients—presunto, chouriço, and orange zest. Adorning the top are slices of the perfectly seared duck breast. Much faster, infinitely easier, and far more sophisticated.

1 TABLESPOON OLIVE OIL

2 DUCK LEGS (ABOUT 1$\frac{1}{4}$ POUNDS), TRIMMED OF EXCESS FAT

KOSHER SALT AND FRESHLY GROUND BLACK PEPPER

6 TO 8 CUPS CHICKEN STOCK (PAGE 243) OR STORE-BOUGHT LOW-SODIUM BROTH

3 OUNCES CHOURIÇO, LINGUIÇA, OR DRY-CURED SMOKED SPANISH CHORIZO, CUT INTO $\frac{1}{4}$-INCH CUBES

1 BONELESS MOULARD DUCK BREAST HALF (ABOUT 1 POUND)

1 SMALL YELLOW ONION, MINCED

2 CUPS CAROLINO, CARNAROLI, OR ARBORIO RICE

$\frac{1}{2}$ CUP DRY WHITE WINE

ONE $\frac{1}{4}$-INCH-THICK SLICE PRESUNTO, SERRANO HAM, OR PROSCIUTTO, EXCESS FAT REMOVED AND CUT INTO $\frac{1}{4}$-INCH CUBES

2 TABLESPOONS FRESH ORANGE JUICE

1 TABLESPOON UNSALTED BUTTER

MINCED FRESH FLAT-LEAF PARSLEY LEAVES, FOR GARNISH

1 TO 2 TABLESPOONS GRATED ORANGE ZEST, TO TASTE

1. Heat the oil in a large skillet over medium-high heat. Season the duck legs well with salt and pepper. When the skillet is hot, add the legs skin side down and sear until lightly browned, about 5 minutes per side. Transfer the legs to a medium pot; drain the fat and set the skillet aside.

2. Add enough of the stock to the pot to cover the duck, bring to a simmer, and cook, covered, over low heat until the meat is tender, 1 to 1$\frac{1}{2}$ hours.

3. Meanwhile, sauté the chouriço in the reserved skillet over medium heat until the fat is rendered, about 5 minutes. Using a slotted spoon, transfer to paper towels to drain.

4. Transfer the duck legs to a plate. When they're cool enough to handle, remove the skin, pull the meat from the bones, and shred into bite-sized

(recipe continues)

pieces. Set aside. Spoon the fat from the top of the stock, and add the remaining stock to the pot. Bring to a simmer over medium-low heat and keep it bubbling gently.

5. Heat the oven to warm, and slip in a wire rack set on a baking sheet.

6. With a razor-sharp knife, score the skin of the duck breast in a crosshatch pattern, being mindful not to cut into the flesh. Pat dry and season with salt and pepper. Wipe out the skillet and heat it over medium-low heat. Add the breast skin side down and sear until crisp, allowing the fat to render slowly, 10 to 15 minutes. Don't rush this—the last thing you want is a mouthful of chewy fat. Flip and sear the other side for 3 to 4 minutes. Transfer the duck to the rack in the oven to keep warm. While in the oven, the breast should reach medium-rare, about 135°F on an instant-read thermometer.

7. Drain all but 3 tablespoons of fat from the skillet, and heat over medium heat. Add the onion and cook, stirring occasionally, until softened, about 5 minutes. Stir in the rice to coat, and cook until translucent around the edges, about 2 minutes. Splash in the wine and continue cooking until it is absorbed. Add a ladleful of hot stock and cook, stirring continuously, until the liquid has almost burbled away. Keep up this rhythm of adding stock, stirring, and cooking for 15 minutes, then stir in the presunto and chouriço.

8. Add the shredded duck to the risotto and resume ladling, stirring, and cooking until the rice slumps gently when mounded and is tender but offers just the slightest bit of resistance in the middle, 5 to 10 minutes more. Stir in the orange juice and butter and season with salt and pepper to taste.

9. To serve, cut the duck breast on an angle into thin slices. Divide the risotto among shallow bowls and arrange the slices of breast on top. Sprinkle with the parsley and orange zest, and rush to the table.

DUCK BREASTS WITH BLACK OLIVES

peitos de pato com azeitonas pretas

SERVES 4 TO 6

This version of the Portuguese classic is an utter 180-degree departure, yet it has all the spot-on flavors of the original. I wanted to get to the heart of the dish—duck, black olives, a wickedly good sauce—without having to go through the tedious process of boning, braising, and then carving a whole duck. Instead, plump breasts are seared to a perfect medium-rare in minutes, and the sauce is whipped up on the stovetop in even less time.

4 OUNCES (ABOUT 3 SLICES)
THICK-SLICED SLAB BACON, CUT
CROSSWISE INTO $\frac{1}{4}$-INCH-WIDE
PIECES

ONE $\frac{1}{8}$-INCH-THICK SLICE PRESUNTO,
SERRANO HAM, OR PROSCIUTTO,
CUT INTO $\frac{1}{8}$-INCH CUBES

5 GARLIC CLOVES, CRUSHED

2 TEASPOONS CHOPPED FRESH
ROSEMARY LEAVES

1 TABLESPOON PLUS 1 TEASPOON
FRESH THYME LEAVES

1 CUP CHICKEN STOCK (PAGE 243)
OR LOW-SODIUM STORE-BOUGHT
BROTH

$\frac{2}{3}$ CUP TAWNY PORT OR MEDIUM-DRY
MADEIRA

$\frac{3}{4}$ TO 1 CUP OIL-CURED BLACK OLIVES,
TO TASTE, PITTED, HALVED, AND
RINSED

4 BONELESS MOULARD DUCK BREAST
HALVES (ABOUT 3 POUNDS TOTAL)

KOSHER SALT AND FRESHLY GROUND
BLACK PEPPER

1. Cook the bacon in a large skillet over medium-low heat, stirring often, until the fat begins to render, about 6 minutes. Add the presunto and garlic and sizzle until the garlic is golden brown and the meaty bits start to crisp, about 6 minutes more. Stir in the rosemary and thyme, pour in the stock and port, and bring to a boil. Cook for a minute, then add the olives and remove the pan from the heat.

2. With a razor-sharp knife, score the skin of the duck breasts in a crosshatch pattern, being mindful not to cut into the flesh. Pat dry and season with salt and pepper. Heat a large dry skillet over medium-low heat. Add the breasts skin side down and sear until crisp, allowing the fat to render slowly, 10 to 15 minutes. Don't rush this—the last thing you want is a mouthful of chewy fat. Flip and sear the other side for 3 to 4 minutes.

3. Meanwhile, bring the sauce back to a boil, then reduce the heat to low. Nestle in the breasts, skin side up, and cook for 4 to 6 minutes for medium-rare, 135°F on an instant-read thermometer. Transfer the duck to a cutting board and let rest for 5 minutes.

4. Slice the breasts on an angle, arrange on plates, and spoon the sauce and olives on top. Devour immediately.

MEATS

CARNES

Cheese-Stuffed Pork Tenderloin

Alentejan-Style Pork with Clams   *Spicy Azorean Garlic-Roasted Pork*

Pork Tenderloin in a Port-Prune Sauce

Pasta Pyramids Stuffed with Pork and Cheese

Grilled Beef Kebabs with Madeira, Bay Leaf, and Garlic

Braised Beef Shanks with Warm Spices

Momma Leite's Braised Beef in Wine and Garlic

Steak "on Horseback," Redefined

Mini Lamb Meatballs   *Lamb Stew with White Beans*

CHEESE-STUFFED PORK TENDERLOIN

lombinho de porco recheado com queijo

SERVES 4

Slathering pork with red pepper paste is hardly new; it's a quintessential pairing in Portugal. But introduce a seductive cheese into the marriage, and things start to get interesting. Luís Caseiro, former chef at Alfama Restaurant in New York City, came up with this clever combination.

ATENÇÃO ◈◈ *Some of the cheese may seep out during roasting: fear not. Simply smear it back in with the tip of a knife after you slice the tenderloins.*

TWO 14-OUNCE PORK TENDERLOINS, FAT AND SILVER SKIN REMOVED, CUT CROSSWISE IN HALF

¼ POUND FIRM CHEESE, SUCH AS NISA, SÃO JORGE, OR PECORINO ROMANO, GRATED

2 TABLESPOONS AMPED-UP RED PEPPER PASTE (PAGE 232)

FRESHLY GROUND BLACK PEPPER

2 TABLESPOONS LARD OR OLIVE OIL

½ CUP DRY WHITE WINE

1½ CUPS BEEF STOCK (PAGE 244) OR STORE-BOUGHT LOW-SODIUM BROTH

CHOPPED FRESH FLAT-LEAF PARSLEY LEAVES, FOR GARNISH

1. Using a metal skewer, poke a channel running the length of each tenderloin half through its center. Widen the channel to about ½ inch in diameter, and carefully stuff the cheese into the pork. Rub the meat with the red pepper paste and season with black pepper. Place the tenderloins in a baking dish, wrap with plastic, and marinate in the fridge for 4 hours, or overnight.

2. Position a rack in the middle of the oven and crank up the heat to 400°F. Remove the pork from the fridge and let sit for 20 minutes.

3. Warm a large skillet over medium-high heat and melt the lard. When it's hot, add the tenderloins and cook, turning occasionally, until well browned all around, 6 to 8 minutes. Transfer to a baking sheet (set the skillet aside), and roast the pork in the oven until the cheese is just beginning to melt and an instant-read thermometer inserted in the center of the meat registers just under 150°F, about 10 minutes. Remove the tenderloins and let rest for 5 minutes.

4. While the tenderloins are roasting, drain off any fat from the skillet, return the pan to high heat, and stir in the white wine. Bring to a boil, scraping up any browned bits from the bottom of the skillet, then add the beef stock and continue boiling until the pan sauce is reduced to 1 cup. Set aside.

5. To serve, cut the pieces of tenderloin in half on the bias. Lay one half in the center of each plate and lean the other against it at a jaunty angle. Drizzle the sauce over the top and garnish with the parsley.

ALENTEJAN-STYLE PORK WITH CLAMS

carne de porco à alentejana

SERVES 6 TO 8

This dish is from the Alentejo, Portugal's vast plains region, but my version bears only a passing resemblance to the original. Portuguese cooks typically fry the marinated cubes of pork loin in lard, making for some tough chewing, even with Portugal's tender pork. The version I was weaned on was braised, requiring hours of cooking so that the meat would soften and break down. I'm indebted to Jean Anderson, author of *The Food of Portugal*, who suggested I use pork shoulder (butt), an excellent choice for juicy, tender morsels—with significantly less time on the stove.

ATENÇÃO ⟫ *This dish is usually served over deep-fried potato cubes. Roasting the cubes in the oven leaves you free to get on with cooking, entertaining, and being a terrific host, without the worry of a major oil spill. Also, the pork needs to marinate at least overnight, so keep that in mind when planning your menu.*

3 POUNDS BONELESS PORK SHOULDER BUTT, CUT INTO 1-INCH CHUNKS

¼ CUP AMPED-UP RED PEPPER PASTE (PAGE 232)

1¾ CUPS DRY WHITE WINE

6 TABLESPOONS OLIVE OIL, OR MORE IF NEEDED

2 MEDIUM YELLOW ONIONS, COARSELY CHOPPED

3 GARLIC CLOVES, MINCED

2 POUNDS YUKON GOLD POTATOES, PEELED AND CUT INTO 1-INCH CUBES

KOSHER SALT AND FRESHLY GROUND BLACK PEPPER

3¼ POUNDS SMALL CLAMS, SUCH AS COCKLES, MANILA, BUTTER, OR LITTLENECKS, SCRUBBED AND RINSED

¼ CUP CHOPPED FRESH CILANTRO LEAVES

1. Toss the pork chunks with the red pepper paste in a medium bowl. Add the wine and toss again. Cover with plastic wrap and refrigerate for at least 24 hours or up to 36 hours.

2. Position a rack in the middle of the oven and crank up the heat to 400°F.

3. Dump the pork into a colander set over a large bowl to drain. Reserve the marinade and pat the pork dry with paper towels. Heat 3 tablespoons of the olive oil in a large pot over medium-high heat until hot. Working in batches, add the pork and cook, stirring occasionally, until browned on all sides, 5 to 7 minutes. Add more oil in between batches, if needed. Transfer the pieces to a plate using a slotted spoon. If the bottom of the pot develops a dark coating, tip in some water in between batches and scrape it up.

(recipe continues)

4. Lower the heat to medium, add the onion, and cook until soft, about 5 minutes. Add the garlic and cook for 1 minute more. Pour in the reserved marinade, return the pork to the pot, and cook, covered, over low heat until the meat is tender, 1 to $1^1/2$ hours. If it looks as if the liquid will burble away, spoon in a bit of water.

5. Meanwhile, toss the potato cubes with the remaining 3 tablespoons oil, season lightly with salt and with plenty of pepper, and scatter in one layer on a foil-lined baking sheet. Roast, flipping them once or twice, until golden brown, about 45 minutes.

6. Discard any clams that feel heavy (which means they're full of sand), have broken shells, or don't close when tapped. Raise the heat under the pork to high, stir in the clams, cover, and cook until they open, 7 to 10 minutes. Toss out any that refuse to pop open. Taste the broth and season with salt and pepper if needed.

7. To serve, remove half the clams from their shells, and return them to the pot. Toss out the shells. Line the bottom of the serving bowls with the potato cubes, top with the pork and clams and broth, and sprinkle with the cilantro. Have a large bowl at the ready for the shells.

SPICY AZOREAN GARLIC-ROASTED PORK

torresmos açoreanos

SERVES 8 TO 10

The name of this recipe is perhaps the most confounding in all of Portugal. In the town of Mealhada, in the central region where roast suckling pig reigns, *torresmos* is a plate of pork cracklings. In other towns, it's short ribs, while in still other places, it's a confit of pork that's eaten for breakfast. In the Azores, especially on the north side of the island of São Miguel, where my family is from, it's the roasted butt section of a pork shoulder. This recipe is an adaptation of my aunt Irena's *torresmos*. Her marinade includes *pimenta moída*, a crushed hot red pepper paste, which you can find at mellôschourico.com (see Sources, page 251), but my version gives the same flavor without the fuss of special ordering. Serve it with Tomato Rice (page 185), with some of the pan drippings stirred in, or with boiled baby red potatoes.

ATENÇÃO ❧ *The pork needs to marinate at least overnight, so keep that in mind when planning your menu.*

½ POUND MEDIUM-HOT RED CHILES, SUCH AS SERRANOS OR JALAPEÑOS, STEMMED AND SEEDED	½ CUP DRY WHITE WINE
10 GARLIC CLOVES	½ CUP DRY RED WINE
¼ CUP SWEET PAPRIKA	ONE 4-POUND BONELESS PORK SHOULDER BUTT, CUT INTO 8 PIECES
KOSHER SALT	3 TABLESPOONS VEGETABLE OIL
	FRESHLY GROUND BLACK PEPPER

1. Combine the chiles, garlic, paprika, and 1 tablespoon salt in a food processor and pulse to form a rough paste. Transfer the mixture to a large bowl and stir in the white and red wines until smooth. Add the pork pieces, turning to coat. Cover the bowl with plastic wrap and refrigerate overnight, or for up to 48 hours.

2. Position a rack in the middle of the oven and crank up the heat to 375°F.

3. Coat the bottom of a roasting pan with the oil. Add the pork, with the marinade, and season with salt and pepper. Roast, uncovered, turning the pork often, until it is evenly browned and an instant-read thermometer inserted into the middle of a piece of pork registers just under 150°F, about 1 hour.

4. Remove the pan from the oven and let the pork rest for 5 minutes. Thinly slice the pieces of pork against the grain and serve immediately.

PORK TENDERLOIN IN A PORT-PRUNE SAUCE

lombinho de porco com molho de porto e ameixas secas

SERVES 6

When I stayed at the quaint Refúgio da Vila, in the tiny town of Portel, I made sure to sign up for their cooking classes. They were held in the airy *cozinha de matança*, or butchering kitchen, where, in years past, livestock went after meeting their maker. This was our first dish of the day. Plums are a specialty of the area, so naturally prunes—aka dried plums—were on the menu.

$^2/_3$ CUP PITTED PRUNES (ABOUT 15)

1 CUP RUBY PORT

$^1/_2$ CUP BEEF STOCK (SEE PAGE 244) OR STORE-BOUGHT LOW-SODIUM BROTH, OR MORE IF NEEDED

A 1-INCH THUMB OF GINGER, PEELED AND GRATED

1 TABLESPOON HONEY

KOSHER SALT AND FRESHLY GROUND BLACK PEPPER

2 TABLESPOONS OLIVE OIL

TWO 1-POUND PORK TENDERLOINS, FAT AND SILVER SKIN REMOVED

1 GARLIC CLOVE, MINCED

3 TABLESPOONS SHERRY VINEGAR

CHOPPED FRESH CILANTRO LEAVES

1. Position a rack in the middle of the oven and crank up the heat to 450°F.

2. Dump the prunes into a small saucepan, add the port, beef stock, ginger, and honey, and bring just to a boil. Reduce the heat and simmer, covered, for 15 minutes. Turn off the heat and let steep for 20 minutes.

3. Pour the prunes and liquid into a blender or food processor and buzz until smooth. Season with salt and pepper to taste.

4. Heat the oil in a large skillet over medium-high heat until hot. Season both tenderloins well with salt and pepper and sear one at a time, turning occasionally, until brown, about 5 minutes. Transfer to a baking sheet and set the skillet aside.

5. Roast the pork until an instant-read thermometer inserted in the center of the meat registers just under 150°F, 15 to 18 minutes. Transfer the tenderloins to a cutting board, tent with foil, and let rest for 5 minutes.

6. Pour off all but a thin film of fat from the skillet. Lower the heat to medium, toss in the garlic, and cook until lightly colored, about 2 minutes. Add the port-prune sauce and stir to pick up the browned bits stuck to the skillet. Pour in the vinegar, and any accumulated juices from the pork, and cook to meld the flavors, 2 to 3 minutes. If the sauce seems thick, add more beef stock. For an elegant take, strain the sauce through a sieve.

7. Cut the tenderloins on the diagonal into $^1/_2$-inch slices. Divide the slices among six plates, drizzle with the warm sauce, and sprinkle with cilantro.

PASTA PYRAMIDS STUFFED WITH PORK AND CHEESE

pirâmides de carne

SERVES 4 AS A MAIN COURSE, 8 AS A STARTER

Pasta entered the culinary vernacular in Portugal sometime during the past fifteen years. Before that, it was found mostly in European-style hotels in the cities as a way of catering to a foreign clientele. Leading the democratization charge has been Italian-born Augusto Gemelli, owner of Restaurante Gemelli in Lisbon. Gemelli is famous for his use of local ingredients cooked in the Italian manner. This dish was inspired by his many fancifully filled pastas.

ATENÇÃO ❧ *If you don't want to fiddle with making the pyramids, just fold the wrappers over to make triangles.*

6 OUNCES CHOURIÇO, LINGUIÇA, OR DRY-CURED SMOKED SPANISH CHORIZO, CUT INTO CHUNKS

3 TABLESPOONS OLIVE OIL

6 OUNCES GROUND PORK

1 MEDIUM YELLOW ONION, MINCED

1 GARLIC CLOVE, MINCED

2/3 CUP REQUEIJÃO CHEESE (SEE PAGE 21) OR WHOLE-MILK RICOTTA

3 TABLESPOONS CHOPPED FRESH CILANTRO LEAVES

KOSHER SALT AND FRESHLY GROUND BLACK PEPPER

TWENTY-FOUR 3-BY-3-INCH WONTON WRAPPERS OR HOMEMADE PASTA SQUARES

6 TABLESPOONS UNSALTED BUTTER

1. Pulse the chouriço in a food processor until finely minced.

2. Heat 1 tablespoon of the oil in a medium skillet over medium-high heat. When it is hot, dump in the chouriço and pork and cook, stirring occasionally to break up any clumps, until the chouriço begins to crisp and the pork is cooked through, 7 to 10 minutes. Scoop into a bowl using a slotted spoon.

3. Lower the heat to medium and add the remaining 2 tablespoons of oil. Dump in the onion and cook, stirring occasionally, until golden brown, 7 to 10 minutes. Add the garlic and cook for 1 minute more. Scrape the mixture into the bowl containing the meat. Stir in the Requeijão and 2 tablespoons of the cilantro, and season with salt and pepper to taste. Set aside.

4. Fill a small bowl with water. Place one wonton wrapper on a work surface, keeping the rest covered with plastic. Dollop a scant tablespoon of the filling in the middle. Dip your finger in the water and dampen the outer ¼ inch of the wrapper all around. Grasp two opposite corners and bring them up to meet. Pull up a third corner, and seal the seams well. Repeat with the fourth

corner, pressing together the seams to make a pyramid. Pinch the top tightly. Place the pyramid on a baking sheet lined with a nonstick baking mat or parchment and repeat with the remaining wrappers and filling.

5. Bring a large pot of water to a gentle boil over medium heat and add 1 tablespoon of salt. Meanwhile, heat the butter in a small saucepan over medium-low heat until fragrant and nut-brown, about 4 minutes. Set aside.

6. Slide the pyramids into the water and cook until tender, 2 to 3 minutes. Using a slotted spoon, lift them from the water, draining well, and transfer them to the serving bowls. Spoon the brown butter over the top, and sprinkle with the remaining tablespoon of cilantro.

GRILLED BEEF KEBABS WITH MADEIRA, BAY LEAF, AND GARLIC

espetada

SERVES 6 TO 8

While on the north side of the island of Madeira, my friend and fellow Lusophile Janet Boileau and I sat down to lunch at a nondescript place practically carved into the side of the mountain. Above us hung a medieval-looking chain. When our kebabs arrived, skewered on a long bay laurel branch, they were hung from the chain, and a plate was slipped beneath to catch the juices. The simplicity of the fire-charred beef, the slight hint of bay from the branch, and the monumental baskets of Fried Cornmeal (page 193) and Madeiran Griddle Bread (page 190) made for one of our most memorable lunches.

3 GARLIC CLOVES, MINCED

$1/2$ CUP DRY MADEIRA WINE

6 TABLESPOONS UNSALTED BUTTER, MELTED

5 TURKISH BAY LEAVES, CRUMBLED, PLUS WHOLE LEAVES FOR GRILLING (OPTIONAL)

KOSHER SALT AND FRESHLY GROUND BLACK PEPPER

3 POUNDS BONELESS BEEF RIB-EYE, BEEF TENDERLOIN, OR SIRLOIN, CUT INTO $1^{1}/_{2}$-INCH CUBES

1. Combine the garlic, wine, butter, crumbled bay leaves, and a pinch each of salt and pepper in a large bowl. Toss the beef in the mixture, and refrigerate for 2 hours.

2. Remove the beef from the fridge and let sit at room temperature for 1 hour.

3. Heat a gas or charcoal grill to high, or heat a grill pan over high heat until hot.

4. Meanwhile, thread the beef chunks and whole bay leaves, if using, onto metal skewers and season well with salt and pepper.

5. Grill the kebabs, turning once and basting with the marinade, until lightly charred, 4 to 6 minutes for medium-rare. Toss out the remaining marinade. Let the skewers rest for a few minutes before serving.

BRAISED BEEF SHANKS WITH WARM SPICES

alcatra à moda de restaurante a colmeia

SERVES 4

Whenever I visit the island of São Miguel, I always stay in the Hotel do Colégio. The service is excellent, the staff is friendly, and the rooms are beautifully appointed. But I hadn't dined at their restaurant, A Colmeia, until recently. There I had what was perhaps the finest—and most scandalous—version of a classic Azorean dish, braised beef from the island of Terceira: finest, because it was so intensely flavored and tender; scandalous because it used not the customary, often dry, rump, but rather beef shanks—an excellent spin on a shopworn staple. Serve this over Puréed Potatoes (page 174).

1 TEASPOON BLACK PEPPERCORNS, CRACKED	KOSHER SALT AND FRESHLY GROUND BLACK PEPPER
1 TEASPOON WHOLE ALLSPICE BERRIES	OLIVE OIL, IF NEEDED
6 WHOLE CLOVES	2 LARGE YELLOW ONIONS, DICED
TWO 3-INCH CINNAMON STICKS	6 GARLIC CLOVES, MINCED
2 TURKISH BAY LEAVES	2½ CUPS BEEF STOCK (PAGE 244) OR STORE-BOUGHT LOW-SODIUM BROTH
A 6-OUNCE CHUNK OF SLAB BACON, CUT INTO ½-INCH CUBES	2 CUPS DRY RED WINE
4 THICK CENTER-CUT BEEF SHANKS (ABOUT 3½ POUNDS TOTAL)	2 TABLESPOONS DARK MOLASSES

1. Tie the peppercorns, allspice, cloves, cinnamon sticks, and bay leaves into a cheesecloth pouch. Set aside.

2. Heat a large ovenproof pot with a tight-fitting lid over medium-low heat until hot. Add the bacon and sizzle to render the fat and crisp the meaty bits, about 10 minutes. Transfer with a slotted spoon to paper towels. Raise the heat to medium-high, season the shanks well with salt and pepper, and sear until very brown, about 5 minutes per side. Don't skimp—deep browning gives the dish more flavor. Transfer to a plate and set aside.

3. Lower the heat to medium. If the pot is dry, drizzle in some oil. Add the onions, and cook until softened, about 7 minutes. Add the garlic and cook for 1 minute more.

4. Meanwhile, position a rack in the lower third of the oven and crank up the heat to 350°F.

5. Add the stock, wine, molasses, and 1 teaspoon salt to the pot and bring to a boil. Turn off the heat, return the bacon, beef, and any accumulated juices to the pot, and nestle in the spice pouch.

6. Cover and braise the beef in the oven, turning several times, until fork-tender, 3½ to 4 hours.

7. Remove the pot from the oven and place it on the stove. Using a slotted spoon, transfer the meat to a plate. It'll fall apart—that's the point. Transfer the bones, too. They contain the marrow, which some people, like me, just lap up. Discard any rubbery bits still clinging to the meat and toss out the spice pouch. If necessary, reduce the cooking liquid over high heat to about 1½ cups. Skim the fat from the sauce and season with salt and pepper to taste.

8. Divide the meat and bones with marrow among four bowls and ladle the sauce on top.

MOMMA LEITE'S BRAISED BEEF IN WINE AND GARLIC

carne assada em vinha d'alhos da minha mãe

SERVES 8 TO 10

This is my mom's version of the traditional Azorean dish. It has a bit of a spicy kick, which is common in the islands. I've tweaked it a bit by searing the beef first for extra flavor, something Portuguese cooks don't usually do. Have a hunk of chewy bread nearby to lap up the *molho*, or gravy.

8 GARLIC CLOVES, CRUSHED

ONE 750-ML BOTTLE DRY RED WINE

3 TABLESPOONS DOUBLE-CONCENTRATE TOMATO PASTE

1 TEASPOON CHOPPED FRESH OREGANO LEAVES

2 TURKISH BAY LEAVES

1 TABLESPOON SWEET PAPRIKA

1 TABLESPOON SWEET SMOKED PAPRIKA

$1\frac{1}{2}$ TEASPOONS CRUSHED RED PEPPER FLAKES, OR MORE TO TASTE

KOSHER SALT

ONE 4-POUND BONELESS CHUCK ROAST, TIED

FRESHLY GROUND BLACK PEPPER

3 TABLESPOONS OLIVE OIL, OR MORE IF NEEDED

2 LARGE YELLOW ONIONS, CHOPPED

$1\frac{1}{2}$ POUNDS CHOURIÇO, LINGUIÇA, OR DRY-CURED SMOKED SPANISH CHORIZO, CUT INTO SEVERAL PIECES

$1\frac{1}{2}$ POUNDS GOLF-BALL-SIZED RED POTATOES, PEELED

$\frac{1}{2}$ POUND BABY CARROTS

CHOPPED FRESH FLAT-LEAF PARSLEY LEAVES, FOR GARNISH

1. Combine the garlic, wine, tomato paste, oregano, bay leaves, both types of paprika, pepper flakes, and 1 teaspoon salt in a large bowl. Add the beef and turn to coat. Cover and marinate in the fridge for at least 4 hours, or, preferably, overnight, turning the beef several times.

2. Position a rack in the lower third of the oven and crank up the heat to 325°F.

3. Remove the bowl from the fridge and transfer the beef and garlic cloves to a plate. Reserve the marinade. Pat the beef dry with paper towels and season well with salt and black pepper. Heat the oil in an ovenproof Dutch oven over medium-high heat and, when it's hot, sear the beef on all sides until well browned, about 5 minutes per side. Transfer to the plate and set aside.

4. Reduce the heat to medium. If the pot is dry, drizzle in more oil. Add the onions and cook, stirring occasionally, until golden brown, about 15 minutes. Add the garlic cloves and cook for 3 minutes more.

5. Pour the marinade and 1 cup of water into the pot and bring to a boil. Nestle in the beef, cover tightly, and braise in the oven, turning and basting every 20 minutes, for 2¼ hours.

6. Add the chouriço, potatoes, and carrots to the pot and cook, covered, until the meat is tender, about 30 minutes more. Transfer the beef to a bowl, ladle some of the cooking liquid over the top and cover with foil to keep warm.

7. Bump up the oven temperature to 400°F and roast the vegetables and sausage, uncovered, until the potatoes are easily pierced with a knife, 15 to 25 minutes more. Transfer the vegetables and sausage to the bowl with the meat. Skim any fat from the sauce in the pot, and reduce the sauce over hight heat if it appears too thin. Toss out the bay leaves.

8. To serve, slice the chouriço on the bias into 2-inch pieces. Center the beef on a platter and ring with the sausage and vegetables. Ladle a bit of the sauce on top, sprinkle with parsley, and serve the rest of the sauce on the side.

STEAK "ON HORSEBACK," REDEFINED

bife com ovo a cavalo, redefinido

SERVES 6

This is a combination of two popular café dishes in Lisbon: *bife com ovo a cavalo*—steak topped with a fried egg, hence the horseback reference—and *bife à Marrare*—steak in a peppercorn cream sauce, named in honor of Marrare das Sete Portas, the luxe early-twentieth-century haunt of artists, writers, and bohemian hangers-on. I've gussied up the presentation by slicing the beef, coiling it on the plates, and topping it with petite quail eggs.

3 SMALL GARLIC CLOVES, THINLY SLICED

THREE $^3/_4$-INCH-THICK BONELESS STRIP STEAKS (ABOUT $2^1/_2$ POUNDS TOTAL)

1 TABLESPOON VEGETABLE OIL, OR MORE IF NEEDED

KOSHER SALT AND FRESHLY GROUND BLACK PEPPER

2 CUPS HEAVY CREAM

$2^1/_2$ TABLESPOONS DIJON MUSTARD

1 TEASPOON BLACK PEPPERCORNS, CRACKED

2 TABLESPOONS UNSALTED BUTTER

6 QUAIL EGGS OR SMALL HEN EGGS

2 TABLESPOONS CHOPPED FRESH FLAT-LEAF PARSLEY LEAVES

1. Pat the garlic onto both sides of the steaks, cover with plastic wrap, and let them sit at room temperature for 30 minutes.

2. Heat the oven to warm and slip in a wire rack set on a baking sheet.

3. Heat a large skillet over medium-high heat until hot, and add the oil. Brush off the garlic from the steaks and generously season the meat with salt and pepper. Working in batches if necessary, sear the steaks, adjusting the heat to avoid burning them, for about 3 minutes per side for medium-rare, about 5 minutes for medium. Transfer the steaks to the rack in the oven to keep warm.

4. Add the cream, mustard, and peppercorns to the skillet and cook, whisking often, until reduced by one quarter, about 5 minutes. Remove from the heat and whisk in any accumulated juice from the resting steaks. Season with salt and pepper to taste.

5. Heat the butter in a medium nonstick skillet over medium heat until the foaming subsides. Crack in the eggs and fry them sunny-side up, 2 to 3 minutes. Season with salt and pepper.

6. To serve, slice the steaks diagonally across the grain into long $^1/_8$-inch-thick slices. Coil the slices on the plates, drizzle with the sauce, crown each with a quail egg, and sprinkle with the parsley.

MINI LAMB MEATBALLS
almôndegas de borrego

When I walked along the burnished cobbled sidewalks of Lisbon and Porto, I'd see ALMÔNDEGAS scrawled on the chalkboard menus of *tascas*, small, family-run eateries. Never having had them growing up, I went on a meatball crusade, sampling them everywhere. What I discovered was they're traditionally made with beef or pork and simmered in a spiced tomato sauce. My friend Teresa Cota Dias, a terrific cook, makes lamb meatballs in a beef sauce with hints of ginger, cumin, and cinnamon that recall Portugal's Moorish past. She serves them over Puréed Potatoes (page 174), but they also work alongside rice or by themselves as a predinner nibble.

FOR THE MEATBALLS

2 POUNDS LEAN GROUND LAMB

$\frac{1}{2}$ CUP DRIED BREAD CRUMBS

1 LARGE EGG, BEATEN

3 GARLIC CLOVES, MINCED

2 TABLESPOONS PEELED, GRATED FRESH GINGER

1 TABLESPOON GRATED ORANGE ZEST

1 TABLESPOON SWEET PAPRIKA

$1\frac{1}{2}$ TEASPOONS GROUND CUMIN

$1\frac{1}{2}$ TEASPOONS GROUND CINNAMON

$\frac{1}{4}$ CUP CHOPPED FRESH CILANTRO LEAVES

2 TEASPOONS KOSHER SALT

1 TEASPOON FRESHLY GROUND BLACK PEPPER

2 TABLESPOONS OLIVE OIL, OR MORE IF NEEDED

FOR THE SAUCE

1 LARGE YELLOW ONION, MINCED

1 TURKISH BAY LEAF

2 GARLIC CLOVES, MINCED

1 TABLESPOON PLUS 2 TEASPOONS ALL-PURPOSE FLOUR

$\frac{1}{2}$ TEASPOON GROUND CUMIN

$\frac{1}{4}$ TEASPOON GROUND CINNAMON

$\frac{1}{2}$ CUP DRY WHITE WINE

2 CUPS BEEF STOCK (PAGE 244) OR STORE-BOUGHT LOW-SODIUM BROTH

KOSHER SALT AND FRESHLY GROUND BLACK PEPPER

CHOPPED FRESH CILANTRO LEAVES, FOR GARNISH

1. Combine the lamb, bread crumbs, egg, garlic, ginger, zest, paprika, cumin, cinnamon, cilantro, salt, and pepper in a large bowl. Wet your hands and knead the mixture, but don't overmix. Scoop up $\frac{1}{2}$ tablespoon of the mixture, roll it into a ball between your palms, and place it on a rimmed baking sheet. Repeat with the rest of the mixture.

2. Heat the oil in a large skillet over medium-high heat. When it's hot, add the meatballs, in 3 or 4 batches, and cook, shaking the pan often to prevent sticking, until evenly browned, 3 to 5 minutes. Transfer to a bowl using a slotted spoon. If too much fat accumulates in the pan between batches, drain it before continuing.

3. After the last batch of meatballs has cooked, drain off all but 2 tablespoons of fat from the skillet. If the pan is dry, drizzle in a bit more oil. Add the onion and bay leaf and cook over medium heat, stirring occasionally, until the onion is golden brown, about 12 minutes. Add the garlic and cook for 1 minute more. Sprinkle in the flour, cumin, and cinnamon and stir until the mixture is fragrant, about 1 minute. Splash in the wine and cook, stirring constantly, until the liquid has almost burbled away, about 1 to 2 minutes. Add the beef stock and cook until the mixture begins to thicken, about 4 minutes. Reduce the heat to low and simmer to thicken the sauce a bit more, 4 to 5 minutes. Season with salt and pepper to taste. Remove the bay leaf.

4. Return the meatballs, along with any accumulated juices, to the skillet and stir to coat. Continue to simmer, lid ajar, until the meatballs are heated through, about 5 minutes. Sprinkle with cilantro and serve immediately. Or, for even better flavor, slip the meatballs into the fridge overnight. Warm in a skillet over low heat before serving.

LAMB STEW WITH WHITE BEANS

borrego ensopado de com feijão branco

SERVES 6 TO 8

This worldly take on a traditional *ensopado*, or stew, is from my friend José Vilela. Although many *ensopados* are often tomato based, this one relies on ingredients and flavors from some of Portugal's former colonies, as well as its many trade routes.

If the doorbell rings, and you're suddenly faced with several more dinner guests, fear not: José often serves this over pasta. His choice? Farfalle. Of course, you can serve the stew over slices of toasted or deep-fried bread, which is traditional.

4 POUNDS LAMB SHOULDER, EXCESS FAT AND SINEW REMOVED, CUT INTO 1½-INCH CUBES

1½ CUPS ORANGE JUICE

6 GARLIC CLOVES, MINCED

A 4-INCH THUMB OF GINGER, PEELED AND GRATED

1 CUP CHOPPED FRESH MINT LEAVES

KOSHER SALT AND FRESHLY GROUND BLACK PEPPER

2 TABLESPOONS OLIVE OIL, OR MORE IF NEEDED

2 TABLESPOONS ALL-PURPOSE FLOUR

3 CUPS BEEF STOCK (PAGE 244) OR STORE-BOUGHT LOW-SODIUM BROTH

1½ CUPS DRIED NAVY BEANS, PICKED OVER, RINSED, AND SOAKED OVERNIGHT IN ENOUGH WATER TO COVER BY 3 INCHES, OR 3 CUPS CANNED CANNELLINI BEANS, DRAINED AND RINSED

8 CARROTS, PEELED AND CUT ON THE BIAS INTO ½-INCH SLICES

3 TURKISH BAY LEAVES

TWO 3-INCH CINNAMON STICKS

1 TABLESPOON CHOPPED FRESH OREGANO LEAVES

1 STAR ANISE

2 TEASPOONS CRUSHED CORIANDER SEEDS

1 TEASPOON GROUND CUMIN

1 TEASPOON GRATED LEMON ZEST

2 TABLESPOONS FRESH LEMON JUICE

2 CUPS CHOPPED CANNED TOMATOES, PREFERABLY SAN MARZANO, DRAINED

CHOPPED FRESH FLAT-LEAF PARSLEY LEAVES, FOR GARNISH

1. Toss the lamb with the orange juice, garlic, ginger, and mint in a large bowl. Let marinate, covered, in the fridge for 4 hours.

2. Dump the lamb into a colander set over a bowl to catch the marinade. Reserve the liquid. Dry the lamb very well with paper towels; if you don't, the pieces will steam, not sear. Generously season the lamb with salt and pepper.

3. Heat the oil in a large pot over medium-high heat until very hot. Working in 3 or 4 batches, sear the lamb pieces, stirring occasionally, until browned, 8 to 10 minutes. Using a slotted spoon, transfer to a bowl.

4. Return all the lamb to the pot, sprinkle with the flour, and stir to combine. Pour in the reserved marinade and the stock. Add the drained soaked beans (if using canned beans, add them in the next step), the carrots, bay leaves, cinnamon, oregano, star anise, coriander seeds, cumin, lemon zest, and lemon juice, cover, and bring to a boil. Reduce the heat to low and simmer for 1¼ hours, stirring occasionally.

5. Spoon in the tomatoes and the canned beans, if using. Continue simmering, uncovered if the stew is thin, until the lamb is tender and the beans are soft but still hold their shape, 15 to 20 minutes more. Toss out the bay leaves, cinnamon sticks, and star anise. Take a taste and season the stew with salt and pepper, if needed.

6. To serve, ladle into bowls and speckle with parsley.

EGGS, VEGETABLES, AND RICE

OVOS, VEGETAIS, E ARROZ

Sausage Tortilla ❧ Eggs Simmered in Tomato Sauce ❧

Scrambled Eggs with Asparagus and Fresh Cod ❧

Fava Bean and Fennel Salad ❧ Orange Salad with Pine Nuts ❧

Spinach with Toasted Bread Crumbs ❧ Seared Broccoli Rabe with Garlic ❧

Sautéed Chestnuts, Onions, and Bacon ❧ Punched Potatoes ❧

Puréed Potatoes ❧ Sweet-Sour Carrots ❧ Crispy Fried Asparagus ❧

My Family's White Beans and Sausage ❧

Black-Eyed Peas with Onions and Red Pepper ❧

Black Olive Risotto ❧ Rice from the Pan ❧ Tomato Rice

SAUSAGE TORTILLA

tortilha com chouriço

SERVES 4 AS A MAIN COURSE, 6 AS A STARTER

Vovó Costa used to serve this to my cousins Barry and Wayne and me right from her big cast-iron skillet for lunch or, if we were lucky, for a late supper on Sunday evenings, if we were allowed to stay up and watch TV. It's terrific served warm as a main course, at room temperature as a starter, or cut into thin wedges to serve 12 as an hors d'oeuvre.

3 TABLESPOONS OLIVE OIL, OR MORE IF NEEDED

$\frac{1}{2}$ POUND CHOURIÇO, LINGUIÇA, OR DRY-CURED SPANISH CHORIZO, CUT INTO $\frac{1}{4}$-INCH COINS

1 MEDIUM YELLOW ONION, CHOPPED

$\frac{1}{2}$ POUND YUKON GOLD POTATOES, PEELED AND CUT INTO $\frac{1}{8}$-INCH SLICES

KOSHER SALT AND FRESHLY GROUND BLACK PEPPER

2 GARLIC CLOVES, MINCED

$\frac{1}{4}$ CUP DICED JARRED ROASTED RED PEPPERS, DRAINED WELL

7 LARGE EGGS

CHOPPED FRESH FLAT-LEAF PARSLEY LEAVES, FOR GARNISH

1. Heat 2 tablespoons of the oil in a 10-inch ovenproof nonstick skillet over medium heat until it shimmers. Add the chouriço and cook until lightly browned, about 5 minutes. With a slotted spoon, transfer to a large bowl. Turn the heat to medium-low and drop in the onion and potatoes. Season with salt and pepper and cook, stirring often, until the onions are translucent and the potatoes are fork-tender, 20 to 25 minutes.

2. Add the garlic and cook for 1 minute more. Transfer the mixture, along with the peppers, to the bowl with the chouriço. Set the skillet aside.

3. Heat the broiler. Beat the eggs in a medium bowl until fluffy and season with 1 teaspoon salt and $\frac{1}{4}$ teaspoon pepper. Pour the eggs over the chouriço-potato mixture and toss to coat.

4. Wipe out the skillet, add the remaining 1 tablespoon of oil, and heat over medium heat. Pour in the egg mixture. Using a rubber spatula, quickly stir to cook the eggs briefly, then jiggle the skillet to settle its contents. Run the spatula around the sides of the skillet to release the *tortilha*. Crank up the heat to medium-high and cook until the edges are set, 3 to 4 minutes.

5. Slide the skillet under the broiler and cook until the top is nicely browned and no puddles of egg remain, 1 to 2 minutes. Slip the *tortilha* onto a large platter and sprinkle with the parsley, or serve it right from the pan, as my grandmother did.

EGGS SIMMERED IN TOMATO SAUCE

tomatada com ovos

SERVES 2 AS A MAIN COURSE

Whenever I want a simple, tasty breakfast, weekend dinner, or late-night supper, I pull out some *tomatada*, a classic Portuguese tomato sauce I always have on hand. This is a riff on a traditional recipe, but instead of firing up the oven for just an egg or two, as the original requires, I make it on the stove. Less than 15 minutes later, I'm sitting down to eat.

1½ CUPS TOMATO SAUCE (PAGE 239)

2 LARGE EGGS

FINE SEA SALT AND FRESHLY GROUND
  BLACK PEPPER

2 SLICES RUSTIC BREAD, TOASTED

1 GARLIC CLOVE, CUT IN HALF

EXTRA-VIRGIN OLIVE OIL

1. Warm the tomato sauce in a small nonstick skillet, covered, over medium-high heat, until it's bubbly and hot, about 5 minutes. Lower the heat to medium, stir, and then make two wells in the sauce with the back of a spoon. Crack an egg into each well and simmer, covered, until the eggs are cooked, 5 to 8 minutes.

2. To serve, lightly rub the toast with the garlic, drizzle with a thin thread of oil, and place on plates. Scoop an egg and some tomato sauce on top of each slice, and season with salt and pepper to taste.

MAN CAN LIVE BY BREAD ALONE

Travel though Portugal, and you'll be dazzled, perhaps dizzied, by the incredible number of dishes in which bread plays a major role. Originally used as a way to stretch meals, bread now remains a part of the cuisine due to flavor. Here's a short list of the most popular bread-based dishes you're likely to find on menus and in homes:

Açorda is a bread soup that can range from loose to dense, depending on where you're dining. It's made by stirring water, broth, or stock into cubed day-old bread. It can be studded with seafood, infused with herbs such as cilantro, or enriched with eggs.

Ensopado is a stew—meat, fish, or shellfish—in which all the luscious juices are sopped up by slices of fresh, toasted, or deep-fried bread lining the bottom of the serving dish.

Sopa seca, or dry soup, is a homey preparation favored in the north. A deep baking dish is filled with bits of the previous days' meals, from meats to vegetables, covered with thick slabs of bread, and doused with stock. Then the whole thing is slid into a piping-hot oven to dry slightly.

Migas (literally, "bread crumbs") is the driest of the bunch. It's made by beating meat drippings, and sometimes leafy greens such as spinach, into crumbled bread. The mixture is then tossed in a hot skillet to form a crust and served as a side dish.

SCRAMBLED EGGS WITH ASPARAGUS AND FRESH COD

espargos verdes à brás com bacalhau fresco

SERVES 4 AS A MAIN COURSE

Ask most Portuguese chefs, and they can pretty much pinpoint the beginning of the country's cooking revolution. It's this dish—well, in its full restaurant glory—from Fausto Airoldi, then chef at Bica do Sapato, in Lisbon. He took a beloved classic of softly scrambled eggs mixed with matchstick potatoes and salt cod, and livened it up with asparagus, fresh cod (gasp!), and an aromatic herb oil. It's one of the dishes most copied in Portuguese restaurants today. For the classic, and a few of the variations, see below.

ATENÇÃO ✺ *You can prepare the asparagus and matchstick potatoes up to 2 hours in advance. For an elegant brunch dish, omit the fish.*

KOSHER SALT

22 MEDIUM ASPARAGUS SPEARS, WOODY BOTTOMS REMOVED

¼ CUP PLUS 2 TABLESPOONS OLIVE OIL, OR MORE IF NEEDED

1 LARGE YUKON GOLD POTATO, PEELED, CUT INTO MATCHSTICKS, RINSED, AND DRIED

1 LARGE YELLOW ONION, CUT IN HALF LENGTHWISE AND SLICED INTO THIN HALF-MOONS

1 TURKISH BAY LEAF

2 GARLIC CLOVES, MINCED

FOUR 5-OUNCE COD FILLETS, SKIN ON

FRESHLY GROUND BLACK PEPPER

ALL-PURPOSE FLOUR, FOR DREDGING

8 LARGE EGGS

FRESH CHIVES, FOR GARNISH (OPTIONAL)

HERBED OIL (SEE PAGE 40; OPTIONAL)

1. Have a bowl of ice water at the ready. Bring a medium saucepan of water to a boil, and add 1 tablespoon of salt. Drop in the asparagus, and blanch until crunchy-tender, 2 to 4 minutes. Remove using tongs and plunge into the ice water to cool. Reserve 16 whole spears. Thinly slice the rest on the bias and transfer to paper towels to drain.

2. Heat the ¼ cup of oil in a large nonstick skillet over medium-high heat until it shimmers. Fry the potatoes in batches, turning with tongs, until golden and crispy, 5 to 7 minutes. Transfer to paper towels, and sprinkle with salt while hot.

3. Lower the heat under the skillet to medium and drizzle in more oil if needed. Drop in the onion and bay leaf and let sizzle until the onion is nicely golden, 10 to 12 minutes. Add the garlic and cook for 1 minute more. Toss out the bay leaf, and slide the skillet off the heat.

(recipe continues)

4. Heat the oven to warm, and slip in a wire rack set on a baking sheet.

5. Heat the remaining 2 tablespoons of oil in another large nonstick skillet over medium-high heat. Dry the cod with paper towels and season well with salt and pepper. Dredge in flour and shake off the excess. When the pan is hot, sear the cod until golden brown and just opaque in the center, 3 to 4 minutes per side. Transfer to the rack in the oven.

6. Add the 16 reserved asparagus spears to the skillet, reduce the heat to low, and cook just to warm them, 1 to 2 minutes. Season lightly with salt and pepper. Remove the skillet from the heat and cover to keep warm.

7. Meanwhile, reheat the onion mixture over low heat, and stir in the sliced asparagus.

8. Beat the eggs in a bowl, and season with $1\frac{1}{2}$ teaspoons salt and $\frac{1}{2}$ teaspoon pepper. Take the skillet with the onion mixture off the heat and pour in the eggs. Return to the heat and stir quickly until the eggs just begin to set. Add the potatoes and continue cooking, stirring occasionally, until the eggs are just softly mounded, 3 to 5 minutes.

9. To serve, make a raft of 4 spears on each plate, dollop the eggs on top, and crown with the fish and a few blades of chives. A drizzle of the herb oil is a nice addition.

VARIAÇÃO ❧ **SCRAMBLED EGGS WITH MUSHROOMS** *cogumelos à brás*

Substitute 1 pound mushrooms, sliced and sautéed in olive oil, for the asparagus.

VARIAÇÃO ❧ **SCRAMBLED EGGS WITH SHRIMP** *camarões à brás*

Substitute $1\frac{1}{4}$ pounds large shrimp, shelled and deveined, for the cod. Sauté the shrimp in olive oil over medium-high heat until just opaque, about 5 minutes.

CLÁSSICO ❧ **SCRAMBLED EGGS WITH SALT COD** *bacalhau à brás*

SERVES 6 • Rinse, soak, cook, and flake 1 pound salt cod (see page 30). Cut and fry $1\frac{1}{2}$ pounds Yukon Gold potatoes as in step 2. Sauté 1 sliced large onion with a bay leaf as in step 3; omit the garlic. Stir the cooked cod and fried potatoes into the cooked onion. Beat the 8 eggs with 3 tablespoons minced fresh flat-leaf parsley, season with a good pinch of salt and a healthy grinding of pepper, add to the onion mixture, and cook as in step 8. Scoop the eggs onto a platter, and garnish with 18 sliced pitted oil-cured black olives and a sprinkling of chopped fresh parsley.

FAVA BEAN AND FENNEL SALAD

salada de favas e funcho

SERVES 4 AS A SIDE

This refreshing salad (see photograph on page 2) is the love child of two favorite Portuguese dishes: a warm fava, chouriço, and cilantro combo and a fennel and fava salad. I nixed the sausage as a way of making this dish both vegetarian-friendly and versatile. It's excellent with fish and poultry—or by itself.

KOSHER SALT

$2^1/2$ POUNDS FRESH FAVA BEANS, SHELLED, OR 1 POUND FROZEN FAVA BEANS (SEE ATENÇÃO, PAGE 56)

2 TABLESPOONS OLIVE OIL

2 SMALL FENNEL BULBS, STALKS REMOVED, CUT INTO $1/2$-INCH-THICK WEDGES

2 SMALL GARLIC CLOVES, MINCED

5 SCALLIONS, WHITE AND LIGHT GREEN PARTS ONLY, THINLY SLICED

1 TABLESPOON WHITE WINE VINEGAR, OR MORE TO TASTE

FRESHLY GROUND BLACK PEPPER

$1/2$ CUP CHOPPED FRESH CILANTRO LEAVES

1. Have a bowl of ice water at the ready. Bring a large saucepan of water to a boil over high heat and add 1 tablespoon of salt. Drop in the fava beans and boil until just cooked through, 2 to 3 minutes. Drain the beans in a colander and slip into the ice water to stop the cooking. When they're cool, drain well. If using fresh favas, nick each bean with a knife and squeeze to pop it out of its tough skin.

2. Heat the oil in a large skillet over medium-high heat until hot. Add the fennel and cook until just edged with brown on both cut sides and beginning to soften, 1 to 2 minutes. Transfer to a bowl using tongs. Lower the heat to medium, sprinkle in the garlic, and cook for 1 minute, then add the favas and warm through, 1 to 2 minutes.

3. Scrape the fava beans and garlic into the bowl with the fennel. Add the scallions and vinegar, toss, and season with salt and pepper to taste. Serve warm or at room temperature. Sprinkle with the cilantro just before taking the dish to the table.

ORANGE SALAD WITH PINE NUTS

salada com laranja e pinhões

SERVES 6 AS A STARTER

Classically, salads in Portugal are lettuce, green-red tomatoes, and sliced onion. If you order one in a restaurant, a caddy of oil and vinegar is plonked down beside you. So I was delighted when I discovered this salad. It combines many of southern Portugal's greatest ingredients: oranges, honey, pine nuts, and smoky presunto.

FOR THE DRESSING

GRATED ZEST OF 1 ORANGE

2 TABLESPOONS FRESH ORANGE JUICE

2 TABLESPOONS WHITE WINE
  VINEGAR

1 TABLESPOON PLUS 1 TEASPOON
  HONEY

1 SMALL GARLIC CLOVE, MINCED

$2/3$ CUP EXTRA-VIRGIN OLIVE OIL

FINE SEA SALT AND FRESHLY GROUND
  BLACK PEPPER

FOR THE SALAD

$1/3$ CUP PINE NUTS

2 TEASPOONS OLIVE OIL

ONE $1/8$-INCH-THICK SLICE PRESUNTO,
  SERRANO HAM, OR PROSCIUTTO,
  MINCED

2 LARGE ORANGES

12 CUPS (ABOUT 10 OUNCES) LOOSELY
  PACKED YOUNG FIELD GREENS

$1/2$ SMALL YELLOW ONION, CUT
  LENGTHWISE IN HALF AND SLICED
  INTO THIN HALF-MOONS

FLOR DE SAL (SEE PAGE 29)

1. Whisk together the zest, orange juice, vinegar, honey, and garlic in a small bowl. Dribble in the oil, whisking constantly until emulsified. Season with salt and pepper to taste. Refrigerate until ready to use. The dressing can be made several hours ahead. Just before serving, give it a good whisk.

2. Toast the pine nuts in a small dry skillet over medium heat, tossing often, until golden brown, about 6 minutes. Turn out onto a plate to cool.

3. Add the oil to the same pan and, when hot, sear the presunto until crisp, 3 to 5 minutes. Drain on paper towels.

4. Meanwhile, cut off and toss out the top and bottom of the oranges and set the fruit on a work surface. Using a paring knife, start at the top of each orange and follow the curve to remove the peel and white pith in wide strips. Working over a bowl, slice between the membranes of the orange sections to release them and let the sections fall into the bowl. Drain off the juice. (It'll make the salad too wet, but it's a treat for the cook.)

5. Combine the greens, onion, and orange sections and toss in a large bowl with enough dressing to suit your taste. Divide the salad among six plates, sprinkle with the pine nuts and presunto crumbs, and finish off with a sprinkling of *flor de sal* and a few grindings of pepper.

SPINACH WITH TOASTED BREAD CRUMBS

migas de espinafres

SERVES 6 AS A SIDE

If my grandmother's *migas* (see page 198)—a moist, stuffinglike dish—is the past, this recipe is entirely today. It's lightened, full of textural contrast, and utterly fresh tasting. No longer needed as a filler to stretch dishes, bread, which took center stage in classic *migas* (see page 159), is now often relegated to a supporting role as bread crumbs in the dish, lending crunch and a toasty, even smoky, flavor. Because of that, the recipe sits comfortably here among the vegetables.

2½ CUPS ¾-INCH FRESH CUBES OF
CORN BREAD (PAGE 188) OR DENSE
RUSTIC LOAF

6 TABLESPOONS OLIVE OIL

PINCH OF GROUND NUTMEG

KOSHER SALT AND FRESHLY GROUND
BLACK PEPPER

5 GARLIC CLOVES, CUT LENGTHWISE
INTO THICK SLICES

2 POUNDS BABY SPINACH, THINLY
SLICED

1. Grind the bread in a food processor until the cubes are coarse irregular crumbs. You need 1¾ cups.

2. Heat a large dry skillet over medium heat, add the bread crumbs, and stir and toss continually until the crumbs begin to dry, about 5 minutes. Drizzle in 2 tablespoons of the olive oil and continue toasting until the crumbs are a deep golden brown and very crisp, 4 to 6 minutes. Season with the nutmeg, salt and pepper to taste, scrape into a bowl, and set aside.

3. Turn down the heat under the skillet to medium-low and warm the remaining 4 tablespoons of oil until it shimmers. Add the garlic and let it sizzle, stirring frequently, until golden brown, 3 to 5 minutes.

4. Add the spinach to the skillet and cook, turning frequently with tongs, until wilted. You may have to work in batches. Pour off any accumulated liquid. Season well with salt and pepper to taste. Stir in half the bread crumbs, spoon the mixture into a serving bowl or onto individual plates, and dust with the remaining crumbs.

VARIAÇÃO **BROCCOLI RABE WITH TOASTED BREAD CRUMBS** *migas de grelos*

Substitute 1½ pounds chopped steamed broccoli rabe for the spinach. Sauté until tender, 3 to 5 minutes.

VARIAÇÃO **COLLARD GREENS WITH TOASTED BREAD CRUMBS** *migas de couve*

Substitute an equal amount finely sliced collard greens, thick center stems and fibrous veins removed, for the spinach. Sauté until tender, about 10 minutes.

SEARED BROCCOLI RABE WITH GARLIC

grelos salteados

SERVES 6 TO 8 AS A SIDE

This is my way of honoring those who have traveled to Portugal, fallen in love with *grelos salteados*—translated on menus everywhere as "sautéed turnip greens"—only to come home and be inconsolable when their local supermarket bunches didn't hold up. It's because Portuguese turnip greens are a wily breed, different from ours (see page 31). Broccoli rabe is a noble substitute.

ATENÇÃO ❧ *For a hit of the Azores, whose island dwellers like things spicier, sprinkle in the optional red pepper flakes.*

¹/₄ CUP OLIVE OIL

6 GARLIC CLOVES, CUT LENGTHWISE IN HALF

PINCH OF CRUSHED RED PEPPER FLAKES (OPTIONAL)

2 POUNDS BROCCOLI RABE, THICK STEMS REMOVED

KOSHER SALT AND FRESHLY GROUND BLACK PEPPER

1. Fit a large pot with a steamer insert and fill with ¹/₂ inch of water. Bring to a boil over high heat.

2. Meanwhile, heat the oil in a large skillet over medium-low heat until it shimmers. Add the garlic and red pepper flakes, if using, and let sizzle, stirring frequently, until golden brown, 3 to 5 minutes.

3. As soon as the water boils, drop the broccoli rabe into the steamer, cover tightly, and steam for 2 minutes. Using tongs, transfer the broccoli rabe to a tea towel and roll it up to absorb excess moisture.

4. Add the broccoli rabe to the skillet and cook, turning frequently with the tongs, until just tender, 3 to 5 minutes. Season with salt and pepper to taste.

SAUTÉED CHESTNUTS, ONIONS, AND BACON

castanhas salteadas com cebolase toucinho entremeado

SERVES 6 TO 8 AS A SIDE

Your first thought was Thanksgiving, wasn't it? Well, the Portuguese don't celebrate the holiday, but they do grow a lot of chestnuts. When something is as vital to the local economy as chestnuts are to the Trás-os-Montes and Alto Douro regions, people find plenty of ways to cook and eat it throughout the year. Although I've had chestnuts in soups, stuffings, breads, and desserts, I'd never had them tossed with onions and bacon, as they are in this elegant dish adapted from a recipe by chef Michel da Costa. It makes sense. The nuts are an excellent foil for the saltiness of the bacon and the caramel sweetness of the onions.

Not surprisingly, it makes for a crowd-pleasing Thanksgiving side dish.

1/2 POUND THICK-SLICED SLAB BACON, CUT CROSSWISE INTO 1/4-INCH STRIPS

1 POUND PEARL ONIONS, A SCANT 1 INCH IN DIAMETER

1 POUND VACUUM-PACKED OR JARRED ROASTED CHESTNUTS WITHOUT SUGAR (SEE SOURCES, PAGE 251)

2 TABLESPOONS HONEY

KOSHER SALT AND FRESHLY GROUND BLACK PEPPER

A FEW SPRIGS OF FRESH FLAT-LEAF PARSLEY, FOR GARNISH

1. Cook the bacon in a large skillet over medium-low heat, stirring often, until the fat has rendered and the meaty bits start to crisp, about 12 minutes. Transfer to paper towels to drain.

2. Meanwhile, fill a bowl with ice water and set aside. Bring a medium saucepan of water to a boil. Drop in the onions and blanch for 30 seconds. Scoop them out with a slotted spoon and plop them into the ice water. To peel, snip off the tips and remove the papery outer layers. Set the onions aside.

3. Raise the heat under the skillet to medium, plonk in the onions, and sauté in the bacon fat, stirring occasionally, until tender and spotted with brown, about 10 minutes. Add the chestnuts, bacon, and honey and toss to warm through, being careful not to break up the nuts—they're fragile. Season with salt and plenty of pepper, then scoop everything into a decorative bowl and garnish with the parsley.

PUNCHED POTATOES

batatas a murro

Portuguese cooks traditionally serve these as an accompaniment to salt cod, but I've broken rank and pair the potatoes with just about any main course. They're so simple to make, not to mention so supremely creamy, that there's not a meat or fish dish I know of that can't benefit from sharing the plate with a few of them. In case you're wondering, *murro* means a "punch," which is what you do to open these babies.

1½ POUNDS GOLF-BALL-SIZED YUKON GOLD POTATOES, PRICKED ALL OVER WITH A FORK

KOSHER SALT

½ CUP OLIVE OIL

3 GARLIC CLOVES, THINLY SLICED

1. Position a rack in the middle of the oven and crank up the heat to 425°F.

2. Rinse the potatoes, blot them almost dry with paper towels, and roll them lightly in salt. Spread them out on a baking sheet and roast until tender when pierced with a knife, 50 minutes to 1 hour.

3. Meanwhile, heat the oil in a small skillet over low heat until it shimmers. Add the garlic and cook until it's golden and the oil is infused with its flavor, 6 to 8 minutes. Remove the pan from the heat.

4. When the potatoes are done, press on them with your fist or a mallet to split, arrange them in a serving bowl, and drizzle with the garlic oil.

PURÉED POTATOES

puré de batata

SERVES 4 TO 6 AS A SIDE

hese are without a doubt the richest, most decadent, most insanely delicious potatoes I've ever had. The Portuguese, who are fanatics for olive oil,
drop all Mediterranean pretense when making puréed potatoes and go right for
the butter. And lots of it. The texture should be soft and polenta-like, with absolutely no lumps whatsoever.

ATENÇÃO ❧ *Don't even think of using a food processor. It'll make the potatoes
gummy. The only tool that helps me to get the same smooth texture as you find in
Portugal is a potato ricer.*

2 POUNDS YUKON GOLD POTATOES,
  PEELED AND CUT INTO 1-INCH
  CUBES

KOSHER SALT

½ POUND (2 STICKS) UNSALTED
  BUTTER, MELTED AND STILL WARM

1 CUP WHOLE MILK, WARMED, OR
  MORE IF NEEDED

PINCH OF GROUND NUTMEG

FRESHLY GROUND BLACK OR WHITE
  PEPPER, DEPENDING ON WHAT THE
  POTATOES ACCOMPANY

1. Plonk the potatoes into a large pot and cover with cold water by 2 inches.
   Add 1 tablespoon salt, cover, and bring to a boil over high heat. Cook until
   tender, 10 to 15 minutes.

2. Drain the potatoes well in a colander. Using a potato ricer or food mill,
   purée the potatoes back into the pot. Or use a handheld masher and mash
   them until perfectly smooth. Pour in the butter and half the milk and whip
   with a whisk. Continue adding more milk until the potatoes ooze lava-like
   when stirred. Add the nutmeg and season with plenty of salt and pepper to
   taste. Serve immediately.

VARIAÇÃO ❧ **PURÉED POTATOES WITH SAFFRON** *puré de batata com açafrão*

Crush a pinch of saffron threads into the warm butter before adding it.

SWEET-SOUR CARROTS

conserva de cenoura

MAKES ABOUT 2½ CUPS AS A SIDE

Conservar means "to preserve," as in the way we put up pickles. But I prefer this technique, adapted from a recipe by my friend Eddie Correia. You get the same flavor without the fuss of canning, because you make the dish one day and eat it the next. You can put this out as a predinner nibble, as they do in the Algarve on Christmas Day, or you can serve it as a refreshing side for grilled dishes, such as Grilled Chicken Slathered in Hot Sauce (page 118).

1 TABLESPOON KOSHER SALT

6 MEDIUM CARROTS, PEELED AND SLICED INTO ⅛-INCH COINS

1 GARLIC CLOVE, MINCED

3 TO 4 TABLESPOONS EXTRA-VIRGIN OLIVE OIL, TO TASTE

2 TABLESPOONS CIDER VINEGAR OR WHITE WINE VINEGAR

1 TABLESPOON CHOPPED FRESH FLAT-LEAF PARSLEY LEAVES

½ TEASPOON CHOPPED FRESH OREGANO LEAVES

1 TEASPOON SWEET PAPRIKA

¼ TEASPOON CRACKED ANISE SEEDS, PLUS (OPTIONAL) MORE FOR SPRINKLING

FRESHLY GROUND BLACK PEPPER

1. Have a bowl of ice water at the ready. Bring a medium pot of water to a boil and add the salt. Drop in the carrots and blanch them until just crisp-tender, 1 to 2 minutes. Using a slotted spoon, slip them into the ice water to cool, then drain them in a colander.

2. Whisk the garlic, oil, vinegar, parsley, oregano, paprika, and anise seeds in a medium bowl. Add the carrots and toss. Cover with plastic and let sit overnight in the fridge. The carrots will last up to a week refrigerated.

3. To serve, remove the carrots from the fridge and let come to slightly cooler than room temperature. Season with salt and pepper to taste, sprinkle with a pinch of anise seeds, if desired, and toss well.

CRISPY FRIED ASPARAGUS

peixinhos da horta

SERVES 6 AS A SIDE OR STARTER, 12 AS AN HORS D'OEUVRE

Peixinhos da horta literally means "little fish from the garden." The reserved Portuguese are unusually playful when it comes to naming their dishes. But this moniker isn't just whimsical, it's also accurate. It describes what green beans—the vegetable used in the classic recipe—look like when cooked: deep-fried slender fish. This version with asparagus was inspired by a dish served by chef José Avillez at a party in the swank town of Cascais, the seaside playground of European royalty in the nineteenth and twentieth centuries.

1 TABLESPOON KOSHER SALT

24 LARGE ASPARAGUS (ABOUT 1 POUND)

¾ CUP PLUS 2 TABLESPOONS
ALL-PURPOSE FLOUR

⅛ TEASPOON BAKING POWDER

¾ CUP VERY COLD SELTZER WATER, OR
MORE IF NEEDED

½ TEASPOON PIRI-PIRI SAUCE
(PAGE 233) OR STORE-BOUGHT HOT
SAUCE, OR TO TASTE

VEGETABLE OIL, FOR DEEP-FRYING

1 CUP CILANTRO AND GINGER
"MAYONNAISE" (PAGE 237);
OPTIONAL, BUT HIGHLY
RECOMMENDED

1. Heat the oven to warm, and slip in a wire rack set on a baking sheet.

2. Have a bowl of ice water at the ready. Bring a medium saucepan of water to a boil, and add the salt.

3. Meanwhile, trim and discard the woody ends of the asparagus. Peel the bottom third of the spears if needed. Slip the asparagus into the water and boil until crunchy-tender, 2 to 3 minutes. Remove using tongs and drop them into the ice water to stop the cooking. Transfer to paper towels to dry.

4. Stir together the flour and baking powder in a small, shallow dish, and season with a pinch of salt. Whisk in the seltzer and piri-piri sauce; don't worry about any small lumps. The consistency should be like thin pancake batter; if the mixture is too thick, pour in more seltzer.

5. Heat 2 inches of vegetable oil in a skillet large enough to hold 5 spears at once over medium-high heat until it registers 350°F on a deep-fat or candy thermometer (see "Small Fry," page 39). Dip 5 spears in the batter and turn to coat. Carefully slide them into the oil and fry until golden brown, 3 to 5 minutes. Using tongs, transfer the asparagus to paper towels to drain. Sprinkle with salt while still sizzling, then place them on the rack in the oven to keep warm. Fry the rest of the spears in the same way.

6. Serve immediately, stacked in a wood pile or standing upright in a low vase, to be plucked out like breadsticks, with the mayonnaise, if using, on the side for dipping.

CLÁSSICO ⊛ Swap 1 pound of green beans, trimmed, for the asparagus. Add 1 beaten egg to the batter. Fry the beans, in batches, until golden brown, about 4 minutes per batch. *Peixinhos da horta* aren't traditionally served with any accompaniment.

MY FAMILY'S WHITE BEANS AND SAUSAGE

feijão branco e chouriço da minha família

SERVES 4 TO 6 AS A MAIN COURSE, 6 TO 8 AS A SIDE

This recipe has been in the Costa side of my family, in one form or another, since at least the beginning of the last century, when my maternal grandmother began making it after she emigrated from the Azores to the States in 1920 as an eighteen-year-old newlywed. Beans are a traditional side dish in Portugal, especially for pork and beef. Whenever I visit my parents, I place an order for these well in advance, because no one makes them better than Momma Leite. But we ignore the side-dish rule and eat them by the bowlful for Sunday supper.

½ POUND THICK-SLICED SLAB BACON, CUT CROSSWISE INTO ½-INCH PIECES

¾ POUND CHOURIÇO, LINGUIÇA, OR DRY-CURED SMOKED SPANISH CHORIZO, CUT INTO ¼-INCH COINS

OLIVE OIL, IF NEEDED

2 LARGE YELLOW ONIONS, DICED

1 TURKISH BAY LEAF

3 GARLIC CLOVES, MINCED

2 TEASPOONS SWEET PAPRIKA

1 POUND DRIED GREAT NORTHERN OR NAVY BEANS, PICKED OVER, RINSED, AND SOAKED OVERNIGHT IN WATER TO COVER BY 3 INCHES

½ TEASPOON CRUSHED RED PEPPER FLAKES, OR MORE TO TASTE

¼ CUP DOUBLE-CONCENTRATE TOMATO PASTE

KOSHER SALT AND FRESHLY GROUND BLACK PEPPER

CHOPPED FRESH FLAT-LEAF PARSLEY LEAVES, FOR GARNISH

1. Heat a large pot over medium-low heat. Add the bacon and cook, stirring often, until the fat has rendered and the meaty bits are crisp, about 15 minutes. Using a slotted spoon, transfer to paper towels.

2. Bump up the heat to medium, add the chouriço, and sear until lightly browned, 7 to 10 minutes. Transfer the chouriço to paper towels.

3. Pour off all but 3 tablespoons of fat from the pot. Or, if the pot is dry, drizzle in some oil. Add the onions and bay leaf and cook, stirring frequently, until deeply golden brown, 20 to 25 minutes; adjust the heat as necessary to prevent the onions from burning.

4. Add the garlic and paprika and cook for 1 minute more. Drain the beans and dump them into the pot, along with the chouriço, red pepper flakes, and 3½ cups water. Bring to a boil, reduce the heat to low, cover, and let burble gently, stirring occasionally, until the beans are tender. Begin checking at 45 minutes, but it may take as long as 1½ hours, depending on your beans; add more water if needed.

5. Fish out and toss the bay leaf. Stir in the tomato paste and bacon and simmer for 10 minutes to thicken the cooking liquid. Season with salt and pepper to taste. Let the beans sit uncovered for 10 minutes to absorb any excess liquid.

6. Scoop the beans into a serving dish and shower with parsley.

VARIAÇÃO ❧ VEGETARIAN WHITE BEANS *feijão branco vegetariano*

Omit the bacon and chouriço. Use 3 tablespoons olive oil to cook the onions.

BLACK-EYED PEAS WITH ONIONS
AND RED PEPPER

feijão frade com cebolas e pimento vermelho

SERVES 6 AS A SIDE

When I was a kid, our family gatherings were so unwieldy they were held in my uncle José's garage or under my dad's grape arbor, where we'd be lined up at long, mismatched tables. My aunts would crouch down beside me, the seams of their dresses screaming over the expanse of their thighs, as they held up bowls, platters, and dishes for my perusal. That's power for a six-year-old. When our family got even larger, we had to rent halls to hold all of us. Somewhere along the way, an aunt, or cousin, or cousin of a cousin brought this dish. I'm eternally grateful to whoever it was.

$1^3/_4$ CUPS DRIED BLACK-EYED PEAS, PICKED OVER AND RINSED

6 FRESH FLAT-LEAF PARSLEY SPRIGS

4 CUPS CHICKEN STOCK (PAGE 243) OR STORE-BOUGHT LOW-SODIUM BROTH, OR MORE IF NEEDED

2 TABLESPOONS UNSALTED BUTTER

1 LARGE YELLOW ONION, CHOPPED

1 MEDIUM SHALLOT, CHOPPED

1 RED BELL PEPPER, STEMMED, SEEDED, AND CUT INTO $^1/_4$-INCH DICE

KOSHER SALT AND FRESHLY GROUND BLACK PEPPER

1. Put the beans and 2 of the parsley sprigs in a medium saucepan, add enough chicken stock to cover by 2 inches, and let soak for 2 hours.

2. Bring the stock to a boil, reduce the heat to low, and simmer, partially covered, until the beans are tender but still hold their shape, 20 to 30 minutes. Add more stock if the pan starts to dry out.

3. Meanwhile, strip the leaves from the remaining 4 parsley sprigs, and finely chop the leaves.

4. Warm the butter in a medium skillet over medium heat until the foaming subsides. Add the onion and shallot and cook, stirring often, until softened, about 7 minutes. Add the bell pepper and cook until crisp-tender, about 2 minutes more.

5. Drain the beans and stir them into the skillet. Season well with salt and pepper. Scoop them into a decorative bowl, toss with the chopped parsley, and serve.

BLACK OLIVE RISOTTO

rizoto de azeitonas pretas

SERVES 4 TO 6 AS A MAIN COURSE, 6 TO 8 AS A STARTER

My friend restaurateur Miguel Júdice gave me this recipe. Well, not exactly. It was part of a vastly complicated, utterly delicious dish from one of his restaurants that I knew would be impossible to cook at home. So I deconstructed it, tossed out some elements that were definitely not Portuguese, and kept the rest. What I like about this, besides its being a snap to make, is that it's a poster child for Portugal's new generation of cooks and cooking: it honors the country but looks beyond its borders. Olives and Carolino rice, both grown in Portugal, are two traditional staples that play nicely against the Italian cheeses.

8 CUPS CHICKEN STOCK (PAGE 243) OR STORE-BOUGHT LOW-SODIUM BROTH

3 TABLESPOONS OLIVE OIL

1 SMALL YELLOW ONION, MINCED

2 CUPS CAROLINO, CARNAROLI, OR ARBORIO RICE

1/2 CUP DRY WHITE WINE

2/3 CUP FRESHLY GRATED PARMIGIANO-REGGIANO, PLUS CURLS FOR GARNISH

1/3 CUP MASCARPONE CHEESE

3/4 CUP PITTED OIL-CURED BLACK OLIVES, RINSED IF OVERLY SALTY, THINLY SLICED LENGTHWISE, PLUS MORE FOR GARNISH

KOSHER SALT AND FRESHLY GROUND BLACK PEPPER

2 TABLESPOONS MINCED FRESH FLAT-LEAF PARSLEY LEAVES

1. Pour the stock into a medium saucepan and bring to a simmer over low heat.

2. Heat the olive oil in a large deep skillet over medium heat until it shimmers. Add the onion and cook, stirring occasionally, until softened, about 7 minutes. Stir in the rice to coat, and cook until translucent around the edges, about 2 minutes. Pour in the wine and continue cooking until it has been absorbed. Add a ladleful of hot stock to the skillet and cook, stirring constantly, until the liquid has almost burbled away. Keep up this rhythm of adding stock, stirring, and cooking until the rice slumps gently when mounded and is tender but offers just the slightest bit of resistance in the middle, 20 to 25 minutes.

3. Stir in a final ladleful of stock, the cheeses, and sliced olives and mix until well combined and very creamy. Season with salt and pepper to taste.

4. To serve, dollop the risotto into warm soup bowls and garnish each one with a few olive slices, curls of cheese, and a sprinkle of parsley. Take to the table immediately.

RICE FROM THE PAN

arroz da panela

SERVES 4 TO 6 AS A SIDE

A heaping bowl of what we casually called *arroz da panela*—a simple rice from the pan—was almost always on my grandmothers' tables at dinnertime. But what I remember most was how the next day they'd shred leftover chicken or chop the rest of Sunday's *carne assada* (roast beef; see page 146) and stir it into the rice. As the days passed, the rice just got richer as they added more liquid and various bits and bobs from the table. When the last grains were polished off, my grandmothers would whip up another huge pot of rice and start all over again.

2 TABLESPOONS OLIVE OIL

1 MEDIUM YELLOW ONION, CHOPPED

1 TURKISH BAY LEAF

1 GARLIC CLOVE, MINCED

6 OUNCES CUBED PRESUNTO, SERRANO HAM, OR PROSCIUTTO; SHREDDED FRESH OR LEFTOVER BEEF, PORK, CHICKEN, OR LAMB; OR SLICED CHOURIÇO, LINGUIÇA, OR DRY-CURED SMOKED SPANISH CHORIZO

1 TABLESPOON DOUBLE-CONCENTRATE TOMATO PASTE

2½ CUPS CHICKEN STOCK (PAGE 243) OR STORE-BOUGHT LOW-SODIUM BROTH

1½ CUPS LONG-GRAIN WHITE RICE

FRESHLY GROUND BLACK PEPPER

KOSHER SALT

2 TABLESPOONS CHOPPED FRESH FLAT-LEAF PARSLEY LEAVES

1. Heat the oil in a medium saucepan over medium heat until it shimmers. Sauté the onion and bay leaf, stirring occasionally, until the onion is golden, 7 to 10 minutes. Add the garlic and cook for 1 minute more.

2. Add whatever combination of meats you wish and cook, stirring occasionally, until warmed through, about 5 minutes. Stir in the tomato paste, then pour in the stock and add the rice and ¼ teaspoon pepper. Bring to a boil, reduce the heat to low, and simmer, covered, until the rice is tender, 20 to 25 minutes. Toss out the bay leaf.

3. Fluff the rice with a fork and season with salt and more pepper if needed, and sprinkle with parsley

VARIAÇÃO ❧ If you like, you can toast the rice in the oil for several minutes, stirring continually, until lightly golden, before adding the onion and bay leaf. This gives a slightly nutty, more complex flavor to the dish.

TOMATO RICE

arroz de tomate

SERVES 4 TO 6 AS A SIDE

This is a simple, traditional side dish I've had in many parts of Portugal. It's always a little different, depending on the region and the cook. Experiment with different herbs, such as thyme, marjoram, and rosemary. You can even use beef stock if it suits your main course. For a quick weekday side dish, toss together any leftover rice with Black-Eyed Peas with Onions and Red Pepper (page 181).

3 TABLESPOONS OLIVE OIL

1 LARGE YELLOW ONION, CHOPPED

1 TURKISH BAY LEAF

2 GARLIC CLOVES, MINCED

5 RIPE PLUM TOMATOES (ABOUT 1 POUND), SEEDED AND DICED

$\frac{1}{2}$ CUP DRY WHITE WINE

$2\frac{1}{2}$ CUPS CHICKEN STOCK (PAGE 243) OR STORE-BOUGHT LOW-SODIUM BROTH, OR MORE IF NEEDED

$1\frac{1}{2}$ CUPS LONG-GRAIN WHITE RICE

KOSHER SALT AND FRESHLY GROUND BLACK PEPPER

$1\frac{1}{2}$ TEASPOONS DOUBLE-CONCENTRATE TOMATO PASTE (OPTIONAL)

2 TEASPOONS CHOPPED FRESH FLAT-LEAF PARSLEY LEAVES

1 TEASPOON CHOPPED FRESH OREGANO LEAVES

1. Heat the oil in a medium saucepan over medium heat until it shimmers. Add the onion and bay leaf and cook until the onion is golden brown, 12 to 15 minutes. Sprinkle in the garlic and cook for 1 minute more.

2. Add the tomatoes and simmer until softened, about 3 minutes. Tip in the wine and let it burble until almost evaporated, 1 to 2 minutes.

3. Pour in the stock and bring to a boil. Add the rice, $\frac{1}{2}$ teaspoon salt, $\frac{1}{4}$ teaspoon pepper, and the tomato paste, if using. Reduce the heat to low and cook, covered, until the rice is tender and all the liquid is absorbed, 20 to 25 minutes.

4. Toss out the bay leaf and shower the rice with the parsley and oregano.

BREADS

PÃES

Corn Bread ❖ Madeiran Griddle Bread ❖ Fried Cornmeal

Presunto and Cheese Loaves ❖ Portuguese Pizza

Grandma Costa's Dressing ❖ Sweet Bread

CORN BREAD

broa de milho

MAKES 2 ROUND LOAVES

I received this recipe from Olga Cavaleiro, owner of O Afonso, a small pastry shop in the tiny town of Tentúgal, in Beira Litoral, famous for its egg desserts. These loaves are dense, with a thick, crackly crust. Olga uses a mix of approximately half cornmeal and half wheat flour, but she says it's possible to increase the proportion of cornmeal for a denser, more crumbly bread. Serve this with any of the heartier soups, poultry, or meat dishes in this book.

2 PACKAGES ACTIVE DRY YEAST

1 CUP WARM WATER (110°F)

3½ CUPS UNBLEACHED BREAD FLOUR, PLUS MORE FOR DUSTING

2 CUPS FINE YELLOW CORNMEAL (PREFERABLY GOYA BRAND)

2 TABLESPOONS KOSHER SALT

1¼ CUPS BOILING WATER

COARSE CORNMEAL, FOR DUSTING

1. Dissolve the yeast in the warm water in a small bowl and let stand until the liquid is foamy, about 10 minutes. Stir in 1½ cups of the bread flour, cover with plastic wrap, and place in a warm spot until doubled in size, about 45 minutes.

2. Dump the fine cornmeal and salt into the bowl of a stand mixer fitted with the paddle attachment. Pour in the boiling water and mix on medium speed until a firm dough clumps together, about 3 minutes. Let sit until the yeast mixture is ready.

3. Switch to the mixer's dough hook, scoop in the remaining 2 cups of bread flour and the yeast mixture, and knead on low, adding more flour, a bit at a time if needed, until the mixture comes together into a firm, elastic dough that cleans the sides of the bowl, about 7 minutes.

4. Line a 13-by-18-inch rimmed baking sheet with parchment and sprinkle with coarse cornmeal; set aside. Turn the dough out onto a lightly floured surface and knead a few times. If the dough is sticking, sprinkle with a bit of flour. Cut it in half and shape each piece into a ball. Cup one ball in both hands and stretch the sides of the dough down and under, making an oval, then turn 90 degrees and repeat, creating a smooth round with a tight surface. Securely pinch the seams closed underneath and turn seam side down. Repeat with the second ball of dough. Dust the loaves heavily with bread flour. Transfer to the baking sheet, cover with a tea towel, and let rise in a warm, draft-free spot until doubled in size, about 45 minutes.

5. Position a rack in the middle of the oven. Place a heavy-bottomed skillet on the floor of the oven, and crank up the heat to 475°F.

6. Uncover the loaves and slide the baking sheet into the oven, then lean back and pour 1½ cups of water into the skillet. Close the door quickly. (The steam will create a lovely crispy crust.) Wait for 5 minutes, and repeat. Bake until the loaves are golden brown and crackly—charred in spots isn't a bad thing— and sound hollow when thwacked on the bottom, 35 to 45 minutes. Transfer to a rack to cool until just warm. These are best devoured the same day.

MADEIRAN GRIDDLE BREAD

bolo de caco

MAKES SIX 6-INCH ROUND BREADS

This is one of the classic sidekicks to the Madeiran specialty Espetada (see Grilled Beef Kebabs, page 143), chunks of beef that have been tossed with olive oil or butter, garlic, and salt, then threaded on a fresh laurel branch and grilled over an open fire. Piping-hot *bolos* are split in half, slathered with garlic butter, cut into fingers, and taken to the table. While in Funchal, Madeira's capital, I met up with a chef who was bored with the pedestrian spread and so concocted his own version, laden with all kinds of liquor. Inspired, I created a softer, less drunken version, a roasted garlic butter with Madeira. Don't be stingy with it; it adds great layers of flavor.

1 SMALL SWEET POTATO (ABOUT 5 OUNCES)

1 TABLESPOON PLUS 1 TEASPOON ACTIVE DRY YEAST

1 TEASPOON PLUS 1 TABLESPOON SUGAR

1¼ CUPS WARM WATER (110°F)

3¼ CUPS ALL-PURPOSE FLOUR, PLUS MORE IF NEEDED

1¾ TEASPOONS KOSHER SALT

1 TABLESPOON UNSALTED BUTTER, AT ROOM TEMPERATURE

OLIVE OIL

ROASTED GARLIC BUTTER WITH MADEIRA (PAGE 241), AT ROOM TEMPERATURE

1. Prick the sweet potato all over with a fork, pop it into the microwave, and zap on high until softened, about 5 minutes. Alternatively, place the potato on a foil-lined baking sheet and roast in a 400°F oven until soft, about 40 minutes. When the potato is cool enough to handle, split it open and scoop out the flesh, and toss out the peel. You should have about ½ cup. Let cool completely.

2. Dissolve the yeast and the 1 teaspoon of sugar in ¼ cup of the warm water in a small bowl and let stand until the liquid is foamy, about 10 minutes.

3. Combine the potato, flour, the remaining 1 tablespoon of sugar, and the salt in a food processor. Whir until the potato is pulverized and no lumps remain. Add the butter and the yeast mixture and pulse until incorporated. With the motor running, pour in the remaining 1 cup of warm water and buzz until the dough just forms a smooth ball that springs back a bit when poked, 30 to 45 seconds. Add more flour a bit at a time if needed.

4. Lightly coat a large bowl with oil. Dump the dough onto a work surface, shape it into a ball, set it in the bowl, and turn to coat. Cover the bowl with

plastic wrap, place it in a warm, draft-free spot, and let the dough double in size, about 1½ hours.

5. Spread a tea towel on a work surface and lightly dust it and the work surface next to it with flour. Plop out the dough and cut it into 6 equal pieces. Roll each piece into a ball with your palm, press it down to a thickness of ¾ inch, and place on the tea towel. Cover with another tea towel and let stand until puffed considerably, 30 to 45 minutes.

6. Position a rack in the middle of the oven and crank up the heat to 350°F.

7. Warm a flat griddle or a large heavy nonstick skillet over medium-high heat for 5 minutes. Slip one hand under the towel, turn a dough circle onto your other hand, and slide it onto the griddle. Cook, pressing down lightly with a spatula to create a golden-brown underside, about 4 minutes. Flip and brown the second side for 2 to 3 minutes. Slip the *bolo* onto a baking sheet and repeat with the remaining circles of dough.

8. Slide the baking sheet into the oven and bake the breads until cooked through, about 15 minutes. Transfer to a rack and cool for a few minutes.

9. Slice the breads horizontally in half and generously slather with the garlic butter. Cut into strips and serve immediately.

FRIED CORNMEAL

milho frito

Along with Maderian Griddle Bread (page 190), *milho frito* is the traditional accompaniment to Grilled Beef Kebabs (page 143), beef threaded on long bay leaf skewers and grilled over an open fire. The classic recipe is nothing more than cornmeal, lard, water, and salt. What makes it delicious is that it's deep-fried. This version gets tons of flavor from stock, cream, and butter. Kale, a common ingredient, and cheese round out the flavor.

ATENÇÃO ✷ *Don't use stone-ground or coarse cornmeal, or the result will be hopelessly mushy.*

OLIVE OIL FOR GREASING, PLUS MORE FOR PANFRYING

¼ POUND COLLARD GREENS OR KALE, THICK CENTER STEMS AND FIBROUS VEINS REMOVED, SLICED CROSSWISE WHISKER-THIN

KOSHER SALT

2 CUPS CHICKEN STOCK (PAGE 243) OR STORE-BOUGHT LOW-SODIUM BROTH

1 CUP HEAVY CREAM

3 TABLESPOONS UNSALTED BUTTER

FRESHLY GROUND BLACK PEPPER

1 CUP FINE YELLOW CORNMEAL (PREFERABLY GOYA BRAND) OR INSTANT POLENTA

½ CUP RICOTTA CHEESE

1. Lightly brush an 8-by-8-inch baking pan with oil, and set aside.

2. Bring a medium pot of water to a boil over high heat. Add the collards and 1 tablespoon salt and cook until the greens are tender, about 10 minutes. Dump into a colander to drain and cool.

3. Meanwhile, add the stock, cream, ¾ cup of water, the butter, 1¼ teaspoons salt, and ¼ teaspoon pepper to the pot and bring to a boil over medium heat. Slowly pour in the cornmeal, whisking constantly. Reduce the heat to low and stir with a wooden spoon until the mixture thickens to the consistency of smooth mashed potatoes and pulls away from the pan, about 5 minutes. Stir in the ricotta until incorporated, about 2 minutes. Add the collards, take a taste, and sprinkle in more salt and pepper if needed.

4. Spread the mixture in the prepared pan and level the top with a greased off-set spatula or the back of a spoon. Let sit until firm, 30 minutes to 1 hour.

5. Cut the cornmeal into 1-by-2-inch rectangles. Brush a large skillet, preferably nonstick, with oil and heat over medium heat. When it's hot, brush the rectangles with oil and sear, in batches, until golden brown, 2 to 3 minutes per side. Transfer to paper towels to drain. Serve warm.

PRESUNTO AND CHEESE LOAVES

pãezinhos de presunto e queijo

MAKES FOUR 6-INCH ROUND LOAVES

Every Saturday when I was growing up, my mother would go to the local Portuguese bakery and buy a dozen chouriço rolls—torpedo-shaped logs stuffed with sausage. By Monday, they were gone, mostly due to me. To dress up my childhood classic, I add presunto and cheese, and sometimes sautéed onions and garlic, to the dough. And I form the rolls into round loaves because I think they look elegant on the table.

1 PACKAGE ACTIVE DRY YEAST

1 TEASPOON SUGAR

1½ CUPS WARM WATER (110°F)

3 LARGE EGGS, AT ROOM TEMPERATURE

¼ CUP OLIVE OIL, PLUS MORE FOR GREASING

4 CUPS ALL-PURPOSE FLOUR, PLUS MORE IF NEEDED

1¼ TEASPOONS KOSHER SALT

TWO ¼-INCH-THICK SLICES PRESUNTO, SERRANO HAM, OR PROSCIUTTO, TRIMMED OF EXCESS FAT AND CUT INTO ¼-INCH CUBES

6 OUNCES CHOURIÇO, LINGUIÇA, OR DRY-CURED SMOKED SPANISH CHORIZO, CUT INTO ¼-INCH CUBES

½ POUND SEMI-FIRM SHEEP'S-MILK CHEESE, SUCH AS NISA, RONCAL, OR MANCHEGO, COARSELY SHREDDED

COARSE CORNMEAL, FOR DUSTING

1. Dissolve the yeast and sugar in the warm water in the bowl of a stand mixer fitted with a dough hook, and let stand until the liquid is foamy, about 10 minutes.

2. Whisk 2 of the eggs and add them to the yeast mixture along with the oil. Whirl on low speed until blended. Scoop in the flour and salt and mix on medium-low speed, scraping down the bowl once or twice, until a smooth, slightly sticky ball that thwacks and cleans the side of the bowl forms, 7 to 10 minutes. Add up to ½ cup flour a bit at a time if needed.

3. Dump the dough onto a lightly floured surface and knead a few times, adding more flour if needed, until supple. Flatten the dough into a large disk, sprinkle with the presunto, chouriço, and cheese, and knead to distribute the pieces evenly. It will seem like a lot, but press on.

4. Place the dough in a large lightly oiled bowl, turn to coat, cover with plastic wrap, and let rise in a warm, draft-free spot until doubled in size, 1 to 1½ hours.

5. Line a 13-by-18-inch rimmed baking sheet with parchment and sprinkle with cornmeal. Lightly dust a work surface with flour, turn the dough out, and knead several times. Cut it into 4 equal parts and shape each piece into

a ball. Transfer the balls to the baking sheet and let rise, covered with a tea towel, until doubled in size, about 1 hour.

6. Meanwhile, position a rack in the middle of the oven and crank up the heat to 425°F.

7. Whisk the remaining egg with 1 tablespoon of water and brush the loaves with the mixture. Bake until the loaves are deeply brown and sound hollow when thumped on the bottom, 20 to 25 minutes. Transfer to a rack to cool completely. The loaves will keep for up to 2 days wrapped in plastic, but you can't beat them on the day they're made.

PORTUGUESE PIZZA

pizza à portuguesa

MAKES 4 INDIVIDUAL PIZZAS; SERVES 4 TO 6

Although associated with Italy, of course, pizza actually has a big following in Portugal. Michael Guerrieri, the Italian-American chef-owner of La Brus"K"etta and longtime Lisbon resident, scatters local ingredients, including kale, *grelos* (similar to broccoli rabe), chouriço, *alheira* (game sausage), ham, and Portuguese cheeses on his delicate, sparse pies—making them decidedly Iberian in flavor.

1 PACKAGE ACTIVE DRY YEAST

1 TEASPOON SUGAR

1⅓ CUPS WARM WATER (110°F)

3½ CUPS ALL-PURPOSE FLOUR, PLUS MORE IF NEEDED

1 TABLESPOON OLIVE OIL, PLUS MORE FOR GREASING AND DRIZZLING

1 TABLESPOON KOSHER SALT

COARSE CORNMEAL, FOR DUSTING

1 POUND FRESH MOZZARELLA, CUT INTO ⅛-INCH SLICES

5 OUNCES CHOURIÇO, LINGUIÇA, OR DRY-CURED SPANISH CHORIZO, CUT INTO ⅛-INCH COINS

1⅓ CUPS TOMATO SAUCE (PAGE 239) OR, IF YOU MUST, STORE-BOUGHT TOMATO SAUCE

6 OUNCES SEMI-FIRM SHEEP'S-MILK CHEESE, SUCH AS SERPA, RONCAL, OR MANCHEGO, FINELY SHREDDED

CHOPPED FRESH OREGANO LEAVES, FOR GARNISH

1. Dissolve the yeast and sugar in the warm water in a small bowl and let stand until the liquid is foamy, about 10 minutes.

2. Dump the flour, oil, and salt into the bowl of a stand mixer fitted with the dough hook. Pour in the yeast mixture and stir on low to moisten the ingredients, then bump up the speed to medium and knead until the dough is supple and soft, 5 to 7 minutes. Add more flour a bit at a time if needed.

3. Transfer the dough to a bowl lightly greased with oil, cover with plastic wrap, and let rise in a warm, draft-free spot until doubled in size, about 1 hour.

4. Position a rack in the middle of the oven, slide in a baking stone or an upside-down baking sheet, and crank up the heat to 550°F. Dust a pizza peel or a rimless cookie sheet with cornmeal and set aside.

5. Divide the dough into 4 equal pieces. Place 3 in the fridge, and roll the fourth on a lightly floured surface into a 10- to 12-inch circle, using a floured rolling pin. Carefully stretch the dough into an oval by draping it over a closed fist and pulling gently with your other hand all around the perimeter. Place the dough on the peel and cover with 5 or 6 slices of mozzarella. (Resist the impulse to overdo the toppings; this is meant to be a sparse,

elegant pie with a crisp crust.) Dot with 8 or 9 chouriço slices, spoon ⅓ cup of the tomato sauce on top, leaving a border, and sprinkle with one quarter of the Serpa cheese. Drizzle the edges with some oil.

6. Position the peel at the far edge of the baking stone and, in one smooth motion, slide it toward you, leaving the pizza on the stone. Bake until the edges are deeply golden brown and the cheese is bubbling, 7 to 9 minutes. Transfer to a wire cooling rack, sprinkle with oregano, and wait several minutes before slicing. Repeat with the remaining dough and toppings.

GRANDMA COSTA'S DRESSING

migas da minha vovó costa

SERVES 6 TO 8

I grew up eating bowls of *recheio,* literally "stuffing." My grandmother made it, and no one, but no one, could match her. It was a moist bread concoction studded with chouriço and bacon. While living in Portugal, I found that none of my friends had ever heard of *recheio.* And no wonder. The mainlanders have their own word for it: *migas.* In their honor, I've changed the name of this recipe.

Serve this alongside beef, pork, roasted chicken, or Thanksgiving turkey.

¼ POUND THICK-SLICED SLAB BACON, CUT CROSSWISE INTO ¼-INCH PIECES

1 POUND CHOURIÇO, LINGUIÇA, OR DRY-CURED SMOKED SPANISH CHORIZO, ROUGHLY CHOPPED

OLIVE OIL, IF NEEDED

2 MEDIUM YELLOW ONIONS, CHOPPED

4 GARLIC CLOVES, MINCED

¼ TEASPOON CRUSHED RED PEPPER FLAKES

⅔ CUP DRY WHITE WINE

3 TABLESPOONS AMPED-UP RED PEPPER PASTE (PAGE 232)

2 TABLESPOONS DOUBLE-CONCENTRATE TOMATO PASTE

12 CUPS ¾-INCH CUBES OF DAY-OLD RUSTIC BREAD

ABOUT 2 CUPS BEEF STOCK (PAGE 244) PLUS 1 CUP WATER, OR 3 CUPS STORE-BOUGHT LOW-SODIUM BROTH

KOSHER SALT AND FRESHLY GROUND BLACK PEPPER

¼ CUP CHOPPED FRESH FLAT-LEAF PARSLEY LEAVES

1. Heat a Dutch oven over medium-low heat. Add the bacon and cook, stirring often, until the fat has rendered and the meaty bits are crisp, 12 to 15 minutes. Using a slotted spoon, transfer to paper towels. Pour off all but a thin film of fat from the pot into a cup and reserve. Bump up the heat to medium-high, add the chouriço, and cook, stirring often, until lightly browned, about 7 minutes. Using a slotted spoon, transfer the sausage to a bowl. Pour off all but 2 tablespoons of fat, adding it to the bacon fat. If the pan is dry, add 2 tablespoons of oil.

2. Lower the heat to medium, add the onions, and cook until soft, 7 to 10 minutes. Add the garlic and pepper flakes and cook for 1 minute more. Splash in the wine, add the red pepper paste and tomato paste, scrape up any stuck-on bits, then let burble for a few minutes to cook the mixture.

3. Turn the heat to low, add the bread and the reserved bacon and chouriço fats, and pour in just enough of the stock-water combination, beating well with a spoon, to make the mixture moist. If you use all the liquid and the pot is still dry, add water as necessary. Fold in the bacon and chouriço and continue beating to lighten the mixture. Take a taste and season with salt and pepper if needed. Scoop the dressing into a bowl and speckle with the parsley.

SWEET BREAD

massa sovada

MAKES ONE 9-INCH ROUND LOAF

My grandmother Leite and aunts Irena, Exaltina, and Lourdes would have marathon assembly-line baking sessions in which they'd make dozens of loaves of *massa sovada* for the family. These weren't the mini loaves you see in Portuguese markets today—they were huge affairs, fifteen inches in diameter.

This slightly sweet bread, with just a hint of cinnamon and lemon, is perfect breakfast and snack fare. I also like to let it stale a bit and make *fatias douradas*, similar to French toast (see the Variação).

½ CUP WHOLE MILK

4 TABLESPOONS UNSALTED BUTTER,
  PLUS MORE FOR GREASING

⅔ CUP PLUS 1 TEASPOON SUGAR

¾ TEASPOON KOSHER SALT

1 PACKAGE ACTIVE DRY YEAST

2 TABLESPOONS WARM WATER (110°F)

3 LARGE EGGS

1 LARGE EGG YOLK

4 CUPS UNBLEACHED ALL-PURPOSE
  FLOUR, PLUS MORE IF NEEDED

¼ TEASPOON GROUND CINNAMON

GRATED ZEST OF ½ SMALL LEMON

1. Heat the milk, butter, the ⅔ cup of sugar, and the salt in a medium saucepan over medium-high heat, stirring frequently, just until steam begins to curl up and bubbles form around the edges, about 5 minutes. Set aside to cool to lukewarm.

2. Meanwhile, dissolve the yeast and the remaining 1 teaspoon of sugar in the warm water in a small bowl, and let sit until the liquid is foamy, about 10 minutes.

3. Plop 2 of the eggs and the yolk into the bowl of a stand mixer fitted with the paddle attachment, and beat until frothy and light, about 1 minute. With the mixer on low, slowly pour in the milk-butter mixture. Switch to the dough hook, dump in the flour, cinnamon, and zest, and pour in the yeast mixture. Mix on medium-low until the dough is supple, 8 to 10 minutes, scraping down the hook and the bowl and adding more flour if needed.

4. Turn the dough out onto a lightly floured work surface and shape into a ball. Place it in a large lightly buttered bowl, cover with plastic wrap, and let rise in a warm, draft-free spot until doubled in size, about 2 hours.

5. Generously butter a 1½-quart round baking dish (6¾ inches in diameter, 3 inches high). Set aside. Punch down the dough, knead several times, and form it into a ball. Cup the ball in both hands and stretch the sides of the

(recipe continues)

dough down and under, making an oval, then turn 90 degrees and repeat, creating a smooth round with a tight surface. Securely pinch the seams closed underneath, and place seam side down in the baking dish. Let rise, covered with a tea towel, in a warm, draft-free spot until doubled in size and well domed, 2 to 3 hours.

6. Position a rack in the lower third of the oven (remove any racks above to give the bread head room) and crank up the heat to 350°F.

7. With a very sharp knife, make a shallow slash across the top of the loaf. Beat the remaining egg and brush it generously over the top. Bake until the bread is a deep mahogany and an instant-read thermometer inserted in the middle registers 190°F, 40 to 50 minutes. Watch closely; overbaking will cause the loaf to be dry. For a shiny crust, brush on more of the beaten egg about 15 minutes before the bread is done. Transfer to a rack to cool for 20 minutes. Remove the bread from the dish, and let cool completely. The loaf will last for 2 or 3 days wrapped well in plastic.

VARIAÇÃO ❧ GOLDEN SLICES *fatias douradas*

Beat 5 large eggs, 1 cup whole milk, and a pinch of salt in a shallow baking dish. Heat 2 tablespoons corn oil or unsalted butter in a large nonstick skillet over medium heat. Cut the day-old sweet bread into 1-inch-thick slices and soak them in the egg mixture, then fry until golden and cooked through, about 3 minutes per side. Sprinkle the slices with confectioners' sugar or cinnamon, or drizzle with honey. Serve for breakfast or, as a nod to tradition, on Christmas Eve as dessert.

SWEETS
AND LIQUEURS

DOCES E LICORES

Sweet Lemon and Black Olive Wafers ❧ Molasses Cookies ❧

Grandma Leite's Sugar Fritters ❧ Rosemary Custard ❧

Silky, Lemony Egg Cream ❧ Rice Pudding Redux ❧

Baked Custard Tarts ❧ Chocolate Mousse ❧

Orange Cake ❧ "Russians" Nut Cakes ❧ Tomato Jam ❧

Sweet Red Pepper Jam ❧ Cherry Cordial ❧ Milk Liqueur

SWEET LEMON AND BLACK OLIVE WAFERS

biscoitos doces de limão e azeitonas pretas

MAKES ABOUT 15 WAFERS

Cookies aren't exactly a specialty of the Portuguese. The traditional ones tend to be crumbly and plain, more like a dunking biscuit. One day at a dinner party, though, I had a sweet thin cookie with a distinctive snap. I immediately made notes in my ever-present little black book; the only thing is, I never asked the hostess for the recipe. I spent months trying to come up with a cookie that matched hers, and finally I've done her proud. But I wanted to ratchet up the recipe, adding two iconic Portuguese ingredients to the mix: olives and lemons.

Serve this alone, as a lovely accompaniment to tea, or, my favorite, as a crunchy bite alongside a scoop of vanilla ice cream or lemon sorbet.

ATENÇÃO ❧ *Sample an olive before you buy them. Strong-flavored ones can give a bitter aftertaste to the cookie.*

1½ CUPS ALL-PURPOSE FLOUR	¼ TEASPOON BAKING POWDER
½ CUP MILD OIL-CURED BLACK OLIVES, RINSED QUICKLY IF PARTICULARLY SALTY, PITTED, AND COARSELY CHOPPED	2 TABLESPOONS GRATED LEMON ZEST
	⅛ TEASPOON GROUND CINNAMON
	PINCH OF KOSHER SALT
¼ CUP SUGAR, PLUS MORE FOR COATING	¼ CUP EXTRA-VIRGIN OLIVE OIL
	1 LARGE EGG, BEATEN

1. Position a rack in the upper third of the oven and crank up the heat to 375°F.

2. Stir together the flour, olives, sugar, baking powder, zest, cinnamon, and salt in a medium bowl. Whisk together the oil and egg, pour the mixture into the dry ingredients, and mix with your hands until the dough no longer looks dry and holds together when squeezed, 1 to 2 minutes.

3. Fill a small bowl with sugar and set nearby. Pinch off 1 rounded tablespoon (about 1 ounce) of dough, roll it into a ball, and coat it well with sugar. Place it in one corner of a sheet of parchment cut to fit your baking sheet, place another piece of parchment on top, and using a rolling pin, roll the ball into a 3½- to 4-inch circle, a scant ¹⁄₁₆ inch thick. The edges will be ragged; that's how they should be. Repeat with 5 more wafers on the same sheet. Lift off the top sheet and slip the parchment with the cookies onto the baking sheet.

4. Bake until the wafers are edged with brown and pebbled on top, 10 to 12 minutes. Slide the parchment onto a wire cooling rack. Repeat with the remaining dough. Once cooled, the wafers will keep in an airtight container for several days, but I doubt they'll stick around that long.

MOLASSES COOKIES

biscoitos de mel

MAKES ABOUT TWENTY-FOUR 3-INCH COOKIES

Madeira is renowned for its *bolo de mel*, a dense, deeply spiced cake rich with almonds, walnuts, and candied fruit and spiked with the eponymous wine of the island. These cookies, a cross between the cake and small spice biscuits called *broas de mel*, have all of the moistness of the former and the portability of the latter.

2½ CUPS ALL-PURPOSE FLOUR

1¾ TEASPOONS GROUND CINNAMON

¼ TEASPOON GROUND CLOVES

PINCH OF GROUND FENNEL

½ TEASPOON BAKING POWDER

½ TEASPOON BAKING SODA

½ TEASPOON KOSHER SALT

½ POUND (2 STICKS) UNSALTED BUTTER, AT ROOM TEMPERATURE

1 CUP SUGAR

1 LARGE EGG

¼ CUP DARK MOLASSES

¾ CUP WALNUT HALVES AND/OR WHOLE BLANCHED ALMONDS

1. Position a rack in the middle of the oven and crank up the heat to 350°F. Line a baking sheet with parchment paper.

2. Whisk together the flour, cinnamon, cloves, fennel, baking powder, baking soda, and salt in a medium bowl. Set aside.

3. In the bowl of a stand mixer fitted with the paddle attachment, or with a hand mixer in a large bowl, beat the butter and sugar until light and fluffy, 5 to 7 minutes. Beat in the egg until incorporated, then pour in the molasses. Add the flour mixture and mix on low speed until just combined.

4. Roll generous tablespoons of the dough between your palms and place them 1½ inches apart on the parchment-lined baking sheet. Press a walnut half or almond into each one. Bake until browned around the edges and dry on top, about 15 minutes. Transfer to a wire rack to cool. Repeat with the rest of the dough.

GRANDMA LEITE'S SUGAR FRITTERS

malassadas da minha vovó leite

MAKES ABOUT 24 FRITTERS

This recipe, adapted from the one my dad's mom used to make in the Azores and then later in Somerville, Massachusetts, has a flood of memories attached to it. I would sleep over at her house, and on Saturdays she'd cook these for my cousins Fatima and Joe and me. Hot out of the cinnamon-sugar bowl is the only way to eat them.

In the Azores, cooks shape these over their knees until they're practically the size of lunch plates, just as my grandmother used to do. I've made them smaller, but beyond that: welcome to my childhood.

FOR THE FRITTERS

1/2 CUP WHOLE MILK

2 TABLESPOONS UNSALTED BUTTER, PLUS MORE FOR GREASING

3/4 TEASPOON KOSHER SALT

1 PACKAGE ACTIVE DRY YEAST

1/3 CUP PLUS 1 TEASPOON SUGAR

2 TABLESPOONS WARM WATER (110°F)

3 LARGE EGGS

3 1/2 CUPS ALL-PURPOSE FLOUR, PLUS MORE IF NEEDED

NONSTICK COOKING SPRAY

VEGETABLE OIL, FOR FRYING

FOR THE CINNAMON SUGAR

1 CUP SUGAR

1/2 TEASPOON GROUND CINNAMON

1. Heat the milk, butter, and salt in a medium saucepan over medium-high heat, stirring frequently, just until steam begins to curl up and bubbles form around the edges, about 5 minutes. Set aside to cool to lukewarm.

2. Meanwhile, dissolve the yeast and the 1 teaspoon of sugar in the warm water in a small bowl, and let stand until the liquid is foamy, about 10 minutes.

3. In the bowl of a stand mixer fitted with the paddle attachment, or with a hand mixer in a large bowl, beat the remaining 1/3 cup of sugar and the eggs on medium-high speed until thick and luscious looking, about 5 minutes. Switch to the dough hook, add the milk mixture, the yeast mixture, and the flour, and mix on low speed until a soft dough forms, about 7 minutes. Add more flour if needed.

4. Turn the dough out onto a lightly floured work surface, and shape into a ball. Place in a lightly buttered bowl, cover with plastic wrap, and let rise in a warm, draft-free spot until doubled in size, about 2 hours.

5. Lightly coat a 13-by-18-inch rimmed baking sheet with cooking spray, and turn out the dough onto the pan. Press it and poke it with your fingers, much as if you were making focaccia, to stretch it until it's about 1/2 inch thick.

Lightly coat the top of the dough with cooking spray, loosely cover the pan with plastic wrap, and let the dough rise until doubled in size, 1 to 1½ hours.

6. Mix together the sugar and cinnamon in a shallow bowl and set aside.

7. Fill a medium saucepan with 3 inches of oil and heat over medium-high heat until it reaches 350°F on a deep-fry or candy thermometer (see "Small Fry," page 39). Using scissors or your hands, cut or pull off a 2- to 3-inch piece of dough. Stretch it into a 4- to 5-inch circle, then lower it into the oil and fry, turning frequently, until just golden brown and cooked through, 45 seconds to 1½ minutes, depending on the size. Drain the fritter on paper towels for 30 seconds then toss in the cinnamon sugar. Repeat with the remaining dough, cooking the fritters one at a time. Devour them warm as soon as they're out of the sugar bowl.

COFFEE COUNTRY

When I lived in Portugal, and on my many other trips there, I had chances to sample its unparalleled coffee. The most popular type is the *bica*, the Lisbon term for a small demitasse cup filled with a hair-raising caffeinated brew similar to espresso. It's so strong that a friend of mine refers to it as "rocket fuel." An ultra-powerful hit is called an *italiana*. Both are usually knocked back in one shot. A small cup with a short pour of milk is called *garoto escuro*; one with a longer pour of milk, *garoto claro*. And the bipartisan cup of half-coffee–half-milk is called *meia de leite*. My preference, though, is a tamer distant cousin, the *galão*, a tall glass filled with hot milk and just a dash of coffee. *Carioca* is coffee made with lots of water, and *abatanado* is made with even more water—both of which the Portuguese are fond of comparing to a cup of American joe.

ROSEMARY CUSTARD

leite-creme com alecrim

SERVES 6 TO 8

Traditionally, *leite-creme*, one of Portugal's countless egg yolk desserts, is made on top of the stove, then poured onto a large platter and sprinkled with sugar. A small metal spatula, usually heart-shaped, is heated like a branding iron and pressed onto the sugar, scorching it and creating a decorative pattern. Chef Albano Lourenço at Arcadas da Capela in the Hotel Quinta das Lágrimas, in Coimbra, tweaks the dessert by first infusing the custard with rosemary, and then giving it the customary French crème brûlée finish of a crystalline crust of caramelized sugar.

4 CUPS WHOLE MILK	¼ CUP CORNSTARCH
THREE 6-INCH SPRIGS FRESH ROSEMARY	PINCH OF KOSHER SALT
1 CUP SUGAR, PLUS 8 TABLESPOONS FOR CARAMELIZING	6 LARGE EGG YOLKS

1. Set out six to eight heatproof decorative bowls or 6-ounce ramekins. Heat the milk and rosemary in a medium saucepan over medium heat until steam begins to curl up and bubbles form around the edges. Remove from the heat, cover, and let steep for 10 minutes.

2. Meanwhile, in a bowl of a stand mixer fitted with the whisk attachment, or with a handheld mixer in a large bowl, whirl the 1 cup of sugar, the cornstarch, and salt together on low speed. Add the yolks, turn up the speed to medium-high, and mix until the mixture lightens and falls from the whisk in a thick ribbon, 2 to 3 minutes.

3. Strain the milk into a medium bowl and discard the rosemary. With the mixer on low, slowly drizzle the milk into the egg mixture. Pour the custard back into the saucepan and cook over medium heat, stirring constantly with a wooden spoon, until the custard thickens to the consistency of a soft pudding, 5 to 10 minutes. Immediately remove from the heat and divide it among the bowls. Cool for 20 minutes, then chill until set, about 2 hours.

4. Now the fun part: caramelizing. If moisture has formed on top of the *leite-creme*, blot it away with paper towels. Sprinkle each custard with about 1 tablespoon of the remaining sugar and pass a kitchen propane torch back and forth over the top until the sugar bubbles and browns, less than a minute. Alternatively, you can slip the bowls under a preheated broiler for 1 to 2 minutes, but watch carefully, because the sugar can burn quickly. Let the custards sit for a minute or two before serving.

SILKY, LEMONY EGG CREAM

ovos moles com natas batidas

SERVES 4 TO 6

The traditional version of *ovos moles*, literally "soft eggs," is a specialty of Aveiro, a lovely small city crossed by canals. The very thick, very eggy sweet is sold in different shapes made of rice paper—fish, boats, and sea shells—that you pop into your mouth. Most famously, the egg sweets are served in miniature wooden barrels just big enough to fit your spoon. This riff on the classic is lighter, more delicate, and less sweet because it has the zip of lemon and is spooned over pillowy whipped cream. It can also be drizzled atop desserts as a decadent sauce.

¾ CUP SUGAR	2 CUPS HEAVY CREAM
GRATED ZEST OF 3 LEMONS	SLICED RIPE STRAWBERRIES
6 LARGE EGG YOLKS	4 TO 6 FRESH MINT SPRIGS, FOR GARNISH (OPTIONAL)

1. Bring the sugar and 1 cup of water to a boil in a small saucepan over high heat—don't stir—and let bubble until an instant-read thermometer registers 230°F. Remove the pan from the heat, add the zest, and let steep for 3 minutes.

2. Meanwhile, in the bowl of a stand mixer fitted with the whisk attachment, or with a handheld mixer in a large bowl, beat the yolks on medium-high until thick and luscious looking, about 3 minutes.

3. Strain the lemon syrup through a fine sieve into a heat-proof measuring cup. Rinse the pan and place back on the stove. Turn the mixer to low and slowly pour in the syrup until incorporated. Scrape the mixture back into the saucepan and cook over very low heat, stirring constantly with a heat-proof spatula, until thickened, 5 to 7 minutes. Pour into a bowl, press plastic wrap against the surface, and let cool completely.

4. Whip the cream to firm peaks. Stir the custard; it may have separated, but fear not. To serve as a dessert, spoon alternating layers of *ovos moles* and whipped cream in dessert glasses and top with a few sliced strawberries and sprigs of mint, if using. To serve as a sauce, whisk the *ovos moles* into the whipped cream to thin the mixture. The *ovos moles* are best eaten the same day.

RICE PUDDING REDUX

arroz doce moderno

SERVES 8

For a country that's deeply religious, Portugal gives her citizens plenty of opportunities to dabble in the sin of gluttony with the staggering volume of its sweets. One of the most famous is rice pudding, made from Carolino rice from the alluvial plains of the Ribatejo. It's a decadent dish, rich with milk, sugar, butter, and cinnamon. This version takes on a modern twist, by being served warm and sandwiched between crackly layers of puff pastry.

ATENÇÃO *You can make the pudding the day ahead and reheat it on low in the microwave. Stir in a bit of milk or cream if it's too thick.*

ALL–PURPOSE FLOUR, FOR DUSTING	PINCH OF KOSHER SALT
1 SHEET (FROM A 17$\frac{1}{4}$–OUNCE PACKAGE) FROZEN PUFF PASTRY (PREFERABLY PEPPERIDGE FARMS BRAND), THAWED	4 CUPS WHOLE MILK, OR MORE IF NEEDED
	$\frac{2}{3}$ CUP GRANULATED SUGAR
$\frac{3}{4}$ CUP CAROLINO, CARNAROLI, OR ARBORIO RICE	2 LARGE EGG YOLKS
ZEST OF $\frac{1}{2}$ LEMON, REMOVED IN LONG STRIPS WITH A VEGETABLE PEELER	CONFECTIONERS' SUGAR, FOR SPRINKLING
A $\frac{3}{4}$–INCH THUMB OF GINGER, PEELED	GROUND CINNAMON, FOR SPRINKLING

1. Position a rack in the middle of the oven and crank up the heat to 400°F. Line a baking sheet with parchment paper and set aside.

2. Lightly dust a work surface with flour, and roll out the pastry to smooth it. Using a pizza cutter or a sharp knife, trim the pastry into an 8-by-8-inch square. Cut the square crosswise and then vertically in half, so you have 4 squares. Cut each in half on the diagonal.

3. Space the 8 dough triangles evenly on the parchment, and bake until well risen and golden, 10 to 15 minutes. Transfer the triangles to a wire rack to cool.

4. Meanwhile, combine the rice, zest, ginger, salt, and 4 cups of water in a medium saucepan. Bring to a boil, lower the heat to medium, and cook, uncovered, until almost all the water has evaporated, about 30 minutes. Adjust the heat as needed so the rice doesn't scorch.

5. About 5 minutes before the rice is ready, heat the milk and granulated sugar in a saucepan over medium heat, stirring occasionally, until wisps of steam curl up and the sugar has dissolved. Turn down the heat to low and keep the milk at a gentle simmer. Beat the egg yolks in a small bowl.

6. Once the water in the pan of rice has almost evaporated, begin adding the hot milk mixture by the ladleful, stirring lazily with a wooden spoon. Keep up this rhythm of adding milk, stirring, and cooking until the rice slumps gently when mounded and all the milk is incorporated. Remove the pan from the heat.

7. Spoon some of the thickened rice mixture into the beaten yolks and quickly stir to incorporate. Drizzle the egg mixture back into the pan, stirring constantly. Return the pan to low heat and cook for 3 minutes. The consistency should be lava-like. Remove the lemon zest and ginger. Let the pudding cool to warm, stirring occasionally. Add more milk, warmed over low heat, if the rice thickens too much.

8. To serve, split open the pastry triangles. Place the bottom halves on plates, spoon the pudding on top, and crown with their mates. Sprinkle with confectioners' sugar and cinnamon.

BAKED CUSTARD TARTS

pastéis de nata

MAKES 24 PASTRIES

The reigning monarch of desserts in Lisbon and, frankly, in all of Portugal, is the *pastél de nata*, or custard tart, the most famous of which can be found in only one place: the Antiga Confeitaria de Belém, on the outskirts of the capital city. Once a sundries shop, the *confeitaria* was converted to a bakery in the early 1800s, and the pastries have been made there ever since. The *pastéis*, rich custard encased in crisp, frilly pastry cups, are served warm with a generous sprinkling of confectioners' sugar and cinnamon.

Everything about the pastries is a secret. During all my "official" visits, trying to suss out the recipe, I was carefully steered away from the vault, behind whose locked doors the elements—tree-trunk-thick logs of puff pastry and the custard—are made. While not "official," this recipe draws upon what I learned, letting me use ingredients and techniques available to the home cook. And it's pretty tasty, too.

ATENÇÃO ❧ *Pastéis de nata are made in individual ⅓-cup forms (see Sources, page 251), which give them their characteristic size and shape and make them eons easier to shape than if made in a muffin tin. If you use a muffin tin (newer ones have a ½-cup capacity), simply press the dough as far up the wells as possible.*

ONE 17¼-OUNCE PACKAGE FROZEN
  PUFF PASTRY (PREFERABLY
  PEPPERIDGE FARMS BRAND),
  THAWED

2 TABLESPOONS ALL-PURPOSE
  FLOUR, PLUS MORE FOR DUSTING

1 TEASPOON KOSHER SALT

GRATED ZEST OF ½ LEMON

1¾ CUPS HEAVY CREAM

1 LARGE EGG

8 LARGE EGG YOLKS

1 CUP GRANULATED SUGAR

½ TEASPOON PURE VANILLA EXTRACT

CONFECTIONERS' SUGAR, FOR
  SPRINKLING

GROUND CINNAMON, FOR SPRINKLING

---

1. Place one still-folded sheet of pastry on a work surface so that a short end is facing you and the thicker fold is to your left. Open the two panels of dough, lightly brush the right panel on both sides with water, and then fold it back into position. Cover with the left panel and press down to seal. Lightly brush the top of the pastry with water, then curl up the short edge and roll up the pastry away from you, as if making a jelly roll. Make sure to keep the spiral very tight. You should have a 3-inch-wide log. Roll it back and forth on the work surface to extend it to 3½ inches. Repeat with the second sheet of pastry. Wrap in plastic and refrigerate.

(recipe continues)

2. Whisk the flour, salt, zest, and ½ cup of the cream in a medium bowl until all the lumps are dissolved. Set aside.

3. Beat the egg and yolks together in a bowl, and set aside.

4. Bring the granulated sugar and ⅔ cup of water to a boil in a small saucepan over high heat—don't stir—and let it bubble until an instant-read thermometer registers 230°F.

5. Meanwhile, heat the remaining 1¼ cups of cream in a medium saucepan over medium-high heat until wisps of steam curl up and bubbles appear around the edges, about 5 minutes.

6. Whisk the hot cream into the flour mixture until smooth, then pour in the hot sugar syrup. Slowly add the egg mixture, whisking continually, then pour the custard back into the medium saucepan and cook over low heat, whisking lazily, until the mixture lightly coats the back of a spoon and registers 170°F on an instant-read thermometer, about 4 minutes. Pour into a bowl, add the vanilla, and let cool completely.

7. Have two muffin tins nearby. Using a serrated knife, trim off the uneven ends of one dough log, sawing in a back-and-forth motion, and discard. Cut twelve ¼-inch slices from the log. Repeat with the remaining log, and refrigerate the slices. Work with only 1 slice at a time. Turn it on its side on a very lightly floured surface. Flatten it into a 3-inch circle with your fingers, and fit it into a well in a muffin tin. Press the dough against the bottom and up the sides, creating a raised lip about ⅛ inch above the pan, if using a tin with one-third cup capacity (see Atenção, page 217). Repeat with the rest of the slices. Prick the shells very well with a fork, and refrigerate the tins for 20 minutes.

8. Position a rack in the middle of the oven, place a baking sheet on the rack, and crank up the heat to 400°F.

9. Fill the tart shells to the top with rice, dried beans, or pie weights. Slip the tins onto the hot baking sheet in the oven (depending on how large your muffin tins are, you may have to bake the pastries in 2 batches) and bake until the edges of the dough are puffed and brown, about 16 minutes. If the pastry starts to color too much, tent the tins loosely with foil. Transfer to a wire rack to cool, leaving the oven on.

10. Empty the rice from the cooled tart shells. Some will stick—no big deal. Use a spoon to gently scrape them out. Fill each shell three-quarters full (2½ tablespoons) with the cooled custard. Bake until the custards barely jiggle in the middle, about 12 minutes.

11. Transfer the tins to the rack to cool for a few minutes, then pop out the pastries and let cool until warm. Dust with confectioners' sugar and cinnamon.

CHOCOLATE MOUSSE
mousse de chocolate
SERVES 6

This indulgence is based upon a mousse I had at Don Dinis, a small, unassuming restaurant in the town of Beja. When we arrived at the unfashionably early hour of 8:00 p.m., the place was almost empty. By the time we left, there was a waiting line—and almost everyone was Portuguese, always a good sign. While we ate, we noticed a big bowl of mousse slowly being emptied. We put in our order early just to be safe. It was so marvelously rich and puddinglike—not a classic mousse at all—I almost couldn't finish my portion.

When serving your guests, make a show of seasoning the dessert with a sprinkle of *flor de sal* and a pinch of crushed pink peppercorns. They'll protest, but persist. The flavor combination is wonderful and quite an eye-opener.

ATENÇÃO ❧ *Because this recipe contains raw eggs, it isn't recommended for pregnant women, young children, the elderly, and the immuno-compromised.*

6 OUNCES BITTERSWEET CHOCOLATE (PREFERABLY 70%), FINELY CHOPPED

$^{1}/_{3}$ CUP WHOLE MILK

8 TABLESPOONS (1 STICK) UNSALTED BUTTER, CUT INTO 8 PIECES, AT ROOM TEMPERATURE

6 LARGE EGG YOLKS, AT ROOM TEMPERATURE

$^{1}/_{4}$ CUP SUGAR

2 LARGE EGG WHITES

FLOR DE SAL (SEE PAGE 29)

FINELY CRUSHED PINK PEPPERCORNS, FOR SPRINKLING

1. Melt the chocolate with the milk in a double boiler over low heat. (If you don't have a double boiler, fit a metal bowl snugly over a small saucepan filled with an inch of water, making sure the bowl isn't touching the water.) Stir with a fork until the milk is incorporated and the mixture is voluptuously glossy. Add the butter one piece at a time, stirring until smooth. Remove from the heat and let cool to room temperature.

2. In the bowl of a stand mixer fitted with the paddle attachment, or with a handheld mixer in a large bowl, beat the yolks and sugar until the mixture is pale yellow and falls in thick ribbons when the paddle is lifted, about 7 minutes. Add the chocolate mixture and whirl on low to combine.

3. Whisk the egg whites in a small bowl until soft peaks form. Using the whisk, stir—do not fold—the whites into the chocolate mixture until incorporated. Pour the mousse into a large bowl. Cover with plastic wrap and refrigerate for 6 hours.

4. To serve, spoon the mousse into individual cups and sprinkle a little *flor de sal* and crushed pink peppercorns on top.

ORANGE CAKE

bolo de laranja

SERVES 10 TO 12

When I lived in Lisbon, a few times a week, I'd trudge up the hill from my apartment and pop into Papas for breakfast, perhaps one of the tiniest restaurants in the city. It seats a mere eight people, and that includes two at the counter. If it wasn't open yet, for the Portuguese regard *horários* (schedules) as nothing more than polite suggestions, I'd wait. My go-to breakfast was this dessert cake. It's dense, moist, and deeply flavored, and, I'm not ashamed to say, the servers tended to have a generous hand when cutting slices.

ATENÇÃO ❧ *Make sure to use a light-colored Bundt pan. A dark one will turn out a cake that sticks and is unpleasantly brown. Since this cake only gets better with age, don't even think about taking a bite until the day after you make it, or even the day after that.*

NONSTICK BAKING SPRAY WITH FLOUR	5 LARGE EGGS
4 TO 5 LARGE NAVEL ORANGES	3 CUPS GRANULATED SUGAR
$3^1/_2$ CUPS ALL-PURPOSE FLOUR	$1^1/_2$ CUPS MILD EXTRA-VIRGIN OLIVE OIL
$1^1/_2$ TEASPOONS BAKING POWDER	CONFECTIONERS' SUGAR, FOR SPRINKLING
$1^3/_4$ TEASPOONS KOSHER SALT	

1. Position a rack in the middle of the oven, remove any racks above, and crank up the heat to 350°F. Coat a 12-cup Bundt or tube pan with baking spray and set aside.

2. Finely grate the zest of 3 of the oranges, then squeeze 4 of them. You should have $1^1/_2$ cups of juice; if not, squeeze the fifth orange. Set aside.

3. Whisk together the flour, baking powder, and salt in a large bowl and set aside.

4. In the bowl of a stand mixer fitted with the paddle attachment, or with a handheld mixer in a large bowl, beat the eggs on medium-high speed until well combined, about 1 minute. Slowly pour in the granulated sugar and continue beating until thick and pale yellow, about 3 minutes. On low speed, alternate adding the flour mixture and oil, starting and ending with the flour, and beat until just a few wisps of flour remain. Pour in the orange juice and zest and whirl for a few seconds to bring the batter together.

5. Pour the batter into the prepared pan and bake until a cake tester comes out with a few moist crumbs clinging to it, about 1¼ hours. If the top is browning too much as the cake bakes, cover lightly with foil. Transfer to a wire rack and cool for 15 minutes.

6. Turn the cake out onto the rack and cool completely, then place it in a covered cake stand and let it sit overnight. Just before serving, dust with confectioners' sugar.

"RUSSIANS" NUT CAKES

russos

MAKES SIXTEEN 2-INCH CAKES

Portuguese desserts are notoriously eggy concoctions and, to be honest, not always to my liking. So the minute I discovered these miniature cakes—a delicate finish to a light luncheon or tea—I set to work learning how to make them from my friend Teresa Cota Dias. Her cakes are filled, not frosted, but I discovered a bakery in Portugal that slathers the buttercream on top, so I adopted its technique.

ATENÇÃO ✍ *If you choose not to use all the ground nuts as decoration, keep them in an airtight container. They're terrific on cereal, yogurt, and* Fatias Douradas *(page 200).*

FOR THE CAKES

NONSTICK BAKING SPRAY WITH
   FLOUR

1 CUP BLANCHED WHOLE ALMONDS

1$\frac{1}{2}$ CUPS WALNUT HALVES

$\frac{1}{2}$ CUP GRANULATED SUGAR

$\frac{1}{8}$ TEASPOON GROUND CLOVES

$\frac{1}{4}$ CUP ALL-PURPOSE FLOUR

1 TEASPOON BAKING POWDER

$\frac{1}{4}$ TEASPOON KOSHER SALT

6 TABLESPOONS UNSALTED BUTTER,
   AT ROOM TEMPERATURE

3 LARGE EGGS, SEPARATED

FOR THE FROSTING

12 TABLESPOONS (1$\frac{1}{2}$ STICKS)
   UNSALTED BUTTER, AT ROOM
   TEMPERATURE

$\frac{1}{3}$ CUP SUPERFINE SUGAR

$\frac{1}{4}$ TEASPOON PURE VANILLA EXTRACT

1. Position a rack in the middle of the oven and crank up the heat to 350°F. Coat an 8-by-8-inch baking pan with baking spray, line the bottom with parchment paper, and spray the paper. Set aside.

2. Spread the almonds and walnuts in a single layer on a rimmed baking sheet and roast in the oven until golden brown, 10 to 15 minutes. Let cool.

3. Buzz the nuts, along with 2 tablespoons of the sugar and the cloves, in a food processor until the mixture is the texture of cornmeal, about 45 seconds. Sift the flour, baking powder, and salt into a small bowl, and stir in 1 cup of the ground nuts. Set the rest aside for decoration.

4. In the bowl of a stand mixer fitted with the paddle attachment, or with a handheld mixer in a large bowl, beat the butter and the remaining 6 tablespoons of sugar on high speed until light and pale yellow, about 5 minutes. Scrape down the mixture occasionally with a spatula. Add the egg yolks one at a time, beating for 1 minute after each addition.

(recipe continues)

5. Whip the whites into glossy, firm peaks in a large bowl. Stir the flour mixture into the yolk mixture, and then gently fold in the whites. Scoop the batter into the prepared pan and smooth the top.

6. Bake the cake until golden brown and a toothpick inserted in the middle comes out clean, about 25 minutes. Transfer the pan to a wire rack and let cool for 10 minutes. Run a knife around the edges of the cake, place a rack on top, and flip. Peel off the parchment, flip once more so the cake is right side up, and cool completely.

7. Switch to the whisk attachment and whip the butter in the clean mixer bowl on medium speed until light and smooth, about 3 minutes. Slowly add the superfine sugar and whip until fluffy, about 6 minutes more. Stir in the vanilla.

8. Slather the top of the cake with the frosting. Sprinkle with as much of the reserved ground nuts as you wish. Using a serrated knife, trim the edges to neaten them, and slice the cake into 16 squares. The cakes can dry out quickly, so wrap them well with plastic if not serving right away.

VARIAÇÃO 🕸 "RUSSIANS" WITH BITTER ORANGE FILLING
russos com laranja amarga

Slice the cake horizontally in half. Spread the bottom layer with a thin layer of bitter orange marmalade, or, for a fancier look, a second batch of frosting mixed with 3 tablespoons of marmalade. Crown with the top layer, and frost and decorate with the plain frosting as above before cutting into squares.

PARA VOCÊ—FOR YOU

Both the Tomato Jam (opposite) and Sweet Red Pepper Jam (page 226) make excellent hostess gifts. Taking a homemade treat when visiting a friend or attending a dinner party is practically a religious dictum in Portuguese families. When I was a kid, my mother and aunts would blanch at the thought of arriving at someone's home with a store-bought gift. It was proof your hostess wasn't worth the bother of making something yourself.

To give the gift the smack of authenticity, tie some decorative string or raffia around the jar, just under the cap, and attach a card with this written on it:

Cara [for a woman] Caro [for a man] _____,
Este pequeno presente, que eu fiz, é uma autêntica receita de Portugal. Aprecie-o!"
("This small gift, which I made, is an authentic recipe from Portugal. Enjoy!")

TOMATO JAM

doce de tomate

MAKES 2 CUPS

Tomato jam is a classic sweet of Portugal. And *sweet* is the operative word. For this recipe, I've decreased the amount of sugar considerably so the meaty tomato flavor shines through. The addition of cinnamon, lemon, clove, and port lends a lovely depth. Use it on toast, alongside cheese, even on burgers.

ATENÇÃO ❧ *If you prefer, you can skip the canning process and simply spoon the jam into impeccably clean jars and refrigerate for up to two weeks.*

2½ POUNDS VERY RIPE TOMATOES, PEELED, SEEDED, AND CHOPPED (SEE PAGE 91)

2¼ CUPS SUGAR

1-INCH PIECE OF CINNAMON STICK

FOUR 3-INCH STRIPS LEMON ZEST, REMOVED WITH A VEGETABLE PEELER

2 WHOLE CLOVES

¼ CUP RUBY PORT

1. Combine the tomatoes and any accumulated juice, the sugar, cinnamon, zest, cloves, and port in a large saucepan. Bring to a strong boil over high heat and skim any foam from the top. Lower the heat to medium-low and simmer, stirring occasionally. As the jam thickens, stir more frequently until it's ready, at least 1 hour. Test to see if the preserve is ready: place a saucer in the freezer for 10 minutes, then dollop a spoonful of jam on top and slip it in the fridge for 2 minutes. If it gels, you're set; if not, continue to cook.

2. While the jam is cooking, place a rack or steamer insert in the bottom of a medium pot and fill with water. Bring to a boil, and immerse two 8-ounce glass canning jars, making sure they're covered by at least 2 inches. Add the metal bands to the pot too. Ladle a cup or so of the hot water into a small bowl and slip in the two canning lids to soften the rubber, about 5 minutes.

3. When the jam's ready, remove the saucepan from the heat and carefully remove and discard the cinnamon, lemon zest, and cloves.

4. Using tongs, remove the jars and bands from the pot, keeping the water boiling. Place a wide-mouth canning funnel over one jar and ladle in the hot jam, leaving ¼-inch headroom. Repeat with the second jar. Wipe the rims with a wet cloth, top with the lids, and screw on the bands. Lower the jars into the pot and make sure they're covered by at least 1 inch of water; if not, pour in more. Once the water returns to a boil, process for 5 minutes. Transfer the jars to a dish towel and let cool completely, at least 4 hours.

5. Test the seals by making sure they're depressed. If the seal didn't take, the jam must be kept refrigerated and eaten within 2 weeks. Properly processed jam will last for 1 year in a cool, dark place. Refrigerate after opening.

SWEET RED PEPPER JAM

doce de pimento vermelho

MAKES 2 CUPS

Red bell pepper is an important ingredient for the Portuguese, especially in the Alentejo, where it's made into a paste used to flavor all types of meats. Never having seen the pepper out of its savory role, I was fascinated to discover this recipe at Quinta de Catralvos, headed up by chef Luís Baena. It was used as a "ketchup" on his McSilva (Mini Salt Cod Sandwiches, page 105), a salt-cod riff on McDonald's Filet-O-Fish, but I found it so good, I serve it alongside cheese, or with grilled game birds, such as pheasant, partridge, and duck; I even stir it into salad dressing. For a simple hors d'oeuvre, spread soft young goat cheese on crusty bread, and top with some jam and a sprinkle of *flor de sal* (see page 29). It's amazing.

ATENÇÃO ❧ *If you prefer, you can skip the canning process and simply spoon the jam into impeccably clean jars and refrigerate for up to two weeks.*

3¼ POUNDS RED BELL PEPPERS (ABOUT 5 PEPPERS)	1¼ CUPS SUGAR ⅔ CUP RED WINE VINEGAR

1. Prepare the canning pot, jars, metal bands, and lids as in step 2 for Tomato Jam (see page 225).

2. Stem and seed the peppers. Cut them into 1-inch-wide strips, and carve away any white bits, or they'll mar the jam's garnet color. Dump into a food processor and pulse to form a purée.

3. Scoop the mixture and its juice into a medium saucepan, then add the sugar and vinegar. Bring to a strong boil over high heat and skim any foam from the top. Reduce the heat to medium-low and allow the mixture to simmer and reduce, stirring occasionally. As the jam thickens, stir more frequently until it's ready, about 1¼ hours, or longer depending on the amount of juice in your peppers. A simple test to tell if the preserve is ready: place a saucer in the freezer for 10 minutes, then dollop a spoonful of jam on top and slip it in the fridge for 2 minutes. If it gels, you're set; if not, continue to cook.

4. Place a food mill fitted with the finest disk over a bowl. When the jam's ready, remove the saucepan from the heat and carefully ladle the jam into the mill, churning the handle to extract as much pulp as possible while leaving behind the fibrous skins. Scrape the bottom of the mill for the last bits. You should have at least 2 cups of jam.

4. Process as in step 4 for Tomato Jam, and check the seals as in step 5.

CHERRY CORDIAL

ginjinha

MAKES ABOUT 5 CUPS

G*inja* is the Portuguese name for the Morello cherry, a sour cherry cultivar native to Europe. *Ginjinha* is the wickedly alluring liqueur made from it. On the north end of Lisbon's Rossio Square, the heart of city life—not to mention the site of a few autos-da-fé in centuries past—is a wedge of a store called A Ginjinha, where they sell nothing but, and where I've been known to dally on occasion. The drink is served either with or without a cherry. Adept at extracting the fruit, the barkeeps mangle not a one as they fish them out. Lacking that skill, I store my *ginjinha* in a wide-mouth jar with a tight-fitting lid.

2 CUPS GRAPPA OR UNFLAVORED VODKA	$^3/_4$ POUND (ABOUT 3 CUPS) FRESH OR FROZEN PITTED SOUR CHERRIES
$1^1/_2$ CUPS DRY RED WINE	1-INCH PIECE OF CINNAMON STICK
$1^3/_4$ CUPS SUGAR	

1. Pour the Grappa and wine into an impeccably clean $^1/_2$-gallon glass jar with a tight-fitting lid. Add the sugar, cherries, and cinnamon and give a good stir. Cover and set the *ginjinha* in a cool, dark spot, stirring every day until the sugar is dissolved.

2. Let the liqueur remain undisturbed for 3 to 6 months for the flavors to marry, after which you can decant it into a wide-mouth glass jar, leaving behind any sediment on the bottom of the steeping jar. The *ginjinha* will keep at room temperature for up to 6 months.

MILK LIQUEUR

licor de leite

MAKES ABOUT 3½ CUPS

Granted, the name doesn't do this astoundingly good liqueur justice. The recipe, from my friend Ana Taveira, is a staple of the Azores and a deliciously sweet finish to a meal. What surprises most people is that even though it's made with milk, it has a crystal-clear amber color. The spark of lemon and the finish of chocolate really round out the creamy flavor. Serve the liqueur as a tipple with dessert or by itself as a digestif.

2½ CUPS GRAPPA OR UNFLAVORED VODKA

2 CUPS WHOLE MILK

2 CUPS SUGAR

2 OUNCES BITTERSWEET CHOCOLATE (PREFERABLY 70%), GRATED

½ LEMON, SEEDED AND CHOPPED, WITH RIND

1. Pour the Grappa and milk into an impeccably clean half-gallon glass jar with a tight-fitting lid. Scoop in the sugar, chocolate, and lemon. Cover the jar tightly and shake well to help the sugar begin to dissolve. It will look curdled; that's as it should be, and it's perfectly safe. Set aside in a cool, dark place and shake or stir well with a clean spoon every day for 10 days.

2. Set a cheesecloth-lined colander over a bowl and pour in the mixture. When the mixture has finished draining, squeeze the cloth to release as much of the liquid as possible, and discard the solids.

3. Line a sieve with a paper coffee filter. Pour in the liqueur and let the mixture drip through to a clean bowl—this can take up to 24 hours. Change the filter when it becomes clogged with the residue from the liqueur. I repeat this step once or twice more after all the liqueur has passed through to clarify it as much as possible.

4. Pour the liqueur into a decanter with a tight-fitting top. It will keep at room temperature for up to 6 months.

SUNDRIES

DIVERSOS

Amped-Up Red Pepper Paste ❖ Piri-Piri Sauce ❖ Piri-Piri Paste ❖
Cilantro Paste ❖ Milk "Mayonnaise" ❖ Tomato Sauce ❖
Lightly Sautéed Onions and Garlic ❖ Roasted Garlic Butter with Madeira ❖
Smoked Paprika Oil ❖ Chicken Stock ❖ Beef Stock ❖
Fish Stock ❖ Shrimp Stock ❖ Home-Rendered Lard

AMPED-UP RED PEPPER PASTE

massa de pimentão forte

MAKES ABOUT 1 CUP

Massa de pimentão, a paste made from heavily salt-cured red bell peppers, is a classic Portuguese staple. Originally from the Alentejo province, the paste is the major flavor component of the region's—and now, the country's—cooking. Every cook has her own version, some made from fresh bell peppers, others from roasted peppers, and still others from paprika.

Because this version is lightly salted and richly seasoned, all you have to do to make dinner is rub a bit of it on beef, chicken, or strong-flavored fish, or toss it with peeled, halved potatoes before roasting. It's that simple.

2 TABLESPOONS SWEET PAPRIKA

2 TABLESPOONS SWEET SMOKED PAPRIKA

$\frac{1}{4}$ CUP DRY RED WINE

8 TO 10 GARLIC CLOVES, TO TASTE

2 TURKISH BAY LEAVES, WELL CRUMBLED

1 TABLESPOON DOUBLE-CONCENTRATE TOMATO PASTE

$1\frac{1}{2}$ TABLESPOONS FRESH LEMON JUICE

7 SPRIGS FRESH CILANTRO

5 SPRIGS FRESH FLAT-LEAF PARSLEY

$1\frac{1}{2}$ TABLESPOONS KOSHER SALT

$\frac{1}{4}$ TEASPOON FRESHLY GROUND WHITE PEPPER

A FEW DASHES OF PIRI-PIRI SAUCE (OPPOSITE) OR STORE-BOUGHT HOT SAUCE, OR TO TASTE

$\frac{1}{4}$ CUP OLIVE OIL

1. Dump both types of paprika, the wine, garlic, bay leaves, tomato paste, lemon juice, cilantro, parsley, salt, pepper, and piri-piri sauce into a food processor or mini chop and pulse until the garlic and herbs are minced. Scrape down any chunky bits from the sides of the bowl.

2. While the motor is running, pour in the olive oil and continue whirring until the paste is slick and homogeneous, 1 to 2 minutes. Use the mixture immediately, or spoon it into a small glass jar with a tight-fitting lid and refrigerate. The paste will keep for up to a month in the refrigerator.

CLÁSSICO ❀ RED BELL PEPPER PASTE *massa de pimentão*

Wash, stem, and seed 3 red bell peppers, and slice them into 1-inch-wide strips. Line a colander with cheesecloth and pour in about an inch of kosher salt. Press some of the strips into the salt and cover with another inch of salt. Continue layering until all the strips are covered. Top with a heavy pan, place the colander in a large bowl, and set aside for 5 days. On the sixth day, fish out the strips and brush off the salt, but don't rinse them. Purée in a food processor, transfer the paste to a clean glass jar, and refrigerate until needed. This is a *much* saltier version than mine, so use a judicious hand.

PIRI-PIRI SAUCE

molho de piri-piri

MAKES ABOUT 1½ CUPS

Portuguese piri-piri sauce, which packs a gut punch of heat, is sprinkled into, smothered over, and smeared onto all types of dishes. Arguably, the most famous is Frango com Piri-Piri (see Grilled Chicken Slathered in Hot Sauce, page 118). So proud are the Portuguese of their potent sauce, it's been advertised as "Portuguese Viagra."

At farmers' markets, old men in their *boné* hats sit behind tables covered with jars of neon-red homemade piri-piri sauce for sale. Some are nothing more than oil infused with the chile peppers, others contain a mixture of crushed fresh peppers and oil, and still others are a combination of oil, vinegar, peppers, and spices. This last version, the one given below, is what comes closest to store-bought piri-piri, and I think the added ingredients give a nice acidic smack to the sauce. The recipe can easily be halved.

Now, while I admire your commitment to making this sauce from scratch, if you can't find peppers with the right punch, there's no shame in using a store-bought hot sauce, such as Frank's RedHot or Tabasco brand pepper sauce.

ATENÇÃO ✎ *Piri-piri peppers are unavailable in North America, but the substitutions suggested below will give a similar wallop of heat. Whenever handling any types of chiles, wear latex gloves, and be assiduously careful not to rub your face, mouth, or eyes. If you do, it'll be a painful experience you're not soon likely to forget.*

3 GARLIC CLOVES, MINCED

⅓ CUP WHITE WINE VINEGAR

6 TO 8 FRESH RED CHILE PEPPERS, SUCH AS CAYENNE, TABASCO, PEQUÍN, OR SANTAKA (SEE PAGE 27), TO TASTE, STEMMED

1 CUP EXTRA-VIRGIN OLIVE OIL

PINCH OF KOSHER SALT

1. Mix the garlic and vinegar in a small bowl and let steep for 20 minutes.

2. Drop the peppers (including their seeds) and the garlic mixture into a food processor and pulse to chop. While the motor is running, pour in the oil, sprinkle with the salt, and whir until smooth. Pour the sauce into a small glass jar with a tight-fitting lid and let steep in the fridge for at least several days, preferably 1 week.

3. Strain the mixture, if you wish, but I never do. The sauce will keep for about 1 month in the fridge. Shake well before using.

PIRI-PIRI PASTE

pasta de piri-piri

MAKES ABOUT 2 CUPS

This recipe was given to me by my friend Edite Vieira, author of *The Taste of Portugal*, who in turn got it from an Angolan. She met him at a country market in the Ribatejo, where he had a vegetable stall. She was shopping for ingredients for her cooking show, and they got to talking. After a bit of coaxing on her part, he scribbled this down for her.

This has a richer taste than Piri-Piri Sauce (page 233) and a thicker consistency, similar to ketchup. I like to spoon it into one of my *tachinos de barro*, small earthenware bowls I bought in the pottery town of São Pedro do Corval, and place it on the table for guests. They can then scoop a bit onto their plate and dip into it. It also makes a sensational dip for Salt Cod and Shrimp Fritters (page 37). If a guest becomes overzealous with the stuff, pour him a glass of milk. The casein works to counteract the burn.

ATENÇÃO ❧ *If your peppers aren't packing the heat you want, add a few dried chiles. Also, feel free to substitute this paste for Piri-Piri Sauce (page 233) in recipes.*

10 TO 12 FRESH RED CHILE PEPPERS, SUCH AS CAYENNE, TABASCO, PEQUÍN, OR SANTAKA (SEE PAGE 27), TO TASTE, STEMMED AND CHOPPED	$\frac{1}{2}$ HEAD OF GARLIC, SEPARATED INTO CLOVES AND PEELED
ZEST OF $\frac{1}{2}$ LEMON, REMOVED WITH A VEGETABLE PEELER, PLUS JUICE OF $\frac{1}{2}$ LEMON	1 CUP WHISKEY
	$\frac{1}{2}$ CUP OLIVE OIL
	$\frac{1}{2}$ CUP WHITE WINE VINEGAR
$\frac{1}{2}$ MEDIUM YELLOW ONION, DICED	1 TABLESPOON HONEY
	1 TABLESPOON SUGAR
	1 TABLESPOON KOSHER SALT

1. Dump the peppers and their seeds, the lemon zest and juice, onion, garlic, whiskey, oil, vinegar, honey, sugar, and salt into a medium saucepan. Bring the mixture to a boil, reduce the heat to low, and simmer, partially covered, until the peppers are completely soft, 1 hour or longer, depending on the type of pepper. Remove the pan from the heat and let cool.

2. Pour the mixture into a blender or food processor and whir until as smooth as possible. Make sure to really grind away to chop the seeds. Spoon the paste into a clean glass jar with a tight-fitting lid. The paste will keep for up to 2 months in the refrigerator.

CILANTRO PASTE

pasta de coentro

MAKES ABOUT 1 CUP

The lightbulb for this paste blinked on in my head while I was eating Açorda Alentejana (see Cilantro Bread Soup with Poached Eggs, page 61) in a small *tasca*. The slap of raw garlic and the cooling herbal flavor of cilantro—two hallmarks of southern Portugal—made me think of Italian pesto. But using roasted almonds and aged Nisa cheese, two other classics of the region, makes this variation entirely Portuguese to my mind. When I passed the idea by some of my friends who are more progressive and (dare I say?) competitive in the kitchen, all of them got that look on their faces that said, "Damn, why didn't I think of that?"

Use the paste as you would pesto: tossed with pasta, spread on a split loaf of buttered bread that's warmed in the oven, stirred into soup, stuffed into a chicken breast before grilling or roasting, or mixed into Requeijão cheese (see page 21) or ricotta cheese for a spread.

½ CUP BLANCHED WHOLE ALMONDS

3 CUPS FRESH CILANTRO LEAVES AND TENDRIL-SOFT STEMS (ABOUT 2 LARGE BUNCHES), RINSED WELL

1 TO 2 GARLIC CLOVES, TO TASTE, SMASHED

½ CUP EXTRA-VIRGIN OLIVE OIL, OR MORE IF NEEDED

⅔ CUP (ABOUT 2 OUNCES) GRATED AGED FIRM SHEEP'S-MILK CHEESE, SUCH AS NISA, SERPA, OR PECORINO-ROMANO

KOSHER SALT AND FRESHLY GROUND BLACK PEPPER

1. Position a rack in the middle of the oven and crank up the heat to 350°F.

2. Scatter the almonds on a rimmed baking sheet and toast until golden, 8 to 10 minutes. Let cool completely.

3. Dump the almonds, cilantro, and garlic into a food processor and whir until the nuts are coarsely ground. Scrape down any chunky bits from the sides of the bowl with a spatula. While the motor is running, drizzle in the olive oil in a fine thread, then pulse until smooth. Add the cheese and buzz several times, but don't overprocess, or the sauce will get clumpy. Tip in a bit more oil if needed. Season with salt and pepper to taste.

4. Use the sauce immediately, or spoon it into an ice cube tray and freeze until hard. Pop out the cubes, and toss them into a freezer bag. They'll keep for up to 3 months.

MILK "MAYONNAISE"

maionese de leite

MAKES ABOUT 1 CUP

This is one of those recipes that require quotation marks, not out of affectation, but because it's not a true mayonnaise. It contains no egg yolks or mustard. It's nothing more than an emulsion of milk and oil. More Brazilian than Portuguese, it's just now beginning to be used on the Continent. The taste is lighter and cleaner than that of an egg-based mayonnaise, allowing other flavors to come through.

Since I was given the recipe, I haven't stopped finding ways to cook with it. The master recipe is only a canvas for additions. Besides the uses in this book, I've smeared the variations on grilled meats and fish, used them as dips and in dressings, spread them on sandwiches, and stirred them into potato salads, much as I do with regular mayonnaise.

ATENÇÃO *Like all emulsions, this can be a bit finicky. Adding the oil in a thin stream and stopping when the right consistency is reached is the key. For almost-foolproof results, a handheld blender is best, but a small regular blender with a narrow jar will do.*

$1/3$ CUP COLD WHOLE MILK

$3/4$ TEASPOON FRESH LEMON JUICE

1 SMALL GARLIC CLOVE

$1/8$ TEASPOON FRESHLY GROUND
   WHITE PEPPER

ABOUT $3/4$ CUP VEGETABLE OIL OR
   ABOUT $1/2$ CUP VEGETABLE OIL PLUS
   $1/4$ CUP OLIVE OIL

KOSHER SALT

Combine the milk, lemon juice, garlic, and pepper in a 2-cup glass measuring cup. Using a handheld blender (see Atenção), buzz for 30 seconds, until frothy. With the motor running, slowly pour in the oil in a fine thread, moving the blender up and down until the mixture thickens lusciously and resembles a soft mayonnaise. You may need slightly less or more oil. Season with salt to taste. The *maionese* will last for up to 1 week in the fridge.

VARIAÇÃO **CILANTRO AND GINGER "MAYONNAISE"**
maionese de leite com coentro e gengibre

Add 1 loosely packed cup well-dried fresh cilantro leaves and tendril-soft stems and a $1^{1}/_2$-inch peeled and grated thumb of fresh ginger to the measuring cup along with the milk, $1^{3}/_4$ teaspoons lemon juice, and the pepper. Omit the garlic. Whir in the oil as directed above, and season with salt. Stir in 1 scallion, cut into thin slices on the diagonal.

(recipe continues)

VARIAÇÃO ⇋ ANCHOVY "MAYONNAISE" *maionese de leite com anchovas*

Add 6 anchovy fillets packed in oil to the measuring cup along with the milk, lemon juice, garlic, and pepper. Whir in the oil as directed above. Omit the salt.

VARIAÇÃO ⇋ CURRY "MAYONNAISE" *maionese de leite com caril*

Add 2 teaspoons of your favorite curry powder to the cup along with the milk, lemon juice, garlic, and pepper. Whir in the oil as directed above, and season with salt. Before using, let this sit for an hour or so in the fridge for the flavor to bloom.

VARIAÇÃO ⇋ TOMATO "MAYONNAISE" *maionese de leite com tomate*

Add 1½ tablespoons double-concentrate tomato paste to the cup along with the milk, garlic, and pepper. Omit the lemon juice. Whir in the oil as directed above, and season with salt. Stir in 1 tablespoon minced oil-packed sun-dried tomatoes.

TOMATO SAUCE

tomatada

MAKES ABOUT 2 CUPS

This recipe is simplicity itself. I make it when fire-engine-red tomatoes are tumbling off tables at the local farmers' market. But in a pinch, you can use good canned tomatoes—many Portuguese prefer them, in fact. For a sauce with the bit of heat favored in the Trás-os-Montes region, as well as in the Azores, drop in the optional chile pepper.

3 TABLESPOONS OLIVE OIL

2 MEDIUM YELLOW ONIONS, CUT IN HALF LENGTHWISE AND SLICED INTO THIN HALF-MOONS

2 SPRIGS FRESH FLAT-LEAF PARSLEY

1 TURKISH BAY LEAF

2 GARLIC CLOVES, MINCED

2 POUNDS VERY RIPE TOMATOES, SEEDED AND CHOPPED, OR ONE 28-OUNCE CAN WHOLE PEELED TOMATOES, PREFERABLY SAN MARZANO, CHOPPED, JUICES RESERVED

2 TO 3 TABLESPOONS DOUBLE-CONCENTRATE TOMATO PASTE, TO TASTE

1 SMALL FRESH MEDIUM-HOT RED CHILE PEPPER, SUCH AS SERRANO, STEMMED, SEEDED, AND CHOPPED (OPTIONAL)

KOSHER SALT AND FRESHLY GROUND BLACK PEPPER

1. Heat the oil in a large skillet over medium heat until it shimmers. Add the onions, parsley, and bay leaf and cook until nicely golden, about 15 minutes. Add the garlic and cook for 1 minute more.

2. Turn the heat to medium-low, stir in the tomatoes and their juices, the tomato paste, and chile pepper, if using, and bring to a simmer. Cook, lid ajar, stirring occasionally, until the tomatoes break down, about 30 minutes.

3. Toss out the parsley and bay leaf, and season the sauce to taste with salt and pepper. If you wish, you can scrape the sauce into a food processor and buzz until smooth. Store the sauce in the fridge in a glass jar with a tight-fitting lid for up to 1 week; it can also be frozen for up to 2 months.

LIGHTLY SAUTÉED ONIONS AND GARLIC

refogado claro

MAKES ABOUT 3 CUPS

This homey onion-garlic mixture, sometimes referred to as *cebolada*, is the undisputed foundation of Portuguese cooking. Not only does it add depth of flavor to dishes, but it contributes texture as well. I find spending up to half an hour sautéing onions takes a chunk out of busy weekday evenings, so I make big batches of the stuff and scoop out what I need when I'm at the stove.

$1/3$ CUP OLIVE OIL

6 MEDIUM YELLOW ONIONS (ABOUT 2 POUNDS), FINELY CHOPPED

2 TURKISH BAY LEAVES

3 SPRIGS FRESH FLAT-LEAF PARSLEY

6 GARLIC CLOVES, MINCED

1. Heat the oil in a large skillet over medium heat until it shimmers. Add the onions, bay leaves, and parsley and cook, uncovered, stirring often, until the onions are fully softened and lightly golden, about 25 minutes. Add the garlic and cook for 5 minutes more. Remove the skillet from the heat and allow the mixture to cool.

2. Discard the bay leaves and parsley, spoon the *refogado* into a glass jar with a tight-fitting lid, and store in the fridge for up to 2 weeks.

VARIAÇÃO ❦ **DARKLY SAUTÉED ONIONS AND GARLIC** *refogado escuro*

MAKES ABOUT 2 CUPS • To make a more complex-flavored darker *refogado*, cook the onions, bay leaves, and parsley, covered, over medium-low heat, stirring often, for 20 minutes. Remove the cover, raise the heat to medium, and continue cooking and stirring until the onions are golden brown, about 20 minutes more. Add the garlic and cook for 5 minutes more.

THE GOLDEN HOUR

Any time you see instructions in this book to cook onions and garlic in olive oil until either golden (*claro*) or golden brown (*escuro*), you can save time by spooning out the corresponding amount of *refogado*, heating it in the pan, and continuing with the recipe.

SIZE OF ONION	AMOUNT OF LIGHT *REFOGADO*	AMOUNT OF DARK *REFOGADO*
1 SMALL (2 INCHES)	$1/4$ CUP	3 TABLESPOONS
1 MEDIUM (3 INCHES)	$1/2$ CUP	SCANT $1/3$ CUP
1 LARGE ($3^3/4$ INCHES)	1 CUP	$2/3$ CUP

ROASTED GARLIC BUTTER WITH MADEIRA

manteiga de alho assado com madeira

MAKES ABOUT $^3/_4$ CUP

The Portuguese love their raw garlic, but sometimes enough is enough. I created this as a way of getting a softer flavor so I could enjoy more of it dripping from hot Madeiran Griddle Bread (page 190), the island's favorite loaf. If you want a bit of raw garlic zing, stir in 1 minced small clove.

2 HEADS OF GARLIC, PAPERY OUTER
    LAYERS REMOVED

2 TABLESPOONS OLIVE OIL

$^1/_4$ CUP DRY MADEIRA

8 TABLESPOONS (1 STICK) UNSALTED
    BUTTER, AT ROOM TEMPERATURE

2 TABLESPOONS CHOPPED FRESH
    FLAT-LEAF PARSLEY LEAVES

GRATED ZEST OF $^1/_2$ LEMON

KOSHER SALT AND FRESHLY GROUND
    BLACK PEPPER

1. Position a rack in the middle of the oven and crank up the heat to 400°F.

2. Slice off the top quarter of each garlic head, exposing the cloves. Drizzle each with 1 tablespoon of the oil, and wrap in foil. Roast until sweet and soft, about 1 hour. Unwrap and let cool completely.

3. Bring the Madeira to a simmer in a small saucepan over medium-low heat and cook until it reduces to 1 tablespoon. Remove from the heat and let cool completely.

4. Squeeze the roasted garlic cloves from their skins into a food processor, add the reduced Madeira, the butter, parsley, and zest, and buzz until smooth. Season with salt and pepper to taste. Scrape the butter into a ramekin, press plastic wrap against the surface, and refrigerate. It will keep for up to 1 week.

SMOKED PAPRIKA OIL

azeite em infusão de colorau fumado

MAKES 1 CUP

So much of Portuguese food is flavored with its unctuous, smoky, paprika-laced sausages. But frankly, I got tired of always having to fry some up to get that flavor—so I came up with this oil. Drizzle it on grilled beef, poultry, or squid (see page 95), as well as on roasted potatoes and onions. I also make a wicked vinaigrette with it that I stir into warm bean or potato salad.

1 CUP EXTRA-VIRGIN OLIVE OIL

3 TABLESPOONS SWEET SMOKED
  PAPRIKA

PINCH OF KOSHER SALT

Combine the olive oil, paprika, and salt in a 1-pint jar with a tight-fitting lid. Shake well and let sit for several days. Pour off the oil and discard the paprika that has settled on the bottom. The oil will keep for several months in a cool, dark place.

CHICKEN STOCK

caldo de frango

MAKES ABOUT 8 CUPS

My grandmother Costa always had a pot of stock simmering on the back of her stove. She wasn't particular about what she tossed in—sometimes it was bits of chicken, other times crispy ends of beef, maybe a splash of wine, and, always, leftover vegetables and wilted herbs. I learned her techniques for cooking with stocks, but I tend not to have her loose approach to their flavors. I like all of my stocks to be distinct and rich. Once you taste them, you'll never reach for a can or carton again.

5 POUNDS CHICKEN LEGS AND THIGHS	1 SHALLOT, HALVED
²⁄₃ CUP DRY WHITE WINE	3 GARLIC CLOVES, CRUSHED
3 CELERY STALKS, CHOPPED INTO 3 PIECES EACH	7 SPRIGS FRESH FLAT-LEAF PARSLEY
3 CARROTS, CHOPPED INTO 3 PIECES EACH	3 SPRIGS FRESH THYME
	1 TURKISH BAY LEAF
3 MEDIUM YELLOW ONIONS, QUARTERED	6 BLACK PEPPERCORNS

1. Dump the chicken pieces in a large stockpot or Dutch oven and pour in 2½ quarts of cold water, or enough to cover. Add the wine and bring to a boil over high heat, then reduce the heat to low so the liquid barely simmers. Skim and discard any foam that floats to the surface, and add the celery, carrots, onions, shallot, garlic, parsley, thyme, bay leaf, and peppercorns. Gently simmer the stock for 2½ hours, being mindful that it doesn't boil.

2. Transfer the chicken to a plate; by this point the meat will have leached most of its flavor into the stock, but it can be munched on if you like. Strain the stock through a sieve into a metal bowl, pressing down on the vegetables and herbs with the back of a ladle to extract all of the juices. Wash the sieve, then line it with cheesecloth or a coffee filter, and strain the stock again. Measure the liquid; if it's more than 2 quarts, pour it into a clean pot and reduce over low heat.

3. Fill a large bowl with ice water. Place the bowl of stock in the ice bath to cool, then refrigerate, uncovered, until completely chilled.

4. Using a spoon, remove the solidified fat from the top of the stock, and save it for other uses, such as sautéing vegetables or flavoring dishes, or discard. Freeze the stock in 1-cup containers or in an ice cube tray. Once frozen, the cubes can be stored for up to 2 months in plastic freezer bags and used as needed. Alternatively, you can store the stock in the fridge for up to 3 days.

BEEF STOCK

caldo de carne de vaca

MAKES ABOUT 8 CUPS

This recipe calls for meaty bones. It's impossible to make a rich, gorgeous stock from what supermarkets call marrow bones. They have practically no meat on them, so your stock will have practically no meat flavor. Ask your butcher for the thin end of the beef shank, rib back bones, or neck bones with lots of meat on them. Barring that, buy 3 pounds of stewing meat and 4 pounds of bones.

2 MEDIUM YELLOW ONIONS, QUARTERED

2 MEDIUM CARROTS, CHOPPED INTO 3 PIECES EACH

1 CELERY STALK, CHOPPED INTO 3 PIECES

1 TABLESPOON VEGETABLE OIL

2 TABLESPOONS DOUBLE-CONCENTRATE TOMATO PASTE

7 POUNDS MEATY BEEF BONES

1 CUP DRY RED WINE

$1/2$ CUP (ABOUT $1/2$ OUNCE) DRIED SHIITAKE MUSHROOMS

3 GARLIC CLOVES, CRUSHED

6 SPRIGS FRESH FLAT-LEAF PARSLEY

4 SPRIGS FRESH THYME

2 TURKISH BAY LEAVES

1. Position a rack in the center of the oven and crank up the heat to 425°F.

2. Toss the onions, carrots, and celery with the oil and tomato paste in a large roasting pan or on a rimmed baking sheet. Scatter the vegetables over the pan and top with the bones. Roast, uncovered, tossing several times, until the meat is deeply browned, 1 to $1^{1}/_{4}$ hours. If the vegetables are browning too quickly, drizzle a few tablespoons of water over them and toss again.

3. Transfer the bones, vegetables, and any juices to a large stockpot or Dutch oven and set aside. Splash the wine into the roasting pan and scrape up the browned bits. If necessary, place the pan over medium heat and heat the wine, scraping the bottom of the pan, to lift off any stubborn bits. Pour the liquid into the stockpot.

4. Add the mushrooms, garlic, parsley, thyme, and bay leaves to the pot and pour in 3 quarts of cold water, or enough to cover. Bring to a boil over high heat, then reduce the heat to low so the liquid barely simmers. Skim and discard any foam that floats to the surface. Gently simmer the stock for $3^{1}/_{2}$ to 4 hours, being mindful it doesn't boil.

5. Strain, cool, and store the stock as in steps 2, 3, and 4 of Chicken Stock (page 243). The stock will keep in the fridge for up to 3 days and in the freezer for up to 2 months.

FISH STOCK

caldo de peixe

MAKES ABOUT 6 CUPS

You can freeze fish bones, heads, and trimmings until you have enough, or you can ask your local fishmonger for scraps. Many stores will place an order if they don't have fish frames on hand. Make sure to rinse the fish well to remove any bits of blood or guts, which can make the stock murky and give it an off taste.

2 POUNDS FISH TRIMMINGS AND BONES FROM LEAN WHITE FISH, SUCH AS HADDOCK, FLOUNDER, COD, OR MONKFISH

1 MEDIUM YELLOW ONION, FINELY CHOPPED

2 MEDIUM CARROTS, FINELY CHOPPED

2 MEDIUM CELERY STALKS, FINELY CHOPPED

8 SPRIGS FRESH FLAT-LEAF PARSLEY

1 TURKISH BAY LEAF

ONE 2-INCH STRIP OF LEMON ZEST, REMOVED WITH A VEGETABLE PEELER

6 WHITE PEPPERCORNS, CRACKED

$^2/_3$ CUP DRY WHITE WINE

1. Dump the fish trimmings and bones, onion, carrots, celery, parsley, bay leaf, zest, and peppercorns in a large stockpot or Dutch oven and pour in 6 cups of cold water, or enough to cover. Add the wine and bring to a boil over high heat, then reduce the heat to low so the liquid barely simmers. Skim and discard any foam that floats to the surface. Gently simmer the stock for 45 minutes, being mindful it doesn't boil.

2. Strain, cool, and store the stock as in steps 2, 3, and 4 of Chicken Stock (page 243). The stock will keep in the fridge for up to 2 days and in the freezer for up to 2 months.

TAKING STOCK OF STOCKS

Stockpots are tall and narrow, which prevents too much liquid from evaporating while a stock simmers. If you're using a Dutch oven, which is wider, watch it to make sure your stock isn't going up in a swirl of steam. If the chicken, beef, or fish pieces start to poke above the liquid, add a bit more water and partially cover the pot to control evaporation.

If you don't have time to make stock from scratch, try this: pour 1 quart of store-bought low-sodium chicken or beef broth into a medium saucepan. Add 1 diced medium yellow onion, 1 chopped medium carrot, 2 dried shiitake mushrooms, 4 sprigs fresh flat-leaf parsley, 2 sprigs fresh thyme, 1 Turkish bay leaf, and a splash of white wine for chicken broth or red wine for beef broth. Bring to a boil over high heat, reduce the heat to low, and simmer, covered, for 30 minutes. Pour the enriched broth through a strainer, and get on with it.

SHRIMP STOCK

caldo de camarão

MAKES ABOUT 4 CUPS

Always buy shrimp in their shells, so you can hoard the main ingredient for this stock. If you're lucky enough to get shrimp with heads, grab them; the heads add so much flavor. As you accumulate the shells, wrap them tightly in plastic, and freeze until you have enough.

2 TEASPOONS VEGETABLE OIL	1 SMALL CARROT, FINELY CHOPPED
1 LARGE LEEK, WHITE PART ONLY, HALVED LENGTHWISE, SLICED INTO THIN HALF–MOONS, AND RINSED WELL	2 POUNDS SHRIMP SHELLS
	$\frac{1}{2}$ CUP DRY WHITE WINE
	1 TURKISH BAY LEAF
1 SMALL CELERY STALK, FINELY CHOPPED	3 WHITE PEPPERCORNS, CRACKED
	3 SPRIGS FRESH FLAT–LEAF PARSLEY

1. Heat the oil in a medium saucepan over medium heat until it shimmers. Add the leek and cook, stirring frequently, until soft and translucent but not browned, about 5 minutes. Add the celery and carrot and cook until soft, about 7 minutes more.

2. Dump in the shrimp shells and cook, stirring frequently, until they turn pink, 3 to 4 minutes. Pour in the wine and cook until the liquid has reduced to about ¼ cup. Pour in 6 cups of cold water and drop in the bay leaf, white peppercorns, and parsley. Bring to a boil over high heat, then reduce the heat to low so the liquid barely simmers. Skim and discard any foam that floats to the surface. Gently simmer the stock for 45 minutes, being mindful it doesn't boil.

3. Strain, cool, and store the stock as in steps 2, 3, and 4 of Chicken Stock (page 243). The stock will keep in the fridge for up to 2 days and in the freezer for up to 2 months.

HOME-RENDERED LARD

banha

MAKES ABOUT 3 CUPS

Before you wince and turn the page, consider this: homemade lard, used in moderate amounts, is actually healthier for you than margarines, spreads, and those bricks of store-bought lard—all of which are loaded with trans fats. Lard is a staple in Portugal, giving dishes a layer of flavor butter and olive oil can't match. Whenever the mood strikes you, substitute an equal amount of lard for olive oil in the savory recipes in this book.

ATENÇÃO 🧩 *Ask your butcher for leaf lard, the fat surrounding a porker's kidneys, which is prized for its purity; fatback will work just as well. Avoid salt pork, which is cured and will make terrible-tasting lard.*

> 2 POUNDS LEAF LARD OR FRESH
>   PORK FATBACK, CUT INTO ½-INCH
>   PIECES

1. Add the lard and ½ cup of water to a medium pot over low heat. Let the mixture burble, stirring often to prevent burning and pressing down on the pieces with the back of a spoon, until the fat has melted and any crispy bits and bobs have sunk to the bottom, 1½ to 2 hours. Let the lard cool for 15 minutes.

2. Line a sieve with cheesecloth, set it over a bowl, and drain the lard. When it is cool but still liquid, pour the lard into a glass jar with a tight-fitting lid. Lightly salt any cracklings—called *torresmos* in central Portugal—left behind in the sieve to snack on. The lard will last for 2 months in the fridge or up to a year in the freezer.

ACKNOWLEDGMENTS

If it takes a village to raise a child, it takes a country to write a cookbook. Or, in this case, six countries. I've been blessed to have the help of people in the United States, Canada, Portugal, England, Austria, and Israel, all of whom added so much to the spirit, accuracy, and tenor of the book.

On home turf, I'd like to thank my parents, Manuel and Ellie Leite, who tolerated, nay, even enjoyed, the endless interrogations and piles of translations foisted upon them and who supported me, comforted me, and just plain loved me through the whole process. A shout-out to the God Squad, all of whom were fans of this book years before I knew I was going to write it. And thanks to David Lindsey Griffin, who helped me realize that being Portuguese was a good thing.

At Clarkson Potter, much-deserved praise goes to my marvelously precise, astonishingly accommodating editor Rica Allannic, multitalented art director Jane Treuhaft, designer extraordinaire Stephanie Huntwork, the ever-patient, always helpful Ashley Phillips, as well as Kate Tyler, Ava Kavyani, Donna Passannante, Patricia Shaw, Janet McDonald, and Joan Denman. Judith Sutton, my dream copy editor, made sure not a period was out of place. Kudos to my photographer and, now, friend Nuno Correia, who traveled all the way from Lisbon for this book; the insanely creative (and sometimes just plain insane) food stylist Susan Sugarman; prop stylist Barb Fritz; and digital tech Hillary Launey, all of whom made the food look better than I ever imagined possible. Thank you to my literary agent, David Black, as well as to Dave Larabell, Gary Morris, and Antonella Iannarino of Taylor-Fladgate, for fighting the good fight.

To my incredibly faithful recipe testers—I owe you all a huge, calorie-busting meal: Leanne Abe, Janet Boileau, Patton Conner, Duane DeMello, Donna Marie Desfor, Tran Doan, Susan Hillery, Susan Komlo Bingaman, Dan Kraan, Cynthia Kruth, Adrienne Lee, Elie W. Nassar, Maria Peplowski, Vicki Ventura, and, especially, the late Dede Eran, who was always the first in the kitchen and the last to leave the table. Also thank you to Emily Halpern and to my longtime kitchen cohort Alice Thompson.

There's no better, more talented work wife than Linda Avery, who kept the lights at Leite's Culinaria burning bright in my absence. Thank you, my dear friend. And everyone should have an assistant as gifted as Nora Singley. She was always a step ahead of me while cleaning up behind me.

A big *obrigado* to Flo Braker, Taylor Cocalis of Murray's Cheese, Shirley O. Corriher, Michael Krondl, Harold McGee, and Peter Reinhart for chiming in with their professional opinions.

The folks at AICEP Portugal Global had a big hand in the making of this book: in America, Miguel Carvalho, Maria da Graca Leite Freitas, and Rui Abecassis, and their partner, Jayme Simões; in Portugal, Eduardo Souto Moura, Ana Sofia Correia de Ahumada, and Maria Inês Oliveira; and in Madeira, Isabel Góis. Ditto to Salomé Relvas of Regional de Turismo de Madeira. A hearty thanks to Marli Monteiro of Centro de Portugal, Paula Oliveira and Helena Ribeiro of Turimo de Lisboa, Marta Sá Lemos of Adeturn, and the staff at ViniPortugal, TAP Portugal, and Azores Express.

Thank you to Toni Allegra, Miguel Avila, Elissa Altman, Monica Bhide, Meg Buchsbaum, Luís Caseiro, Tarcísio Costa and Miguel Jerónimo of Alfama Restaurant, Terry Costa, Barbara Fairchild, Ellen Fitzgerald, Cherie Furtado, Carlotta Florio Johnson, Ellen Kroner, Bob Pidkameny, Angela Costa Simões, Howard Sklar, Kate Stiassni, and Kristin Zangrilli. And I can never thank Linda Bartoshuk and Miriam Grushka enough for giving me my taste buds back.

In Portugal, I'm indebted to my brilliant Portuguese teacher and translator Cristina Vasconcelos; friends and hosts Ana Maria Albuquerque Taveira and Filipe Le Velly de Sousa Lima; Elvira André; Paulo Amado and Rita Cupido of Edicões do Gosto; Adrian Bridges and Robert Bower of Taylor, Fladgate & Yeatman; Teresa Cota Dias and Diogo Leite de Castro; Duarte Calvão; Eddie Correia; Pedro do Carmo Costa; Jorge Duque and João Frere of ecoterra; Maria Emília "Mani" Ferreira Pinto and her husband, Pedro; Cecília Gouveia; Amy Herrick and Luís Vasconcellos e Souza; Carrie Jorgensen of Cortes de Cima; David Lopes Ramos; Angela Moreira; Manuel Murteira Martins; Teresa Paiva; José Queimado; Pedro Rodrigues; Pilar Serras; Teresa Torres; Ana Viera Soares; José Vilela; Mimi Vasconcelos; and Leonor Xavier.

Then there are all the chefs, cooks, and restaurateurs who let me prattle on in bad Portuguese: Fausto Airoldi, Antonio Miguel Amaral, José Avillez, Luís Baena, Miguel Castro e Silva, Olga Cavaleiro, Antonieta Cocheirnha Tarouca, Michel da Costa, Olivier da Costa, Filipe dos Ramos, João Encarnação, Nuno Faria, Fernando Fernandes, Augusto Gemelli, Fernando Neves, Miguel Rodrigues, Henrique Sá Pessoa, Vitor Sobral, Ilda Vinagre, and especially Miguel Júdice.

In England, thanks to the marvelously generous Portuguese radio host, writer, and author Edite Vieira, who always came to my rescue, with a recipe, advice, or insight. In Vienna, I tip my hat to José C. Fernandes de Andrade, and, in Israel, to Clementina Garrido.

Last, to my dear Alan Dunkelberger, who is German/Italian by birth but who's now Portuguese by dint of consumption. I thank you for eating your way through every one of these recipes at least thrice, and I will never forgive you for not having gained a pound.

SOURCES

For a list of up-to-date suppliers and Portuguese products made exclusively for and by Leite's Culinaria, contact sources@leitesculinaria.com.

SALT COD, SAUCES, OLIVE OIL, AND OTHER PORTUGUESE FOODS

Portuguesefood.com
(508) 916-8781 (inquiries only)
www.portuguesefood.com
Best bets: olive oils, cheeses, sausages, and piri-piri sauces

La Tienda
3601 La Grange Parkway
Toano, VA 23168
(800) 710-4304
www.tienda.com
Best bets: salt cod, hams (from acorn-fed pigs), serrano ham

The Spanish Table
1426 Western Avenue
Seattle, WA 98101
(206) 682-2827
www.spanishtable.com
Best bets: olive oils and smoked paprika

MEATS AND SAUSAGES

Lopes Sausage Company
304 Walnut Street
Newark, NJ 07105
(973) 344-3063
Best bets: chouriço, linguiça, Spanish chorizo, morcela (blood sausage), and farinheira

Mello's North End Manufacturing
63 North Court Street
Fall River, MA 02720
(800) 673-2320
www.melloschourico.com
Best bets: chouriço, linguiça, morcela (blood sausage), and pimenta moída

Amaral's
c/o Lisbon Sausage Company, Inc.
433 South Second Street
New Bedford, MA 02740
(800) 262-7257 (inquiries only)
www.amarals.com
Best bets: chouriço, linguiça, pickled peppers, and corn flours

Niman Ranch
1600 Harbor Bay Parkway
Suite 250
Alameda, CA 94502
(888) 206-3327
www.nimanranch.com
Best bets: pork tenderloins

CHEESES

Murray's Cheese
254 Bleeker Street
New York, NY 10014
(888) 692-4339
www.murrayscheese.com
Inventory changes; call for current selection

Artisanal Premium Cheese Center
500 W. 37th Street
New York, NY 10018
(877) 797-1200
www.artisanalcheese.com
Inventory changes; call for current selection

igourmet.com
(877) 446-8763
www.igourmet.com
Best bets: cheeses, preserves, and piri-piri sauce

CHESTNUTS

Girolami Farms
11502 East Eight Mile Road
Stockton, CA 95212
(209) 931-0158
www.chestnutsforsale.com

SEA SALT

Belamandil
c/o Sea Salt Superstore
10711 Evergreen Way,
Suite A
Everett, WA 98204
(866) 999-7258
www.seasaltsuperstore.com

Zingerman's
422 Detroit Street
Ann Arbor, MI 48104
(888) 636-8162
www.zingermans.com

HERBS AND SPICES

Penzeys Spices
12001 W. Capitol Drive
Wauwatosa, WI 53226
(800) 741-7787
www.penzeys.com

PASTÉIS DE NATA FORMS AND CATAPLANAS

Tucha Gifts
105 Ferry Street
Newark, NJ 07105
(973) 589-3681

Note: *Italicized* page numbers indicate photographs.